GREAT S...
FOR YOUNG ... W9-BWR-404
FROM THE STAGE

CRAIG SLAIGHT is the Director of the Young Conservatory at the American Conservatory Theater in San Francisco. Prior to joining the A.C.T. company, Mr. Slaight was the head of the acting and directing program at the Los Angeles County High School for the Arts. He also served on the Theater faculty at the acclaimed Interlochen Center for the Arts. In addition to his commitment to developing and training young actors, Mr. Slaight spent ten years in Los Angeles as a professional director. Mr. Slaight holds a degree in Theater and English from Central Michigan University.

JACK SHARRAR is the Registrar for the American Conservatory Theater, where he also teaches acting, directing and voice. He has directed young performers in more than 35 plays and musicals, and is the author of *Avery Hopwood, His Life and Plays*. Mr. Sharrar holds a Ph.D. from the University of Utah.

i

GREAT SCENES
FOR YOUNG ACTORS
FROM THE STAGE

Craig Slaight
Jack Sharrar
Editors

SK
A Smith and Kraus Book

iii

A Smith and Kraus Book
Published by Smith and Kraus, Inc.

PN
2080
.G4
1991

Cover design by David Wise
Text design by Jeannette Champagne

Manufactured in the United States of America

First Edition: May 1991
10 9 8 7 6 5 4 3 2 1

Publisher's Cataloging in Publication
(Prepared by Quality Books Inc.)

Great scenes for young actors from the stage / Craig Slaight, Jack
Sharrar, editors. --
 p. cm.
 Includes bibliographical references.   *R00898 / 5301*
 ISBN 0-9622722-6-4

 1. Drama--Collections. 2. Acting. I. Slaight, Craig, 1951-
II. Sharrar, Jack, 1949-

PN2080   808.82
                        91-60869

Smith and Kraus, Inc.
Main Street, P.O. Box 10, Newbury, Vermont 05051
(802) 866-5423

DEDICATION

For Nora and Renee, and to our students past and present.

ACKNOWLEDGMENTS

The editors would like to thank Arthur Ballet, Michele Bernier, Edward Hastings, Timothy Mason, Dennis Powers, James Prideaux, Susan Stauter, and the students and staff of the American Conservatory Theater for their help in preparing this collection. We also thank Smith and Kraus for believing in this project. Our special thanks to Julie Harris for her inspiration and support.

Then, perhaps, the actor is a messenger, searching for the human passions of a character, deep into history, deep into imagination and poetry, far into the desert. As a conscientious and loyal messenger, he should return, clad in magnificent tatters, and tell of what he saw and of what he has lived during his voyage. He should tell this to the very audience which invested him with this marvelous mission: to use simple and splendid designs, in order to bring to life a human being among us here and now.

—Ariane Mnouchkine
Le Théâtre Du Soleil

x

CONTENTS

FOREWORD Julie Harris xv

INTRODUCTION Craig Slaight and Jack Sharrar xvii

Section I - Scenes for 1 Man and 1 Woman

AND THEY DANCE REAL SLOW IN JACKSON Jim Leonard, Jr. 1

*ANTIGONE Jean Anouilh, translated by Alex Szogyi 7

BILLY LIAR Keith Waterhouse and Willis Hall 11

BLUE DENIM James Leo Herlihy and William Noble 17

THE CHOPIN PLAYOFFS Israel Horovitz 24

*LA DISPUTE Marivaux, translated by Timberlake Wertenbaker 28

DOES A TIGER WEAR A NECKTIE? Don Petersen 31

IN A NORTHERN LANDSCAPE Timothy Mason 36

*THE LADY'S NOT FOR BURNING Christopher Fry 40

LILY DALE Horton Foote 44

LOVERS (WINNERS) Brian Friel 49

LU ANN HAMPTON LAVERTY OBERLANDER Preston Jones 56

NICE PEOPLE DANCING TO GOOD COUNTRY MUSIC Lee Blessing 61

OUT OF GAS ON LOVERS LEAP Mark St. Germain 66

CONTENTS

THE RISE AND RISE OF DANIEL ROCKET Peter Parnell 73

STREET SCENE Elmer Rice 78

TRIBUTE Bernard Slade 83

WHAT I DID LAST SUMMER A.R. Gurney, Jr. 87

WOMEN AND WALLACE Jonathan Marc Sherman 91

Section II - Scenes for 2 Women

*ANTIGONE Jean Anouilh, translated by Alex Szogyi 98

ASCENSION DAY Timothy Mason 103

COURTSHIP Horton Foote 108

*LA DISPUTE Marivaux, translated by Timberlake Wertenbaker 116

LEMON SKY Lanford Wilson 120

LYDIE BREEZE John Guare 124

MY SISTER IN THIS HOUSE Wendy Kesselman 129

THE RIMERS OF ELDRITCH Lanford Wilson 133

SENIORITY Eric Ziegenhagen 136

*WHO WILL CARRY THE WORD? Charlotte Delbo 142

A YOUNG LADY OF PROPERTY Horton Foote 148

CONTENTS

Section III - Scenes for 2 Men

ALBUM David Rimmer 152

*ANOTHER COUNTRY Julian Mitchell 164

BLUE DENIM James Leo Herlihy and William Noble 169

THE CHOPIN PLAYOFFS Israel Horovitz 176

*THE CONTRAST Royall Tyler 180

THE DIVINERS Jim Leonard, Jr. 187

ENTER LAUGHING Joseph Stein 192

ORPHANS Lyle Kessler 198

SCOOTER THOMAS MAKES IT TO THE TOP OF THE WORLD
Peter Parnell 208

*SPRING AWAKENING Frank Wedekind, translated by Tom Osborn
215

Section IV - Scenes for Groups

ASCENSION DAY Timothy Mason 221

THE CHOPIN PLAYOFFS Israel Horovitz 226

*SPRING AWAKENING Frank Wedekind, translated by Tom Osborn
232

WHAT I DID LAST SUMMER A.R. Gurney, Jr. 237

CONTENTS

THE YOUNG AND FAIR N. Richard Nash 242

PERMISSIONS ACKNOWLEDGMENTS 251

* Indicates Advanced Scenes

FOREWORD

Here I am on February 23, 1991, waiting in my dressing room to begin a matinee performance of *Lucifer's Child* by William Luce, at the Eisenhower Theatre, Kennedy Center, and thinking about all the young people who will become, and who are becoming, and who *are* our actors of the future and trying to remember what it was like for me as an actor when I was just starting out on "The Road to Broadway" and distant stages. With this book, *Great Scenes for Young Actors from the Stage*, the young actor has been given a very important introduction to dramatic literature and a wonderful guide to inspire and awaken curiosity and broaden horizons. In these pages are the creative tools the actor can use to study his craft. My love to you all! I look forward to seeing your work!

—Julie Harris

INTRODUCTION

We have long felt that there was a need for a new scene book for young actors. The following collection represents some of the best scenes in dramatic literature that reflect life's experience through the eyes of the young and offers a broad range of roles from the classics to the contemporary. Students are encouraged to expand their technique beyond their immediate life experiences and open themselves to a dynamic cross-section of culturally diverse dramatic characters. We have provided the necessary starting point to explore each scene, including a brief overview of the play, a few words setting the scene in context, and, in some instances, special notes that may help focus study of the scene. No scene work should be undertaken without first reading the entire play from which the scene is taken, however. With this in mind, we have only selected scenes from published plays. Young actors and teachers will find enough quality material here to guide them through their study of acting from beginning to advanced work for many years.

—Craig Slaight
Jack Sharrar
San Francisco
March 1, 1991

GREAT SCENES
FOR YOUNG ACTORS
FROM THE STAGE

AND THEY DANCE REAL SLOW IN JACKSON
by Jim Leonard, Jr.
Elizabeth (15) - Skeeter (15)

The Play: A chilling memory play, the story deals with Elizabeth Ann Willow, a young girl confined to a wheelchair, crippled at birth from cerebral palsy. Through a fascinating series of both real and dream sequences, the play goes in and out of time to show Elizabeth living with this affliction in the fictitious small town of Jackson, Indiana. In addition to seeing Elizabeth with her mother and father, we also see her struggles with friends and the townspeople of Jackson (played by a chorus of four actors) as she attempts to live a normal life and be treated like any other person. Ultimately, the prejudices and unfeeling ignorance of the people of Jackson are more than Elizabeth can overcome, and she sinks into a reclusive state of madness.

The Scene: Skeeter Robins is one of the few young people in town who has shown Elizabeth kindness and accepted her, regardless of her condition. Except for the fact that Elizabeth is in a wheelchair, this is not unlike the first real talk between any fifteen-year-old girl and boy. As the scene begins, Elizabeth and Skeeter are arriving at Reverend Peester's home for confirmation class.

Special Note: The playwright specifically cautions that the only physical indications of Elizabeth's condition should be that she cannot move her legs. There should be no other attempt to portray her condition.

AND THEY DANCE REAL SLOW IN JACKSON

[(Elizabeth enters on the above line as the Kid is crossing off. She's on the stage floor level, but there's no interaction whatsoever between Elizabeth and the Kid.] Elizabeth is fifteen now. When Skeeter turns to say "hi" he becomes himself at fifteen too.)

ELIZABETH: Hi, Skeeter.

SKEETER: Hi. Uh, hey, you want some help with that thing?

ELIZABETH: I'm all right.

SKEETER: Sure? *(Skeeter wheels her around some small obstruction or something or just plain helps wheel her to the area that'll serve as the minister's house—not that she needs any help.)*

ELIZABETH: I'm fine, just—well, thank you.

SKEETER: *(Overlapping.)* No, here, let me give you a hand.

ELIZABETH: Thanks a lot, Skeeter.

SKEETER: *(Shrugs.)* S'nothing.

ELIZABETH: Where's Reverend Peester at?

SKEETER: He left. His wife's down in the basement, I think. In the reck room, I think. I hear she's been hitting the bottle down there. You want me to get her?

ELIZABETH: No!

SKEETER: Sure?

ELIZABETH: I just wondered where Mr. Peester was at.

SKEETER: Store.

ELIZABETH: Nothing's open on Sundays is it?

SKEETER: IGA is. Probably just Cokes and crap like that's all he wants. He'll be back in a minute, I imagine.

ELIZABETH: My mother says Coke's not very good for you.

SKEETER: Yeah?

ELIZABETH: It does something strange to your stomach, she says. It eats it away.

SKEETER: Yeah, my dad says the same thing about cigarettes and he smokes like a chimney.

ELIZABETH: Really?

SKEETER: No shit. Shoot I mean...

ELIZABETH: How long is this supposed to last tonight?

SKEETER: Dunno. Never been to a communion class before.

2

AND THEY DANCE REAL SLOW IN JACKSON

ELIZABETH: Confirmation.

SKEETER: Huh?—

ELIZABETH: Confirmation.

SKEETER: Yeah, well Peester'll be back in a minute.

ELIZABETH: You're fifteen, Skeeter Robins?

SKEETER: Yeah, I am. Gonna get me a car in another year.

ELIZABETH: Same as me! Fifteen, I mean.

SKEETER: Yeah, I'm thinking I might get me one of them GTO's. A red one.

ELIZABETH: Like Billy Taylor's you mean!

SKEETER: Yeah, cherry bomb red! How you know what kind of car Billy drives?

ELIZABETH: I seen him out the window.

SKEETER: No shit?

ELIZABETH: He drives by all the time.

SKEETER: I seen you at your window sometimes.

ELIZABETH: I've seen you too, Skeeter.

SKEETER: You have?

ELIZABETH: *(Smiling.)* Sure.

SKEETER: *(Truly curious.)* Elizabeth, is your mom a bitch?

ELIZABETH: *(Surprised.)* No!

SKEETER: I just wondered. I mean it'd be kind of creepy being cooped up inside most of the time if she bitched at you. Man, I'd deep six myself if I had to spend too much time with my mom.

ELIZABETH: I get out of the house, Skeeter. I go to school you know. Five days a week.

SKEETER: Don't you hate school?

ELIZABETH: I love it.

SKEETER: You like going to school out at that looney bin place?

ELIZABETH: It's not a looney bin, Skeeter. We got teachers and class rooms and bath rooms and books; we just only don't have many students. See, me and Zelda Graves—you know she's my best friend— and we're in the same class. We both got Mrs. Fowler.

SKEETER: She a bitch?

ELIZABETH: Huh uh! She gives me A's.

AND THEY DANCE REAL SLOW IN JACKSON

SKEETER: Good for you, Elizabeth.

ELIZABETH: I got an A+ on my last report.

SKEETER: Great.

ELIZABETH: About Israel.

SKEETER: Yeah?

ELIZABETH: You want to hear about it? *(Skeeter shrugs.)* You sure?

SKEETER: Yeah. Sure. Sure, go on and tell me about Israel, Elizabeth.

ELIZABETH: *(Excited.)* Well, see in Israel—that's where Jesus was born—

SKEETER: Yeah.

ELIZABETH: And he lived over there on the desert and all...you could probably do all kinds of things out there because it's so flat, huh...? National Geographic had pictures of it, and they're growing farms in that sand ten times bigger than any farm in Jackson. At least that!

SKEETER: Right over Calvary?

ELIZABETH: Uh huh. They're growing wheat and corn right on it!

SKEETER: Damn!

ELIZABETH: This tall at least!

SKEETER: Something, huh?

ELIZABETH: Something!

SKEETER: I might like living on a farm. Be kinda the way I figure it. Bet better'n Shepherd Street anyways.

ELIZABETH: I like our street.

SKEETER: Yeah, well you don't have to play ball on it! Shepherd Street ain't for shit when it comes to setting up bases, Elizabeth Ann.

ELIZABETH: We play baseball out at the institute.

SKEETER: *(Not believing her.)* Come on...

ELIZABETH: Yeah, we do! We got enough room for bases at least, Skeeter Robins. Zelda, she's a pitcher, and I play short stop. You want to see something, you oughta see Zelda pitching when she's mad.

SKEETER: That little shrunk up girl?

ELIZABETH: She's not shrunk up, Skeeter! She's just little is all.

SKEETER: I don't know. She looks to me like somebody left her in

4

the dryer too long.

ELIZABETH: Oh, Skeeter...

SKEETER: Pretty hot with the ball, huh?

ELIZABETH: Zalda's the best one on the team, I think.

SKEETER: How's she, uh, how's she get it down there so's people can hit at it? In their chairs and all, I mean.

ELIZABETH: *(Matter of fact.)* We got a rule that you gotta let the batter hit it.

SKEETER: That's not baseball then!

ELIZABETH: *(Challenging.)* Why don't you come look?

SKEETER: Maybe I will!

ELIZABETH: You wanta come tomorrow?

SKEETER: Uh, tomorrow I gotta go to the doctor.

ELIZABETH: How bout after that?

SKEETER: After that I got the dentist.

ELIZABETH: Oh...

SKEETER: Yeah...I got rotten teeth. Too much Coke...

ELIZABETH: I wish the minister'd get here...

SKEETER: *(Gladly changing the subject.)* Hey, have you looked at these things? Some of em're longer than hell. You don't feel wretched do you?

ELIZABETH: No.

SKEETER: Yeah, well you will in an hour or so. *(He sits or kneels near her, showing her the little catechism book.)* Look at this one, will ya? It's just plain nuts is what it is. Whacky as shit!

ELIZABETH: Like our baseball games, huh?

SKEETER: I'm sorry...

ELIZABETH: S'okay...

SKEETER: I mean, I'm really sorry, huh?

ELIZABETH: *(Forgiving.)* S'all right, Skeeter Robins.

SKEETER: *(Renewed.)* Here's the question. It's right there after all that introduction type garbage...

ELIZABETH: *(Reading.)* "How many things must you know that you may live and die in the blessedness of God's grace?"

SKEETER: Yeah, yeah, that the one! Jesus, the guy who wrote these things must beat up on old ladies for fun! This stuff is warped!

ELIZABETH: *(Pleased.)* You want me to read it again? "How many things must you know that you may live and die in the blessedness of God's grace?"

SKEETER: Three. First, the greatness of my sin and...wretchedness! *(On the word "wretchedness" Skeeter tilts Elizabeth's chair up on its back wheels and goes running off stage with her like her chair is a car. She loves it.)*

ELIZABETH: Skeeter!

ANTIGONE
by Jean Anouilh
translated by Alex Szogyi
Antigone (18) - Hemon (19)

The Play: Jean Anouilh's retelling of Sophocles' *Antigone* (the second tragedy in the Oedipus Cycle) was motivated by the Nazi occupation of Paris during World War II. The parallels between the tyranny of Hitler's rule and that of Creon's Thebes are at once evident. Eteocles and Polyneices, the sons of the late Theban King Oedipus, and the brothers of Antigone and Ismene, have recently killed one another in a civil war to gain control of Thebes. Their uncle Creon has become King. Creon has decreed that Polyneices, whom he believes provoked the war, be left unburied—his spirit left to roam eternally. Antigone considers this edict a sacrilege and defies her uncle by covering her brother's body with earth. When Creon learns of the deed, he is unyielding, and he condemns his neice to be buried alive. This act brings about the suicide of Creon's son, Hemon (Antigone's fiance), and Creon's wife, Eurydice. Creon is left to face the tribulations of life alone. Ultimately *Antigone* explores questions concerning human responsibility to family, government and personal honor.

The Scene: Antigone has sent for Hemon so that she can apologize for a quarrel they had he night before. Hemon does not yet know that she has defied Creon's edict and buried her brother's body. Antigone professes her love for Hemon and then breaks off their relationship, much to Hemon's bewilderment.

Special Note: A comparison of Alex Szogyi's translation of Anouilh's *Antigone* with Lewis Galantiere's version and Sophocles' original Oedipus' Cycle may prove helpful to a full exploration of the text.

ANTIGONE

HEMON: You know very well I forgave you as soon as you slammed the door shut. Your perfume was still there and I had already forgiven you. *(He holds her in his arms, he smiles, he looks at her.)* Who did you steal this perfume from?

ANTIGINE: From Ismene.

HEMON: And the lipstick, the powder, the beautiful dress?

ANTIGONE: From Ismene, also.

HEMON: Why did you make yourself so beautiful?

ANTIGONE: I'll tell you. *(She huddles a little closer to him.)* Oh! my darling. How stupid I was. A whole evening spoiled. A beautiful evening.

HEMON: We'll have other evenings—Antigone.

ANTIGONE: Perhaps not.

HEMON: And other fights too. Happiness is full of quarrels.

ANTIGONE: Happiness yes... Listen, Hemon.

HEMON: Yes.

ANTIGONE: Don't laugh at me this morning. Be serious.

HEMON: I am serious.

ANTIGONE: And hold me. Tighter than you ever have before. So that all your strength may be pressed into me.

HEMON: There. With all my strength.

ANTIGONE *(in a breath)*: That's good. *(They remain for a moment without a word, then she begins softly.)* Listen, Hemon.

HEMON: Yes.

ANTIGONE: I wanted to tell you this morning... The little boy that we would have had together...

HEMON: Yes.

ANTIGONE: You know, I would have defended him against everything.

HEMON: Yes, Antigone.

ANTIGONE: Oh! I would have squeezed him so tight he would never have been afraid, I swear it, not of the oncoming night, nor of the shadows... Our little boy, Hemon! He would have had an insignificant mother, her hair badly combed—but better than all the real mothers in the world with their big bosoms and big aprons. You believe that don't you?

8

ANTIGONE

HEMON: Yes, my love.

ANTIGONE: And you believe too, don't you, that I would have been a true wife?

HEMON *(holds her)*: I have a true wife.

ANTIGONE *(cries out suddenly, huddling close to him)*: Oh! you loved me, Hemon, you did love me, are you really sure you did love me, that evening?

HEMON *(cradles her gently)*: Which evening?

ANTIGONE: Are you quite sure that at the ball when you came to me in my corner, you didn't go to the wrong girl? You're sure that you've never regretted it since, never thought, even deep down, not even once, that it was Ismene you should have asked for?

HEMON: Idiot!

ANTIGONE: You love me, don't you? Do you love me as a woman? Your arms enfolding me aren't lying to me, are they? Your great big hands placed on my back don't lie, nor your smell, nor your good warmth, nor all this great confidence I feel when I put my head on the hollow of your neck?

HEMON: Yes, Antigone, I love you as a woman.

ANTIGONE: I'm dark and thin. Ismene is rosy and golden as a fruit.

HEMON *(murmuring)*: Antigone...

ANTIGONE: Oh! I'm blushing with shame. But this morning I must know. Tell me the truth, please. When you think I will belong to you, do you feel that a great empty space is being hollowed out of you...

HEMON: Yes, Antigone.

ANTIGONE *(breathy, after a time)*: I feel that way. And I would have been very proud to have been your wife, your true wife, on whom you would have placed your hand in the evening, when you were sitting down, without giving it a thought, as upon something belonging to you, *(She has drawn away from him, she has taken another tone.)* There. Now, I am going to tell you just two things more. And when I have said them, you must leave without any question. Even if they seem to you to be extraordinary, even if they hurt you. Swear to me.

HEMON: What else have you to say to me?

ANTIGONE: Swear first that you'll leave without saying anything.

9

ANTIGONE

Without ever looking back. If you love me, swear it.

HEMON *(after a moment)*: I swear it.

ANTIGONE: Thank you. Now then. Yesterday first. You asked me before why I had worn one of Ismene's dresses, this perfume and this lipstick. I was stupid. I wasn't very sure that you really wanted me and I did all that in order to be a little more like other girls, to make you want me.

HEMON: So that was why?

ANTIGONE: Yes. And you laughed and we quarreled and my bad temper got the best of me. I ran away. *(She adds in a lower voice.)* But I had come to you last evening, so that you would make love to me, so that I might become your wife before. *(He draws back, he is about to speak, she cries out.)* You swore to me not to ask why. You swore to me, Hemon! *(She says in a lower voice, humbly.)* Please... *(And she adds, turning away, hard.)* Besides, I am going to tell you. I wanted to be your wife last night because that is how I love you, very strongly, and that—I'm going to hurt you, oh my darling, forgive me!— that never, never can I marry you. *(He remains stupefied, mute: she runs to the window, she cries out.)* Oh Hemon, you swore it! Go away, leave right away without saying anything. If you speak, if you take one step toward me, I'll throw myself out this window. I swear it, Hemon. I swear it to you on the head of the little boy that we have had together in a dream, the little boy that I shall never have. Now go, quickly. You will find out tomorrow. You will find out in a while. *(She ends with such despair that HEMON obeys and goes off.)* Please leave, Hemon. That's all you can still do for me, if you love me.

BILLY LIAR
by Keith Waterhouse and Willis Hall
Billy (19) - Barbara (19)

The Play: Set in a dreary industrial town in the North of England, *Billy Liar* depicts the life of Billy Fisher, an imaginative teenager who is viewed by many in his community as little better than an idle, dishonest liar. But the play is more than a comedy about a boy who tells lies; it is a play that touches the very essence of all who long to escape the complacency of a mundane world. Billy, an undertaker's clerk, creates a world of fantasy far from his lower-middle class background—so much so that at times it is difficult to discern fact from fiction. His family is at a loss to understand him or control his habits; to them he is a hopeless good-for-nothing. Billy becomes engaged to three different girls simultaneously. When one offers him the opportunity to run away in search of a better life, he retreats into his dream world, preferring fantasy to reality.

The Scene: Billy has asked Barbara, his second fiancee, over for a visit—somehow he needs to get her engagement ring back so he can return it to Rita, the girl he first asked to marry him. Billy has some confessions to make, too.

11

BILLY LIAR

[BILLY: Barbara, I'm glad you asked me that question. About my sister.]

[BARBARA: What is it?]

[BILLY: Sit down, darling. *(BARBARA sits on the couch.)* Darling, are you still coming to tea this afternoon?]

BARBARA: What is it?

BILLY: Sit down, darling. *(BARBARA sits on the couch.)* Darling, are you still coming to tea this afternoon?

BARBARA: Of course.

BILLY: Because there are some things I want to tell you.

BARBARA: What things, Billy?

BILLY: You know what you said the other night—about loving me? Even if I were a criminal.

BARBARA: Well?

BILLY: You said you'd still love me even if I'd murdered your mother.

BARBARA: *(Suspiciously.)* Well?

BILLY: I wonder if you'll still love me when you hear what I've got to say. You see—well, you know that I've got a fairly vivid imagination, don't you?

BARBARA: Well, you have to have if you're going to be a script-writer, don't you?

BILLY: Well, being a script-writer, I'm perhaps—at times—a bit inclined to let my imagination run away with me. As you know. *(BARBARA is even more aloof than usual.)* You see, the thing is, if we're going to have our life together—and that cottage—and little Billy and little Barbara and the lily pond and all that... Well, there's some things we've got to get cleared up.

BARBARA: What things?

BILLY: Some of the things I'm afraid I've been telling you.

BARBARA: Do you mean you've been telling me lies?

BILLY: Well not lies exactly... But I suppose I've been, well, exaggerating some things. Being a script-writer... For instance, there's that business about my father. Him being a sea captain. On a petrol tanker.

12

BILLY LIAR

BARBARA: You mean he's not on a petrol tanker?

BILLY: He's not even in the navy.

BARBARA: Well, what is he?

BILLY: He's in the removal business.

BARBARA: And what about him being a prisoner-of-war? And that tunnel? And the medal? Don't say that was all lies?

BILLY: Yes. *(BARBARA turns away abruptyly.)* Are you cross?

BARBARA: No—not cross. Just disappointed. It sounds as though you were ashamed of your father.

BILLY: I'm not ashamed. I'm not—I'm not!

BARBARA: Otherwise why say he was a prisoner-of-war? What was he?

BILLY: A conscientious ob... *(He checks himself.)* He wasn't anything. He wasn't fit. He has trouble with his knee.

BARBARA: The knee he's supposed to have been shot in, I suppose.

BILLY: Yes. Another thing, we haven't got a budgie, or a cat. And I didn't make the furniture... Not all of it, anyway.

BARBARA: How may other lies have you been telling me?

BILLY: My sister.

BARBARA: Don't tell me you haven't got a sister.

BILLY: I did have. But she's dead. If you're still coming for your tea this afternoon they never talk about her. *(BARBARA remains silent, her head still turned away.)* You remind me of her... If you're not coming, I'll understand... I'm just not good enough for you, Barbara... If you want to give me the engagement ring back—I'll understand.

BARBARA: *(Turning towards him.)* Don't be cross with yourself, Billy. I forgive you.

BILLY: *(Moving to kiss her.)* Darling...

BARBARA: *(Moving away.)* But promise me one thing.

BILLY: That I'll never lie to your again? *(BARBARA nods.)* I'll never lie to you again. Never, I promise... Darling, there is one thing. I have got a grannie.

BARBARA: I believe you.

BILLY: Only she's not blind. She's not very well, though. She's upstairs. Sleeping. She might have to have her leg off.

BILLY LIAR

BARBARA: *(Kissing him.)* Poor darling.

BILLY: *(Moving quickly towards the cocktail cabinet.)* Would you like a drink?

BARBARA: Not now, pet.

BILLY: *(Opening the cabinet.)* Port. To celebrate.

BARBARA: All right. Well, just a tiny one.

BILLY: I'm turning over a new leaf. *(Unnoticed to BARBARA he pours the drinks and taking a tablet from the "passion pill" bottle, places it in her glass. He crosses with the glasses and sits beside her on the couch.)* That's yours, darling.

BARBARA: *(Sitting on the edge of the couch she sips the port.)* Let's talk about something nice.

BILLY: Let's talk about our cottage.

BARBARA: Oh, I've seen the most marvellous material to make curtains for the living-room. Honestly, you'll love it. It's a sort of turquoise with lovely little squiggles like wine-glasses.

BILLY: Will it go with the yellow carpet?

BARBARA: No, but it will go with the grey rugs.

BILLY: *(Taking her in his arms.)* I love you, darling.

BARBARA: *(Moving away.)* I love you.

BILLY: Do you? Really and truly?

BARBARA: Of course I do.

BILLY: Are you looking forward to getting married?

(BARBARA takes an orange from her handbag and peels it and eats it during the following dialogue.)

BARBARA: I think about it every minute of the day.

BILLY: Darling... *(He again attempts unsuccessfully to kiss her.)* Don't ever fall in love with anybody else.

BARBARA: Let's talk about our cottage.

BILLY: *(Simulating a dreamy voice.)* What about our cottage?

BARBARA: About the garden. Tell me about the garden.

BILLY: We'll have a lovely garden. We'll have roses in it and daffodils and a lovely lawn with a swing for little Billy and little Barbara to play on. And we'll have our meals down by the lily pond in summer.

14

BILLY LIAR

BARBARA: Do you think a lily pond is safe? What if the kiddies wandered too near and fell in?

BILLY: We'll build a wall round it. No—no, we won't. We won't have a pond at all. We'll have an old well. An old brick well where we draw the water. We'll make it our wishing well. Do you know what I'll wish?

BARBARA: *(Shaking her head.)* No.

BILLY: Tell me what you'll wish first.

BARBARA: Oh, I'll wish that we'll always be happy. And always love each other. What will you wish?

BILLY: Better not tell you.

BARBARA: Why not, pet?

BILLY: You might be cross.

BARBARA: Why would I be cross?

BILLY: Oh I don't know... You might think me too...well, forward. *(He glances at her face but can see no reaction.)* Barbara...? Do you think it's wrong for people to have—you know, feelings?

BARBARA: Not if they're genuinely in love with each other.

BILLY: Like we are.

BARBARA: *(Uncertainly.)* Yes.

BILLY: Would you think it wrong of me to have—feelings?

BARBARA: *(Briskly and firmly.)* I think we ought to be married first.

BILLY: *(Placing his hand on BARBARA's knee.)* Darling...

BARBARA: Are you feeling all right?

BILLY: Of course, darling. Why?

BARBARA: Look where your hand is.

BILLY: Darling, don't you want me to touch you?

BARBARA: *(Shrugging.)* It seems...indecent, somehow.

BILLY: Are you feeling all right?

BARBARA: Yes, of course.

BILLY: How do you feel?

BARBARA: Contented.

BILLY: You don't feel...you know—restless?

BARBARA: No.

BILLY: Finish your drink.

BARBARA: In a minute. *(She opens her handbag and offers it towards him.)* Have an orange.

(BILLY snatching the bag from her he throws it down and oranges spill out across the floor.)

BILLY: You and your bloody oranges!

BARBARA: *(Remonstratively.)* Billy!... Darling!

BILLY: *(Placing his head on her shoulder.)* I'm sorry, darling. I've had a terrible morning.

BARBARA: Why? What happened?

BILLY: Oh, nothing. The usual. Family and things. Just that I've got a headache.

BARBARA: I'm sorry, pet. You know, you ought to see a doctor.

BILLY: I've seen doctors—specialists—I've seen them all. All they could give me was crêpe bandage. *(BARBARA, unimpressed, licks her fingers.)* You know, my darling, I think you have feelings, too. Deep down.

BARBARA: *(Examining her hands distastefully.)* Oooh, sticky paws!

BILLY: Wipe them on the cushion. *(He rises as a thought strikes him.)* You can go upstairs if you want. Use our bathroom.

BARBARA: Thank you.

BLUE DENIM
by James Leo Herlihy and William Noble
Arthur (15) - Janet (15)

The Play: First produced on Broadway in 1958, *Blue Denim* is a compassionate drama concerning the communication problem between the younger and older generations. The plot centers around Arthur Bartley, son of a retired Army Major, his mother, sister, friend Ernie, and his girl friend, Janet, and concerns the crisis that develops when Arthur finds out that he and Janet are about to become parents. Arthur is scared and alone; he can't turn to his parents for help, they just don't seem to speak the same language. When Arthur and Janet decide that an abortion is the only answer to the problem, Arthur turns to his friend Ernie for advice on how to handle the situation. Ernie advises against such action and urges Arthur to talk to his parents. They boy tries to do so, but is unable to make himself understood; his parents seem unwilling to truly listen. Ultimately, the play depicts the insecurity of youth and the failure of many parents to ever really come to know their children.

The Scene: Arthur and Ernie have been playing cards and generally hanging out in Arthur's basement. When Arthur's girl friend, Janet, appears, Ernie feels like the third man out. Ernie storms out, leaving Arthur and Janet alone.

Special Note: While the issues and concerns of *Blue Denim* remain timely, the language is that of the late 1950's when the play was written. Because of this, the play may be best served when set during that period.

BLUE DENIM

JANET: You sore?

ARTHUR: Naw!

JANET: For breaking up the game, I mean.

ARTHUR: Well, okay then! *Why?*

JANET: I just don't like to see you—the way you act when Ernie's around.

ARTHUR: And how's that?

JANET: Oh—*pretending* so!

ARTHUR: Who's pretending? Ernie and me happen to like a couple of beers and a hand of poker. Why do you have to act like somebody's mother?

JANET: I'm sorry. *(As he does not answer)* I'm sorry, Arthur.

ARTHUR: Why don't you call me Art, like everybody else?

JANET: All right. I'm sorry, Art.

ARTHUR: Forget it.

JANET: *(Searching for a topic)* Want to go down to the drugstore?

ARTHUR: For what?

JANET: I don't know—Coke, soda...

ARTHUR: On top of beer!

JANET: Oh. *(A rather strained pause. JANET joins ARTHUR near the punching bag. She makes him uneasy. He goes to the table, gathers the cards. JANET hits the punching bag with her fist)* Ow!

ARTHUR: Janet. What'd you mean, when you said you wished your father was different? *(As she does not answer)* The way he's so funny about lipstick and stuff? And doesn't like you to date guys?

JANET: I wish I lived downtown with Norma! I'm going to, the minute I graduate!

ARTHUR: What the hell, lots of parents are old-fashioned and raise cain with their kids. 'Specially girls.

JANET: Yes, but *my* father *doesn't* raise cain. He says: "How can you *hurt* me this way? How *can* you?" And then he—cries.

ARTHUR: Cries?

JANET: *(Nodding)* Real tears.

ARTHUR: But your dad's a grown-up man, a college professor!

JANET: I know. And he makes me feel so *sorry* for him. I—

18

(Looking around desperately) Does your radio still work?

ARTHUR: O'course. Why shouldn't it?

JANET: *(Switching it on)* Good. Let's find some real crazy music!

ARTHUR: You won't find anything at that end. *(Dailing for her)* How's this? Not very crazy, though.

(Dance music comes on)

JANET: It's fine—Arthur, dance with me.

ARTHUR: You know I can't!

JANET: It's no big mystery. *(Walking to him, taking charge)* Now—just walk in time to the music! *(After a moment)* It'll never work if you keep on being so stand-offish. Here, like this! *(Walks into his arms. As he draws back)* No, goofy, closer! *(She presses tightly against him. After a moment)* You catching on?

ARTHUR: *(Breathlessly)* Yeah, I—think so. *(Acutely conscious of her)* We—we better stop pretty soon, huh?

JANET: You're doing fine. Everybody's self-conscious at first.

ARTHUR: *(Painfully)* No—I think we better— *(He breaks from her, hurries to the radio and turns it off)*

JANET: What's the matter?

ARTHUR: Nothing. I told you—I'm no good at that stuff.

JANET: You'll never learn if you won't try!

ARTHUR: Too bad Ernie isn't here. He goes to dances all the time. Real ones, downtown.

JANET: I wanted to dance with you, not Ernie.

ARTHUR: I'd give anything if I could be like him.

JANET: Now why?

ARTHUR: He's really got a smooth tongue on him. I admire that. With me things get all twisted up...

JANET: Arthur, what sort of things?

ARTHUR: Things I wonder about— One thing, it bothers me a lot. I tried to tell Mom about it once, but...

JANET: But what?

ARTHUR: Aw, every time my mother looks at me I feel like she's seeing something small and pink and wrapped up in a blanket.

JANET: *(Moving closer to him)* Try telling me, Art.

BLUE DENIM

ARTHUR: See...I've got this feeling I ought to be somebody—special!

JANET: Who doesn't? I want to be a poet, and what's sillier than that?

ARTHUR: Yeah, but you got what it takes. I'm just—ordinary.

JANET: Ordinary! You think I'd hang around with you if I didn't think you were going to be—special?

ARTHUR: You do?

JANET: O'course. That's why you and I can talk.

ARTHUR: I guess we do talk better than most people. All the kids at school—even Ernie...I mean, I figured it out, I don't really *know* anybody at all. Not even my own folks. Does that sound bats?

JANET: Not to *me*!

ARTHUR: Hunh?

JANET: It seems to me the only people who really know each other are—people in love.

ARTHUR: Maybe so.

JANET: Arthur, how d'you suppose it feels to be in love with someone?

ARTHUR: Don't ask me!

JANET: *(Bravely)* Because—because I think *I'm* in love. With you.

ARTHUR: You...! *(Sharply)* Whadd'ya want to kid like that for?

JANET: I'm not!

ARTHUR: You are. And I thought we were talking serious.

JANET: Well, if that's your attitude, I'm sorry I told you! *(JANET starts to leave but ARTHUR'S voice stops her)*

ARTHUR: Janet! Weren't you kidding? *(She turns slowly to face him, shakes her head)* But Lordie, Janet...

JANET: Don't worry about it. At my age it's perfectly natural to have crushes on people.

ARTHUR: Yeah, but—why me?

JANET: Frankly, I don't know. You're not the handsomest boy in the world.

ARTHUR: Thanks!

JANET: You see, I'm very objective about you, Arthur. My mistake was I told you. Norma says never let a boy know you really like him.

BLUE DENIM

ARTHUR: Norma doesn't know everything.

JANET: She knows plenty!

ARTHUR: *(Stunned)* When did you find out? I mean, about me?

JANET: *(Turning to him, excited)* I can tell you the exact second. It was this morning. Remember the English test? I saw you trying to decide whether or not to copy from Billy Robinson's paper... Turning sideways, leaning back... And all you had to do was look over! But you didn't. I started to laugh. At least I thought I was—but I was starting to cry. Now, almost everything you do is funny...and at the same time...*not* funny. *(She turns away)* Well—*say* something!

ARTHUR: I don't know what to say!

JANET: I guess you don't—

(She wanders away from him)

ARTHUR: *(Joining her, taking her arm)* Don't be—mad.

JANET: I'm not mad.

ARTHUR: Yes you are.

JANET: I really made a fool of myself, didn't I?

ARTHUR: No. God no. If you feel like that, and if—

JANET: Norma was right.

ARTHUR: No! *(He kisses her quickly, awkwardly. Then, laughing self-consciously)* Our noses got in the way.

JANET: *(Softly)* Goofy. Like this.

(She tilts her head slightly, kisses him on the lips)

ARTHUR: *(Joking breathlessly)* You seem to know a lot about kissing.

JANET: *(Also breathless and joking)* Enough to keep my nose out of the way. *(They stand holding each other at arm's length, each on the verge of hysteria. Then JANET draws a sharp breath. As though this were a signal, they move suddenly together and cling)* Arthur... *(Into his shoulder)* I bet you like me a lot more than you think you do!

ARTHUR: Maybe—I do. *(She draws back, smiles at him, then self-consciously pushes away and wanders to the table, where she sits)* I feel—funny. Do you?

JANET: Kind of.

(ARTHUR sits at the table)

BLUE DENIM

ARTHUR: Janet. I want to ask you something personal. Only don't get sore.

JANET: I won't.

ARTHUR: Well—a guy's bound to *wonder*!

JANET: *(Pleased)* You're jealous!

ARTHUR: You're crazy!

JANET: Yes you are! Well, you don't have to worry, Arthur.

ARTHUR: You've never?—Not that I'd *blame* you, understand, I'm broad-minded.

JANET: I've thought about it for a long time, though. *(Flaring)* And that's perfectly biologically normal, too! Lots of countries' kids our age are already married and raising families.

ARTHUR: Sure they are.

JANET: *(Quietly)* With me, I always get to a certain point—listening to somebody's line and kissing, and petting—then I get scared or disgusted and... *(A helpless gesture)* Do you think I've got a sex blockade or something?

ARTHUR: O'course not! *(Then treading softly)* You simply didn't love those other guys.

JANET: Arthur. Have you slept with lots of girls?

ARTHUR: Oh, the—the regular amount for a guy fifteen, I guess.

JANET: Is it—was it like you thought it'd be?

ARTHUR: *(After a moment's deliberation)* More or less.

JANET: When it happened, were you in love with those girls?

ARTHUR: Hell, no! *(Explaining)* A man doesn't have to be.

JANET: That's not fair! *(Suddenly)* Art, let's not talk about it any more!

ARTHUR: *(Following)* What's the matter?

JANET: I think if we talk about it, it's going to spoil something.

ARTHUR: Okay, Jan.

JANET: *(Sitting on the cot, frowning, her tone violent)* I wish I was eighteen right this minute and knew all about everything!

ARTHUR: 'F you were, you wouldn't like *me* any more.

JANET: I suppose. *(Looking at him)* That's so hard to believe, though...

22

BLUE DENIM

(They stare at each other for a long moment)

ARTHUR: You're so— *(Unable to find a fine enough word)* Why didn't I know before what you were like?

(They kiss tenderly, then nuzzle, forehead to forehead)

JANET: *(After a moment, softly)* Are your eyes closed?

ARTHUR: Yes.

JANET: I love you, Arthur!

ARTHUR: *(Crooning)* Janet, little Janet, Jan...

JANET: Arthur... Teach me how to love you?... *(He draws back and looks at her, slowly comprehending her meaning)*

ARTHUR: Jan, you don't mean?—

(JANET reaches up, covers his eyes with her hand so that he can't see her face)

JANET: Yes, Arthur. *(Then, to ARTHUR'S mortification and surprise, he starts to cry, knuckles fiercely at his eyes)* Why, dearest... What's the matter?

ARTHUR: *(Sharply)* Nothing! Don't look at me. *(After a moment he draws a long, shuddering breath, wipes his eyes, and tries to smile at her)* Now, why'd I do a crazy thing like that?

JANET: Is it my fault?

ARTHUR: *(Strongly)* No!

JANET: Then what?...

ARTHUR: *(Whispering, panic-stricken, his face averted)* Janet—I don't know about anything!

JANET: What do you mean?

ARTHUR: I made it all up. About other girls.

JANET: *(Tenderly, her voice shaking slightly)* Why, you—you big phoney!

(She breaks into a slight hysterical laugh. After a moment they are laughing together, briefly, softly, with panic underneath. Then ARTHUR'S breath goes out of him in a long sigh. He kisses her, straining his body against hers.)

23

THE CHOPIN PLAYOFFS
by Israel Horovitz
Fern (16) - Irving (16)

The Play: This is play number three in a trilogy by Mr. Horovitz based on stories by Morley Torgov. At the heart of the play is a piano contest between Irving Yanover and Stanley Rosen, two sixteen-year-old boys living in Sault Ste. Marie, Ontario, Canada in 1947. More precisely, the "playoffs" occur between the Rosen and Yanover families for their position in the Jewish community, between the two boys in their private struggles to each win the heart of Fern Phipps, a very Protestant girl (much to the horror of the two very Jewish families), and between Fern and the boys as she attempts to make the right decision and please everyone. The play snaps and crackles with these individual playoffs as the boys battle, the parents battle, the boys battle with the parents, and Fern becomes the ultimate judge on the entire proceedings. Added to the mix of children and parents, Horovitz weaves two brilliant characters: Ardenshensky, an old Jew, and Uncle Goldberg, Irving's old Jewish uncle (both roles played by the same actor). Here the wisdom of age and a sense of the struggle between the old world and the new offers a balance and much fun. As Fern promises her heart to the winner of the playoffs, the play serves almost as a boxing ring (Horovitz even calls for a prizefight bell to ring the transitions between scenes). The play concludes with lessons for everyone. Young and old alike question the decisions made in youth that will effect one's life forever.

The Scene: Fern Phipps has a problem. She is in love with both Irving Yanover and Stanley Rosen. In additon, she is a Protestant girl in love with two Jewish boys. The Yanovers and the Rosens are counseling hard for Irving and Stanley to not see Fern. Each boy, on the other hand, is determined to win Fern's affection. They take every opportunity offered to discredit each other, at times even fist fighting, something at this point in the play Fern has forbidden. In this scene, Fern has been bruised by Stanley's uncaring treatment of her in front of his parents. Irving sees this as an opportunity to get closer to Fern.

Special Note: Mr. Horovitz cautions actors to avoid any stereotypical behavior with the characters in this play. In addition, Yiddish or Eastern European accents - "or stereotypically 'Jewish' intonation" should be avoided.

THE CHOPIN PLAYOFFS

(Fern enters, goes to Irving)
FERN: Do you know how truly insulting this whole thing has been for me?
IRVING: I have an idea...
FERN: You *don't*, Irving! You weren't there! Stanley Rosen actually said to me, "Get out of here before my parents see you!"...
IRVING: Oh, well, Rosen's an animal. We've established this as a fact of life...
FERN: It's all because I'm not Jewish, you know...
IRVING: Oh, God, well, why do you think that, Fern?
FERN: Oh, come on Irving Yanover. You think I'm some kind of dumb dippy? I know about Jewish parents.
IRVING: How?
FERN: You forget who my ultimate best friend is.
IRVING: Rosie Berkowitz talks about it?
FERN: Constantly. I shouldn't be telling you this, but Rosie has a crush on Andrej Ilchak...
IRVING: Yuh, so? The Ilchaks are wonderful, wonderful people...
FERN: Yuh, but Andrej's Urkrainian, and Rosie's mother and father hate Ukrainians...
IRVING: My parents don't. I mean, you can't lump everybody together, you know. All Jews aren't exactly like the Berkowitzes...
FERN: Be careful what you say, Irving...
IRVING: I know she's your ultimate best friend...
FERN: That's not what I was going to say.
IRVING: What were you going to say?
FERN: Mrs. Berkowitz and your mother had a long conversation about me, recently...
(A beat)
IRVING: Let's just drop the whole subject, Fern. You're not going out with my parents. You're going out with me...
FERN: I don't want to drop the whole subject! My parents don't have prejudiced bone in their bodies...
IRVING: Oh, yuh, well, how come you never tell them it's me who's calling, hmmm?

THE CHOPIN PLAYOFFS

FERN: I do so!

IRVING: Come on, will you? You think I'm a dope? You think I can't tell?

FERN: It's my father. He really hates Jews...

IRVING: He does? Oh, God, that's terrible.

FERN: How about *your* father?

IRVING: My father's no problem. It's my mother. You're not the first non-Jewish girl I've loved, you know...

FERN: I know. You told me...

IRVING: My mother tried to get me to promise that I wouldn't go out with you...

FERN: Did you?

IRVING: Promise? Uh uh...

FERN: Did you stand up to her?

IRVING: Sort of. I stood up...

FERN: And?

IRVING: I, uh, ran out...

FERN: Oh, God, this is hard for me to admit out loud. You've got to take this in the right spirit, Irving...

IRVING: Of course I will...

FERN: My father said, "There's never been a Jew in our family, not since the beginning of time..."

IRVING: *(After a long, long, long pause; clench-jawed)* That is the worst thing I have ever heard in my entire life, and I have heard some horrible, horrible, *horrible* things...

FERN: Oh, yuh, well, how do you think I felt when Stanley Rosen shoved me out the door with a blue pin-stripe suitcoat, saying, "Get out of here before my parents see you!"

IRVING: Oh, yuh, well, Rosen, sure, he's brain-damaged...

FERN: Stanley Rosen is not brain-damaged, Irving Yanover! He is my *friend*! It's not him, it's his *parents*, and *my* parents and *your* parents...

IRVING: I guess.

FERN: I *know*...

IRVING: You've talked to Rosen.

THE CHOPIN PLAYOFFS

FERN: He feels awful...

IRVING: He smells pretty bad too...

FERN: What?

IRVING: Just kidding...

FERN: You're *always* kidding!

IRVING: Our parents are wrong. You are a wonderful, wonderful person, Fern and I care for you...

FERN: You are, too, Irving, and I care for you, too...

IRVING: There is absolutely nothing wrong with our going out together!

FERN: Absolutely nothing...

IRVING: Our parents are acting unreasonably...

FERN: Totally... All we're doing is *going out together, right*?

IRVING: And they're acting completely insane! Imagine if we got *married*?

FERN: My father would kill me!

IRVING: My mother would kill *herself*!

FERN: Do you ever really think about us...in the future...together... *married*?

IRVING: Us? I do, Fern. I think about it a lot...

FERN: I just got goose bumps.

IRVING: Me, too...

FERN: I want to be kissed.

IRVING: Yes.

FERN: No arms, no hands...

IRVING: What about lips?

FERN: Lips are fine.

IRVING: Fern. Fernnnn...oh, Fern...

FERN: Irving. Irving...oh, Irvingggg...

(Irving and Fern kiss a long, passionate kiss—no hands, no arms, of course. We hear: Chopin, being played by a piano, on tape.)

LA DISPUTE
by Pierre Carlet de Chamblain de Marivaux
translated by Timberlake Wertenbaker
Egle (18) - Azor (18)

The Play: Marivaux has long been considered the fourth most popular playwright at the *Comédie-Française* (after Moliere, Corneille, and Racine). In a recent volume, playwright Timberlake Wertenbaker has made available an exciting English translation of Marivaux's enchanting *La Dispute*. The "dispute" is over whether it was man or woman who was the first to be unfaithful in love. Some eighteen years ago this dispute took place at the court of the King, a man of science who decided to recreate an environment that would be like the beginning of the world when man and woman first encountered each other. The experiment consisted of selecting four new born babies (two girls and two boys), placing them in four separate homes in the forest, with each raised by guardians Mesrou and his sister Carise (both black, unlike the four babies). This very day is the first opportunity each of the four children, now eighteen, are permitted out of their respective environments thus allowing the FIRST meeting to take place between man and woman. The play first introduces each boy to each girl, provides encounters between the two girls, then the two boys, and ultimately all four together. What begins as a delightful discovery, soon turns to selfishness and jealousy. In the end, *La Dispute* remains unresolved.

The Scene: Egle is thrilled to be out to discover the wonders beyond the confines of the estate she's lived on for eighteen years. She has been left here alone by Carise. Azor, experiencing similar reactions to this new world, has been left here alone by Mesrou. Here is the very first boy-girl encounter in the play. Step one of the experiment begins with this scene, the fourth scene of twenty that make up the play.

Special Note: The editors have selected this scene for advanced students and encourage in-depth examination into period and style.

LA DISPUTE

(Egle is alone for a moment, then Azor appears, facing her.)

EGLE: I'm so beautiful I'll never tire of looking at myself. *(She sees Azor.) (Frightened)* Oh. What's this? Another person just like me. No, no, don't come any closer. *(To herself.)* The person laughs. The person seems to be admiring me. *(To Azor.)* Wait, please. Don't move. *(To herself.)* And yet, the person looks at me with such a gentle expression. *(To Azor.)* Can you speak?

AZOR: Yes. It was the pleasure of seeing you that had made me speechless.

EGLE: The person hears me and answers me in a very pleasant manner.

AZOR: You enchant me.

EGLE: Good.

AZOR: You delight me.

EGLE: I like you too.

AZOR: Why then do you forbid me to come any closer?

EGLE: I'm no longer forbidding you with as much conviction as before.

AZOR: Then I'll come closer.

EGLE: Yes, I would enjoy that. No, wait. I'm so agitated.

AZOR: I obey you because I'm yours.

EGLE: The person obeys me! Well then, come a little closer. You can't really be mine if you stay so far away. Ah, yes. It's you. *(To herself.)* The person's very well put together. Do you know, you're almost as beautiful as I am.

AZOR: Being so close to you is making me die of happiness. I want to give myself to you. I don't know what I feel, I don't know how to say it.

EGLE: That's how I feel.

AZOR: I'm happy. I'm fainting.

EGLE: I'm sighing.

AZOR: It doesn't matter how close I am to you, I still can't see enough of you.

EGLE: That's what I think too. But I don't know how we can see more of each other. It's impossible for us to be any closer.

29

LA DISPUTE

AZOR: My heart wants your hands.

EGLE: Here: take my hands. My heart gives them to you. Are you any happier now?

AZOR: Yes, but not more at peace.

EGLE: Nor am I, we're alike in all things.

AZOR: Oh, no, there's such a difference between us. The whole of me can't even compare with your eyes. They're so soft.

EGLE: But yours are lively.

AZOR: You're so pretty, so delicate.

EGLE: Yes, but I assure you it wouldn't suit you to be as pretty as I am. I wouldn't want you to be any different from the way you are. It's another kind of perfection. I don't deny mine, but you must keep yours.

AZOR: I won't change then.

EGLE: Ah, tell me, where were you before I knew you?

AZOR: In a world of my own. But I won't ever go back there since you don't live there and I want to have your hands with me forever. I can no longer manage without them, nor can my mouth deprive itself of kissing them.

EGLE: And my hands can no longer be deprived of the kisses of your mouth. Shh. I hear a noise. These must be the people from my world. Hide behind this tree or they'll be frightened. I'll call you.

AZOR: But I can't see you from behind that tree.

EGLE: All you need do is look into that water. My face is there, you'll see it.

DOES A TIGER WEAR A NECKTIE?
by Don Petersen
Linda (18) - Conrad (20)

The Play: Set in a rehabilitation center for juvenile narcotic addicts, *Does a Tiger Wear a Necktie?* presents a powerful, compassionate, and sometimes humorous slice of the lives of a group of troubled young people and the teachers who attempt to help them. Among the many characters at the center are Mr. Winters, a patient English teacher; Dr. Werner, a gentle but persistent psychiatrist; Bickham, a cocky, pugnacious youth who has little chance of being released (he tracked down his wayward father and beat him bloody); Linda, a young black prostitute; and Conrad, a shy but earnest young black man who appears to be the only one in the group who has any hope of rehabilitation and release. Numerous excellent supporting and smaller roles add texture and depth to this absorbing, dramatic work, which featured Hal Holbrook as Winters and Al Pacino as Bickham (Tony Award) in the original Broadway production.

The Scene: Linda and Conrad have just made love in Mr. Winter's classroom, where they put together a makeshift bed of newspapers, a blanket, and a pillow. Linda has been telling Conrad how he reminds her of a trick she once turned—a trick who liked to talk afterwards.

DOES A TIGER WEAR A NECKTIE?

CONRAD: You're some baby, aren't you?

LINDA: You bet your sweet, I am.

CONRAD: How much was you shootin' then?

LINDA: Oh, I don't know—about 30 bucks a day.

CONRAD: How long you been shootin'?

LINDA: Four years I been strung out. Four years next month. I started three days after my fourteenth birthday.

CONRAD: You ever think you could make it? Kick it, I mean.

LINDA: Are you kiddin'. I'm eighteen years old.

CONRAD: What's that got to do with it? Some people make it.

LINDA: Come off it! Who's been feedin' you?... Some silly-ass psychiatrist out here?

CONRAD: Nobody's feedin' me nothing', but I was talking' with Doctor Werner the...

LINDA: *(Disgustedly)* Werner? You takin' therapy from *him*?

CONRAD: *(Defensively)* Yeah. What about it?

LINDA: Look, I had Werner last time I was here. Did you ever really *look* at that cat?

CONRAD: Sure. Why?

LINDA: Dig it! How's he gonna help you?

CONRAD: Don't kid yourself, girl. That old boy is pretty hip. That man's *educated*! He told me, if I could just start *living* with myself, facin'-up to life.

LINDA: *(Laughs sarcastically)* Yeah? I heard that song. Face up to your childhood...your past...all that jazz. I went through that routine with Werner last year. I opened up for that lip-lickin' creep. I told him everythin' I know. Did it do me any good? Well, you see me here, don't ya? Look, man, talk about *facin'*! Well, then, face it! You're a junkie...no past, no present, no future.

CONRAD: *(Earnestlty)* But I ain't gonna be no junkie *all* my life. I'm gettin' discharged real quick now. Maybe I'll make it...maybe I won't, but one of these days I'm gonna quit.

LINDA: Yeah, me too! I'm gonna stop shootin' and whorin' and lay back in a neat little crib and watch "Life Can Be Beautiful" on the television.

DOES A TIGER WEAR A NECKTIE?

CONRAD: Don't knock it, honey. You wouldn't mind that.

LINDA: *(Starts to get up. He stops her.)* Squash it, man! I'm goin'.

CONRAD: You wouldn't mind settlin' down in that apartment, would you? You wouldn't mind living like real people in the real world. Havin' nice clothes and a place to sleep, and a little car to go ridin' around with on Sunday afternoon. You wouldn't mind holing up with one guy for a change. You wouldn't mind none of those things... neither would I. I'm a junkie all right, but at least I don't lie about it.

LINDA: I'm not lyin'. You're the liar. You're lying to yourself. You ain't gonna kick the habit and neither am I. We *had* it. We had it the day we was born.

CONRAD: If I really believed that, I'd cut my throat right now.

LINDA: Got a knife? Give it to me. I'll cut it for you... Might just as well save you the trouble. Listen, you creep, you chump, we had "junkie" stamped across our ass the day we was shoved from our old lady's guts.

CONRAD: Oh, yeah? Lotsa people start off that way but...

LINDA: *(Interrupts.)* When I was born, my mama didn't even have a bed for me. You know where I slept? I slept in a waste basket layin' on its side stuffed with newspapers. That's right, trash-basket stuffed with trash.

CONRAD: You wanna go on layin' there? Is that what you want? Layin' in that trash?

LINDA: *(Rises. Ignores him.)* When I was five years old, my old man ran out on my old lady and left her with me and my three brothers. When I was ten, my mama dumped me in a movie house on 42nd Street, while she went out hustlin'. I used to sit there and let the old perverts feed me popcorn and feel me up. That's right, my mama was on the street, and I was hustlin' for popcorn in the movie houses.

CONRAD: *(Crosses and takes her arm.)* We all got sad stories! Everybody on this island's got a sad story. I know that, don't you think I know that?

LINDA: *(Pulls away.)* No, you don't know! You don't know nothin'! Here! *(She goes to Winters' desk for her wallet.)* Here, take a look at this! *(She flips open her wallet and hands it to Conrad.)* That's my

33

mama! She died when I was twelve. They said it was syph! Syphilis my mama died of...that's what the doctor said. *(She grabs the wallet and points at the picture.)* Sheeeeit! *(She throws the wallet on the floor.)* Let me tell you somethin'. My mama was just plain worn out...that's what *she* died of. At 28 she looked 45...and she didn't have a trick left in her. *(Moves away from him.)* And, when she pulled stakes and left me all alone at 12 years old, it was one lousy relative after another. They didn't want me, and I didn't want them. So...so, you creep, when I took my first shot at 14...when I first took off at that grand old age of 14...it was the nicest...it was the wonderfullest thing that ever happened to me. *(Whirls on him.)* You talk about *real*. When I climbed aboard that horse...that beautiful white horse, I *became* real. Real for the first time in my cruddy, stinkin' life.

CONRAD: *(Goes to her and takes her by the shoulders.)* Look, girl, I'm sorry for your life...I really am, but I have to tell you you're lyin'. No junkie is *real*! No junkie, you hear me?!

LINDA: *(She breaks free with one arm and swings at him.)* You bastard! You dirty bastard...let go of me! *(He holds her by her shoulders, as she pounds on his chest.)*

CONRAD: That's right...you fight, but you're still lyin'! I'm sorry I got you all worked up. I'm a little scared, see, and I guess I took it out on you.

LINDA: *(She turns to him.)* What are ya scared of?

CONRAD: Leavin' here, I guess. Look, I know you don't think it's possible, but I really wanna make it this time. I really do.

LINDA: *(Softened by his candor.)* I didn't say it was *im*-possible. I said... *(Nervously.)* I said... aw, forget it. I'm going'...you stay here.

CONRAD: *(He takes her in his arms. She turns her head away.)* Linda. Linda, honey, I...I... Lookee, here, I like you an awful lot.

LINDA: *(Softly.)* Come on, let loose. I gotta go.

CONRAD: No, listen. Couldn't we...that is, I'm only gonna be here for a little while and...well, couldn't we be friends?

LINDA: *(She pulls loose and faces away from him.)* No. I don't want no friends. I don't need any, and I don't want none.

CONRAD: *(Pleadingly.)* Maybe you don't...but *I* do.

LINDA: *(She turns on him.)* Look, boy...I can't help you...and you can't help me. Nobody can help nobody! So what's the use? *(She moves toward the door.)*

CONRAD: Please...just tomorrow night. *(She stops.)* Just once more.

LINDA: *(Facing the door.)* No.

CONRAD: *(He goes to her, takes her shoulders in his hands and tries to kiss her neck.)* Please. Just once. You'd do that for *anybody*, wouldn't ya?

LINDA: *(She whirls around and pushes him away from her. She has tears in her eyes.)* No! I don't want to! You dig it?! I don't want to get used to *you* or anything else. You understand me?!

CONRAD: *(He stares at her for a moment. Then:)* Yeah. Yeah, I understand. *(She opens the door.)* Just a minute...you forgot something. *(He goes to his coat on Winters' desk and takes out a carton of cigarettes.)*

LINDA: What?

CONRAD: *(Holds out the carton.)* Here, you forgot your cigarettes... one carton for one trick.

LINDA: *(Angrily, with tears in her eyes.)* *You* keep 'em! The trick was on the house. I don't want your *cigarettes*...or *nothing else* you got! *(She runs out of the classroom, goes down the hall and exits R. Conrad stands shirtless, facing the door.)*

IN A NORTHERN LANDSCAPE
by Timothy Mason
Emma (16) - Thorson (19)

The Play: The northern landscape of the title in Timothy Mason's haunting memory play is a farming community in Minnesota in the late 1920's. The story concerns the love between a brother and sister and the shocking, untimely consequenses that result. Samuel and Emma are the children of Matthew and Charlotte Bredahl. Mr. Bredahl teaches Philosophy at the local college, the same college that Samuel attends. The mother is devoted to her family, her poetry, and is guided and comforted by the Bible, which she quotes from generously. Samuel and Emma's life is like the landscape, bleak and isolated. The inability to find connections with any of their contemporaries drives them closer together as the story is told in flashback. We first see Samuel's horrific fate at the jaws of a pack of wild dogs, then the charred remains of the family home, a chilling metaphor for the shell of the family that is left after Samuel's death. The play crosses back and forth between time over a two-year period to reconstruct the events that led to such an end. But the story is never a simple matter of "what went wrong," or "who was right." Throughout the play we struggle to understand the complexities of the Bredahl family, which is not unlike any family. The philosophy that drives the father is no more reassuring to Samuel and Emma than the words offered in the mother's Bible lessons. What seems to Emma and Samuel as pure and right and constant is the love they share. The chemistry between the siblings ignites a passion in them which destroys them before they can understand it. It is this twist of fate and honesty that brings the condemnation of the community and ultimately leads to Samuel's death and the collapse of the family. When it is over, the townspeople are forgiving, the evil has stopped, but what remains can never be the life Emma, Charlotte, or Matthew would have wanted. In the end, we are left to question the strength of our own convictions, if not the very texture of our lives.

The Scene: Emma's rabbit has recently been killed by wild dogs. Anders Thorson, a college student in Mr. Bredahl's class, has just come in from burying the rabbit. It is obvious that Thorson is interested in Emma. It is perhaps not so obvious, but never-the-less true, that Emma is not interested in him.

IN A NORTHERN LANDSCAPE

(The lights become cold and angular. After a moment, Anders Thorson, dressed in a heavy winter overcoat and wearing a fur cap with earflaps, backs hurriedly out of the kitchen door. He obviously has just recently come indoors, and is still showing signs of the cold.)

THORSON: *(Shouting through the kitchen door.)* I'm sorry, Emma. I didn't mean to track up your kitchen. I'll...I'll take them off out on the porch. *(He exits out the screen door and returns a few moments later without his heavy boots. Alone in the room, he seems ill at ease, as well as cold. Eventually he moves to the closed kitchen door and talks through it.)* The earth was like flint. Well, hard as rock, anyway. I had to chip away at it for almost an hour, even to dig such a shallow grave as that one was. *(Emma enters from the kitchen, wearing an apron. Her hands are covered with flour and bits of dough, which she is wiping off with a cloth.)* I didn't get more than a foot down, I'm afraid—I just couldn't manage any more—but anyway they should be safe from the dogs now.

EMMA: I appreciate it, Anders.

THORSON: It's strange, having such a hard frost so early in December. They're not burying *anyone*, you know. Not for months to come. They send 'em to the big ice house in Dundas, to wait for the thaw. Up in the loft they are, I've seen 'em. It's strange. The earth just isn't ready for them, so there they are in a row, covered up with stiff white sheets, just waiting. And that row just keeps getting longer. People got to be strong out here, but they just aren't strong enough, it seems. I don't like what's happening, two hangings in two months, and that old woman from Faribault who set herself on fire, it's unnatural. My brother told me about one of them, one of those that hanged herself—she was just a little girl, Emma, fifteen years old maybe, and my brother said that when they found her in the barn, they could tell that the rope had broke twice. Two times it broke and three times she strung it up agian, the rope getting shorter and shorter, but the third time it worked. That bread sure smells good.

EMMA: She must not have had anything to live for... What a terrible thing, not to have anything to live for. Oh, if only I could have sat beside her, and held her, and talked away the darkness from her eyes. Only fifteen. Just a child, really.

THORSON: And it's not just your rabbits. Already they're calling it

37

IN A NORTHERN LANDSCAPE

an epidemic. Some disease killing off all the rabbits, and those that do live—you don't dare eat their meat. I mean, not that *you* would, but lots of people keep 'em for their meat, live off of them in the winter, but now nobody dares. It's strange. I'm sorry about your rabbits, Amma.

EMMA: I'm not. Oh, of course, I'm *sad*—very sad to lose those sweet quiet things. But I know they're in heaven now.

THORSON: Rabbits?

EMMA: Of course, Anders. What more perfect creatures for heaven than those soft, silent, gentle beasts. Don't laugh, now, Mr. Thorson, I mean it. Not a sound they make. And they always look to me so ancient—like some creature that is from some other age, and with some other wisdom than ours... I think you *are* smiling at me, thinking I'm foolish, aren't you?

THORSON: I am in love with you, Emma.

EMMA: *(After a beat, stern.)* Hush.

THORSON: What? I'm leaving school at the end of this semester, Emma. It's not the place for me, I know that now. I used to resent it... I used to resent your father *and* Sam, I thought they were just acting superior. Well, they *were* superior, it seemed. *(Brief, nervous laugh.)* Not just in their minds, but everything about them, I always felt so clumsy when I was with them, they made me feel like a fool, like a big clumsy dull witted giant, but I'm not all that big, I know that now. I'm just average, but whenever I'm With Sam he makes me feel huge and ugly and slow. Like some big side of beef, you know? And I hated it, I almost hated him for that, *and* your father. Like when I would laugh and your father would look at me the way he does, looking out at me from under those eyebrows, not moving a muscle. Just looking. It would make me go all red...and then...very, very cold. Like I just wanted to wait for the day when *I* could look at *him* like that. But not any more, no...no I know now that I'm just as good as they are, no better, no worse, just different from them, that's all. Golly, Sam is so...sort of graceful almost, when he moves. It used to make me sick to watch him with you, compared to him I felt like an oaf, you know? But not now. I'm leaving school at the end of the semester, in January... Your father was right all along, he didn't mean any harm, he was right about me not belonging there. I've already got

IN A NORTHERN LANDSCAPE

a part-time job in sales, and there'll be a full-time sales job with a good salary waiting for me at the end of January, I'll really be making some money, Emma. And I know now that I'm not such a worthless sort as they used to make me feel. I'm all right, don't you think, Emma? They didn't mean any harm, did they? *(Long silence. Emma looking at Thorson.)* Emma?

EMMA: Please don't talk that way.

THORSON: You used to do it to me, too, the same thing. Making me feel... *(Pause.)* I am in love with you.

EMMA: Stop that talk! *(Beat.)* I am very happy for you, Anders, in your plans for the future. The future does not much concern me, but I think that now you have something to live for, and that's really all any of us needs, isn't it? I wish you all of the best.

THORSON: That's not what I'm saying... Don't you care for me, Emma?

EMMA: And now *I* have a job, too—isn't it grand? Whoever would have thought that Emma Bredahl would be a working girl? Mr. Ferguson was sceptical at first, I could tell, but Sam taught me so very well, teaching me everything he knew about the job, so I could take over for him when he returned to college. I may not have a college education—neither of us will, will we, Anders—but we'll both be working, isn't that a nice thought? *(Small pause.)* The future does not much concern me—not nearly so much as now does. But you have found something, I hope, and I have found something... You see, Dilsey didn't have anything to live for after the dogs got to Jack, so it's just as well she and her babies went to heaven. *(Samuel enters from the second-level L. door, and stands unnoticed at the top of the stairs.)*

THORSON: What do you live for, Emma? That job at Ferguson's?

EMMA: *(After a pause.)* It's a secret. *(Thorson sees Samuel standing at the top of the staircase.)*

THORSON: *(After a pause.)* I think maybe this house is too full of secrets. *(Small pause.)* Remember what I told you, Emma. Think about it. *(He backs towards the screen door.)* Please. *(He turns towards the screen door but turns back just as he reaches it. He looks up at Samuel again, and at Emma.)* I left the shovel leaning against the shed.

(Thorson exits.)

39

THE LADY'S NOT FOR BURNING
by Christopher Fry
Richard (19) - Alizon (17)

The Play: A rich, poetic and humorous comedy in verse, Fry's *The Lady's Not For Burning* is a magical fantasy set in 15th-century England. Thomas Mendip, a disillusioned soldier recently discharged from service, arrives in a small village and announces to the Mayor that he has killed a man, Matthew Skipps, and that he demands to be hanged for the offense. The Mayor, Hebble Tyson; Margaret, his sister; Tappercoom, the Judge; and the Chaplain will hear none of it, however; they are more interested in punishing witches—namely Jennet Jourdemayne, a beautiful, enchanting creature whom they believe has turned old Skipps into a dog. Jennet denies the charge; she may speak to her dog in French, but she is not a witch. Nevertheless, the Judge sentences her to death. Thomas comes to her defense: why kill a lovely, guiltless woman who does not want to die, and let go free a guilty man who does want to die? Margaret's sons, Humphrey and Nicholas, don't want to see Jennet die either; they are each vying for her attentions. It is Jennet and Thomas who fall in love, however. Along the way, Humphrey's pure fiancee, Alizon, elopes with the man she really loves—the Mayor's equally pure orphaned clerk, Richard. When old Skipps finally turns up, not dead or bewitched but very drunk, a happy ending is ensured.

The Scene: Thomas has been speaking to Richard of Jennet's charms, when Alizon arrives and professes her love for the young clerk.

Special Note: Try not to fight the graceful rhythms of the verse, which help to communicate the intentions of the characters.

THE LADY'S NOT FOR BURNING

(ALIZON enters quickly, shuts door and the sounds cease.)

ALIZON: *(Just inside door.)* Richard!

RICHARD: Alizon!

ALIZON: I've come to be with you.

RICHARD: Not with me. I'm the to-and-fro-fellow. Tonight. You have to be with Humphrey.

ALIZON: I think I have never met Humphrey. I have met him less and less the more I have seen him.

RICHARD: The crickets are singing well with their legs tonight.

ALIZON: *(Below chair L.)* It sounds as though the night air were riding on a creaking saddle.

RICHARD: You must go back to the others.

ALIZON: Let me stay. I'm not able to love them. Have you forgotten what they mean to do tomorrow?

RICHARD: How could I forget? But there are laws and if someone fails them...

ALIZON: I shall run away from laws if laws can't live in the heart. I shall be gone tomorrow.

RICHARD: *(To her.)* You make the room suddenly cold. Where will you go?

ALIZON: Where will you come to find me?

RICHARD: Look, you've pulled the thread in your sleeve. Is it honest for me to believe you would be unhappy?

ALIZON: When?

RICHARD: If you marry Humphrey?

ALIZON: Humphrey's a winter in my head. But whenever my thoughts are cold and I lay them against Richard's name, they seem to rest on the warm ground where summer sits as golden as a humblebee. So I did very little but think of you until I ran out of the room.

RICHARD: Do you come to me because you can never love the others?

ALIZON: Our father God moved many lives to show you to me. I think that is the way it must have happened. It was complicated, but very kind.

RICHARD: *(Makes slight turn away, then back again.)* If I asked you

41

THE LADY'S NOT FOR BURNING

if you could ever love me, I should know for certain that I was no longer rational.

ALIZON: I love you quite as much as I love St. Anthony, and rather more that I love St. John Chrysostom.

RICHARD: But putting haloes on one side, as a man could you love me, Alizon? *(Kneels on her R.)*

ALIZON: I have become a woman, Richard, because I love you. I know I was a child three hours ago. And yet I love you as deeply as many years could make me, but less deeply than many years will make me.

RICHARD: *(Kisses her.)* I think I may never speak steadily again, what have I done or said to make it possible that you should love me?

ALIZON: Everything I loved before has come to one meeting place in you, and you have gone out into everthing I love.

RICHARD: Happiness seems to be weeping in me, as I suppose it should, being newly born.

ALIZON: We must never leave each other now, or else we should perplex the kindness of God.

RICHARD: The kindness of God itself is not a little perplexing. What do we do?

ALIZON: We cleave to each other, Richard. That is what is proper for us to do.

RICHARD: But you were promised to Humphrey, Alizon. *(Crosses to her L.)* And I'm hardly more than a servant here, tied to my own apron-strings. They'll never let us love each other. *(Turns back to her.)*

ALIZON: Then they will have to outwit all that ever went to create us.

RICHARD: *(Taking her hands in his.)* So they will. I believe it. Let them storm. We're lovers in a deep and safe place and never lonely any more... Alizon, shall we make the future, however much it roars, lie down with our happiness? Are you ready to forego custom and escape with me?

ALIZON: Shall we go now, before anyone prevents us?

RICHARD: *(Moves to U.L. door and back to ALIZON.)* I'll take you to the old priest who first found me. He is as near to being my father as putting his hand into a poor-box could make him. He'll help us. Oh, Alizon, I so love you. *(Kisses her, takes her R. to below door U.R.)* Let yourself quietly out and wait for me somewhere near the gate but in a shadow. I must fetch my savings. Are you afraid?

ALIZON: In some part of me, not all; and while I wait I can have a word with the saints Theresa and Christopher: They may have some suggestions.

RICHARD: Yes, do that. Now: like a mouse. *(Gives her a quick kiss. ALIZON exits U.R. and off. RICHARD goes to the window.)* Only let me spell no disillusion for her, safety, peace, and a good world, as good as she has made it!

LILY DALE
by Horton Foote
Lily (18) - Will (late teens/early 20's)

The Play: *Lily Dale* is the third of nine plays that comprise the Orphans' Home Cycle by one of America's most prolific playwrights, Horton Foote. Mr. Foote is the recipient of two Academy Awards, one for his film *Tender Mercies* and one for the screen adaptation of Harper Lee's *To Kill a Mockingbird*. Set in Texas, Foote's nine-play cycle deals with the life journey of Horace Robedaux beginning in 1902, when at the age of twelve his father dies, to 1928, when his twelve-year-old son (Horace, Jr.) must deal with the death of his maternal grandfather. The characters are rich and the language often poetic but always true to the heart. *Lily Dale* finds Horace in Houston, attempting to reconnect with his mother (now remarried) and his sister (the title character). When Horace arrives he discovers his mother hesitant, his stepfather insensitive and uninterested in including him in the family, and his sister selfish and spoiled. The stepfather in fact early on demands that Horace leave. Horace, however, becomes ill, which delays his departure. As Horace recovers he attempts to reconcile his father's death by learning about him from his mother and sharing with Lily Dale the early experiences of their lives together. These efforts meet with resistance from both mother and sister who prefer to move on with their lives and bury the past. Horace feels compelled to deal first with the unsettled past before he is able to finally become a man. After his recovery, and after forcing a reconciliation with his past and his family, Horace leaves Houston to return to his boyhood home of Harrison. The illness has left his body and his troubled soul.

The Scene: Will Kidder has asked Lily Dale to marry him. Lily has accepted but insists on waiting a year. Although Will has won Lily's hand and the approval of her mother and the strict and conservative stepfather, he is impatient. As the scene begins, Lily is at the piano playing (badly) while Will attempts to distract her with affectionate advances.

Special Note: The editors urge the actors to read the first two plays in Foote's nine-play cycle, *Roots in a Parched Ground* and *Convicts* (*Lily Dale* is number three). These plays provide wonderful background information on the character of Lily Dale and the Robedaux family.

LILY DALE

LILY DALE: Will, behave yourself. Mama and Brother may come in at any moment, not to mention Mr. Davenport. You know he's very old fashioned. He would be furious if he knew Mama had left us alone in the house unchaperoned. Now you go over there and sit down and behave yourself. *(He doesn't move. Lily Dale stands up.)* Will...

WILL: I'm not leaving your side until you promise to marry me.

LILY DALE: I promised to marry you, a year from now.

WILL: *(Stands and comes towards her. Lily Dale backs up.)* I don't want to wait a year.

LILY DALE: You told Mama you would. That was our agreement when we beame engaged. *(A pause.)* Why are you going back on your word? Why are you doing that to me? And stop looking at me that way. You are making me very nervous. Now go sit down in that chair over there *(She points to the slipper chair D. of the piano.)* or I'm leaving here and I'm going to find Brother and Mother and tell them I won't stay here alone with you because you have not behaved like a gentleman.

WILL: *(Takes another step towards her, she stops him by pointing at the chair. Will stops, shrugs, laughs and goes to the chair and sits.)* Is this how a gentleman behaves?

LILY DALE: Yes. Thank you. *(She goes back to the piano and begins to play.)*

WILL: Lily Dale?

LILY DALE: *(Stops playing.)* What?

WILL: Something is wrong with you.

LILY DALE: Nothing is wrong with me. Now be quiet and let me practice. *(She plays again.)*

WILL: Lily Dale?

LILY DALE: What?!!!

WILL: Something is troubling you.

LILY DALE: Oh, I don't know, Will. I'm very nervous. I think it's Brother's being here. He's been so sensitive and touchy. And it's not easy, four of us living on this one floor. Mr. Davenport has been so silent and morose, too, not his usual jolly self, and poor Mama, she's just torn into little pieces trying to make peace between us all.

45

LILY DALE

WILL: It will soon be over. He's leaving tomorrow.

LILY DALE: I must say it will be a relief to have the house back to ourselves. Brother just doesn't fit in. We all try. I do, Mama does, Mr. Davenport and Brother, too, but he just doesn't fit in. Now you fit in. Isn't that funny? You're here five minutes and you cheer everybody up, and Mr. Davenport begins to talk like a normal human being, but once you leave we're silent and gloomy and unhappy. *(A pause.)* I had this dream about Brother again last night. I dreamt he was dead and this time I didn't cry. I said a terrible thing. I said, "It's about time." And Mama said, "We'll bury him in our family plot here in Houston." And I said, "No, we won't. I'll not have him buried with you and Mr. Davenport and me. I want him buried with his father where he belongs." Wasn't that terrible for a sister to have a dream like that about her brother?

WILL: You probably ate something that didn't agree with you for supper.

LILY DALE: No, I didn't. I'm always having terrible dreams. I dreamt once last week that I was a very old woman and I was a famous concert pianist and I had come to Houston to give a concert and before the concert, I looked out through the curtain into audience and I called and I said, "Is Will Kidder there?" "No," they said. "He is dead." "What did he die of?" I asked. "A broken heart," they said.

WILL: Shoot... don't worry about that dream. I'm not ever going to die of a broken heart.

LILY DALE: Will...

WILL: What?

LILY DALE: Look the other way. I want to tell you something.

WILL: Where shall I look?

LILY DALE: Anywhere away from me. *(He does so.)* I don't want to get married.

WILL: *(He looks at her, she turns away.)* Why?

LILY DALE: Don't look at me, please.

WILL: *(Turning away, again.)* Why?

LILY DALE: Because you're going to hurt me if we do.

WILL: How am I going to hurt you?

46

LILY DALE

LILY DALE: You know.

WILL: Oh. *(A pause.)* Why do you think I will hurt you? Who told you I would?

LILY DALE: Sissy Douglas.

WILL: She's a fool.

LILY DALE: I asked Mama about it, too.

WILL: What did she say?

LILY DALE: She didn't want to talk about it. *(A pause.)* She said Papa didn't hurt her, but some women told her they were hurt by their husbands.

WILL: *(He goes to her and touches her gently.)* I'm not going to hurt you.

LILY DALE: How do you know?

WILL: I just do. *(She cries. He holds her.)* Lily, what's the matter?

LILY DALE: I'm scared. I want to marry you, but I'm scared.

WILL: Now I told you...

LILY DALE: I'm scared that I'll have a baby. I know that hurts when you do and I'll die while I'm having the baby. Mama say it's the worst pain in the world. She said she prayed to die the whole time she was having her children.

WILL: Don't you want to have children?

LILY DALE: I do, but I'm scared to, Will. I'm scared of the terrible pain, and I might die and...

WILL: We don't have to have them then.

LILY DALE: You mean you can get married and not have children? *(She pulls away and looks at him.)*

WILL: Yes.

LILY DALE: How?

WILL: There are ways. Pete and your mama are married, have been for ten years now, and they have no children.

LILY DALE: Pete and Mama? Oh, my God, Will! What are you saying? Are you saying that Pete and Mama...!?

WILL: Honey, they're married.

LILY DALE: But they're too old, Will.

WILL: No, they're not. Your mama is only 38. She could still have

47

LILY DALE

a child, if she wanted to.

LILY DALE: My God Almighty, Will!! *(She goes to couch, begins to cry again.)* I wish you wouldn't tell me things like that. God knows what kind of terrible dreams I'll start having now.

WILL: Honey, I only told you so you could understand that married people don't always have to have children if they don't want to. *(He sits with her.)*

LILY DALE: I don't want to, I mean, I want to, but I'm scared to.

WILL: Then we'll never have them.

LILY DALE: Do you promise?

WILL: I promise. Does that make you happy?

LILY DALE: Yes, it does. It certainly does. *(She hugs him.)* You are so sweet. You are the sweetest person in this whole world.

WILL: *(Returning hug.)* You're mighty sweet yourself. *(They hug for a few moments. Lily giggles as Will puts his hand on her leg. She pushes it away. More hugs and giggles.)*

LOVERS (WINNERS)
by Brian Friel
Joe (17) - Maggie (17)

The Play: *Lovers* consists of two one-act plays: *Winners* and *Losers*. *Winners* is about a young Irish couple on an afternoon just before final examinations. Joe is trying to study, but Maggie keeps distracting him, and their talk soon turns to the future and their imminent marriage. Maggie is pregnant, perhaps only a month. Two rather dispassionate narrators sit at the side of the stage and offer commentary on the lives of the lovers. Before long it becomes clear that the couple will be killed in an accident by the end of the day. Yet the couple are "winners," for we learn much about life and love through them. *Losers*, the companion piece, is about a pair of much older lovers.

The Scene: Joe has been studying for his final examinations while he waits for his girlfriend, Maggie. Joe is an excellent student although not brilliant; he is hard working and industrious. Maggie, while intelligent, is no scholar; she is scattered. They are in love and are to be married in two weeks' time.

Special Note: Focus attention on developing the character relationship rather than trying to master an Irish dialect, which is not necessary to the scene.

LOVERS (WINNERS)

(JOE glances up from his work and scans the land below him. No sign of MAGGIE. He returns to his book. Now MAGGIE creeps up behind him and pounces on his back, trying to push him to the edge of the hill so that he will roll down. They wrestle for a few seconds.)

JOE: Come on! Cut it out, will you! That'll do!

MAG: Ha! You leaped like a rabbit!

JOE: I was looking for you. Where were you?

MAG: Waiting for you. You're late.

JOE: I was here at ten exactly.

MAG: I've been here for at least half an hour.

(She throws herself on the ground in exaggerated exhaustion, produces cigarettes, and begins talking. During most of this episode JOE is studying, or trying to study. But occasionally he tunes in to her prattle. By throwing in an occasional word he gives her the impression he is conversing with her.)

JOE: Did you walk it?

MAG: The bike's lying at the foot of the hill.

JOE: I didn't see it.

MAG: Sure you're half blind! God, my tongue's hanging out for a reek after that! *(Inhales and exhales with satisfaction.)* Aaaah, bliss! Sister Pascal says: You may search the lists of the canonized but you will search in vain for the saint that smoked. Maybe you'll be a saint, Joe.

JOE: Let's get started.

MAG: I read in a book that there are one million two hundred thousand nuns in the world. Isn't that fierce? Imagine if they were all gathered in one place—on an island, say—and the Chinese navy was let loose at them—cripes, you'd hear the squeals in Tobermore! I have a wicked mind, too. D'you ever think things like that, Joe? I'm sure you don't. I think that women have far more corrupt minds than men, but I think that men are more easily corrupted than women.

JOE: We'll get a couple of hours done before we eat.

MAG: *(With excessive disgust)* Food!—I don't care if I never see another bite ever again. My God, I thought I was going to vomit my guts out this morning! And this could keep up for the next seven months, according to Doctor Watson. The only consolation is that *you're* all right. It would be wild altogether if you were at it too. Sympathetic sickness, they call it. But it's only husbands get it. Maybe you'll get it this day three weeks—the minute we get married—God wouldn't that be a scream! D'you know what Joan O'Hara told me? That all the time her mother was expecting Oliver Plunket, her father never lifted his head out of the kitchen sink. Isn't it crazy! And for the last three days he lay squealing on the floor like a stuck pig and her mother had to get the police for him in the end. I love this view of Ballymore: the town and the fields and the lake; and the people. When I'm up here and look down on them, I want to run down and hug them all and kiss them. But then when I'm down among them I feel like doing that *(she cocks a snook into JOE'S face)* into their faces. I bet you that's how God feels at times, too. Wouldn't you think so?

JOE: I don't know how God feels.

MAG: Why not?

JOE: Because I'm not God.

MAG: Oh, you're so clever! Well, I'll tell you something: there are occasions in my life when *I* know how God feels.

JOE: Good for you.

MAG: And one of those occasions is now. *(Puffing her cigarette regally.)* At this moment God feels...expansive...and beneficent...and philanthropy.

JOE: Philanthropic.

MAG: *(After momentary setback)* And we will not be put into bad humor by grubby little pedants.

JOE: Look, Mag: we came up here to study. What are you going to do first?

MAG: French. And then maths. And then Spanish. And then English language and literature. And after lunch geography and the history of the world. I have planned a program for myself. The important thing about revising for an examination is to have a method. What are you starting with?

JOE: Maths.

MAG: Then what?

LOVERS (WINNERS)

JOE: That's all.

MAG: Only maths?

JOE: Huh-huh.

(She considers this absurd idea for a second. Then, because JOE is wiser in these things than she, she readily agrees with him.)

MAG: Then that's what I'll do too. *(Really worried)* My God, if the volume of a cone doesn't come up, I'm scootrified! Not that I care—I can afford to go down in one subject. *(Pause.)* Joe...

JOE: What?

MAG: What's the *real* difference between language and literature?

JOE: You're not serious, Maggie?!

MAG: Don't—don't—don't tell me... I remember now... One is talking and the other is...books!

JOE: Talking...?

MAG: That's it.

JOE: That's no definition! Language is—

MAG: Don't say another word. I have it in my head. But if you start lecturing, I'll lose it again. I have my own way of remembering things. Joe, last night again Papa asked me to let him get the flat painted for us before we move in.

JOE: *(Doggedly)* I said I'll paint the flat.

MAG: That's what I told him. And I was thinking, Joe...

JOE: What?

MAG: If we put a lace curtain across the kitchen window, we wouldn't actually *see* down into the slaughterhouse yard.

JOE: And if we wore earplugs all the time, we wouldn't actually *hear* the mooing and the shooting!

MAG: *(Softly to herself)* And even if a curtain did make the room darker, it'll still be lovely.

JOE: I signed the lease yesterday evening.

MAG: *(Absolutely thrilled)* It's ours now? We own it?

JOE: Old Kerrigan was so busy working he wouldn't take time off to go into the office; so we put the document on the back of a cow that was about to be shot and that's where we signed it. Cockeyed old miser!

52

LOVERS (WINNERS)

MAG: He's not!

JOE: What?

MAG: Cockeyed.

JOE: I'm telling you. And crazy, too. In a big rubber apron and him dripping with blood. And cows and sheep and bullocks dropping dead all around him.

MAG: Oh God, my stomach!

(JOE realizes that his tale is successful. He gets up on his feet to enact the scene. MAG listens with delight and soon gets drawn into the pantomime.)

JOE: "Drive them up there! Another beast. Come on! Come on! I haven't all day. And what's bothering you, young Brennan? Steady, there! Steady! Bang! Bang! Drag it away! Slit its throat! Slice it open! Skin it!"

MAG: Stop—stop!

JOE: "Another beast! Get a move on! What am I paying you fellas for?" You told me to call about the flat, Mr. Kerrigan. "Steady—bang! Bang! Damnit, I nearly missed—bang!—that's it. Drag him off. What are you saying, young Brennan? The lease? Oh, the lease! Oh, aye. Here we are." *(JOE produces an imaginary document from his hip pocket.)* "Best flat in town. Hell, it's all blood now." *(JOE wipes the imaginary document on his leg.)* "Come on! Another animal! There's a fine beast for you, young Brennan! Look at those shanks! Bang! Bang! Never knew what hit him! I sign here, son, don't I?" *(JOE pretends to write; but the pen does not work and he flings it away.)* "Hell, that doesn't write."

MAG: Bang! Bang!

JOE: "Keep behind me, young Brennan. This is a dangerous job."

MAG: Let's sign it in blood, young Brennan.

JOE: "Finest view in town. And the noise down here's great company. Bang! Bang!"

MAG: Like living in Dead Man's Creek.

JOE: There's a bullock that looks like the president of Saint Kevin's. Bang! Bang!

MAG: A sheep the image of Sister Paul. Bang! Bang!

53

LOVERS (WINNERS)

JOE: Drag 'em away!

MAG: Slice 'em open.

JOE: Joan O'Hara's white poodle, Tweeny.

MAG: Bang! And Philip Moran's mother.

JOE: Bang! Bang! Doctor Watson.

MAG: A friend. Pass, friend, pass.

JOE: Skinny Skeehan, the solicitor.

MAG: Bang-bang-bang-bang! Look—reverend mother!

JOE: Where?

MAG: To the right—behind the rocks!

JOE: *(Calling sweetly)* Mother Dolores.

MAG: *(Answering sweetly)* Yes, Joseph?

JOE: *(Viciously)* Bang-bang-bang!

(MAG grabs her stomach and falls slowly.)

MAG: Into thy hands, O Lord—

JOE: Bang!

(The final bullet enters her shoulder.)

MAG: O shite—!

(MAG rolls on the ground, helpless with laughter.)

JOE: The town clerk—bang! All the teacher—bang!

MAG: The church choir—

JOE: Bang! Everyone that lives along snobby, snotty Melville Road—bang-bang-bang-bang-bang!

MAG: A holy-cost, by God.

(JOE listens attentively. Silence.)

JOE: Everything's quiet. Now we'll have peace to study . Back to the books.

MAG: I'm sore all over. *(Searching)* Give us a fag quick.

JOE: *(Bashfully)* I'm afraid—I—sort of—sort of lost my head there, ma'am.

MAG: Does your mother know you act the clown like that?

JOE: Does your father know you smoke? Look at the time it is! I came here to work.

(He goes back to his books. He is immediately immersed.)

MAG: Joe...

LOVERS (WINNERS)

JOE: What?

MAG: The flat's ours now?

JOE: Isn't that what I'm telling you.

MAG: You're sure you wouldn't like the top floor in our house?

JOE: Positive.

MAG: *(After a moment's hesitation)* So am I. I just wanted to know if you were, too.

JOE: Goodbye.

MAG: It's only that Papa'll be lonely without me. For his sake, really. But he'll get over that. And it's just that this is the first time he'll ever have been separated from me, even for a night. But he'll get over it. All parents have to face it sooner or later. *(Happily)* Besides, I can wheel the pram over every afternoon. *(She looks at JOE, lost in his books: and again she has the momentary dread of the exam.)* I'm like you, Joe. When I concentrate, you could yell at me and I wouldn't hear you.

(She opens a book—almost at random. Looks at the sky.)

It's going to be very warm...

(She takes off her school blazer, rolls up the sleeves of her blouse, and stretches out under the sun.)

If we didn't have to work, we could sun-bathe.

(Pause)

MAG: That Easter we were in Florence, I kept thinking about your father and how good the sun there would have been for his asthma. I read in a book that asthma is purely psychosomatic and that a man with asthma has a mother-fixation. Crazy the things they dig up too. I'm glad Papa's not a doctor or he'd be watching me for symptoms all the time. Your parents are such wonderful people, Joe. I'm crazy about them. And I'm going to treat my own parents with...with a certain dignity. My God, the things they said to me—they seared my soul forever—

(And without drawing a breath she hums a few bars of a popular song. She has a book before her eyes—but her eyes are closed.)

LU AN HAMPTON LAVERTY OBERLANDER
by Preston Jones
Lu Ann (17) - Billy Bob (17)

The Play: This is play number two in Preston Jones's *A Texas Trilogy*, a series of plays all set in Bradleyville, a small town in West Texas. In the first act, Lu Ann is seventeen, in the second act twenty-seven, and in the third act thirty-seven. During the journey she has had two marriages: one ending in divorce and one ending in a tragic auto accident killing the husband. She has one daughter who, by the end of the play, is a teenager. Before the play is over, Lu Ann is left to take care of her alcoholic brother and her mother who has suffered a stroke. The play begins with the hope of an aspiring young lady eager to conquer the world and leave small-town existance to those with no dreams. As the play proceeds, and as life hands Lu Ann significant obstacles, we see her spirit weaken and finally cave in. Even though we see three periods of a particular life, we feel for the universal cycle of the life we all handle—from marriage, to raising children. The dramatic strength of the play lies in the spirit of its people and the attempted, but failed struggle to be successful, happy, and live a challenged and vital life. The fact that Lu Ann doesn't achieve what she wants provides a heartfelt glimpse at a universal human struggle.

The Scene: This is the first scene in the play. Lu Ann is a cheerleader for the local high school team. Billy Bob, Lu Ann's boyfriend, is on the basketball team. They've just returned from school after a pep-rally. Billy Bob's hair is dyed green.

Special Note: Please pay attention to the playwright's careful spellings indicating the regional dialect. If you follow these notations you will accomplish all the accent necessary to good character study.

LU ANN HAMPTON LAVERTY OBERLANDER

BILLY BOB: *(Offstage.)* Lu Ann! Lu Ann! Wait up, will ya! *(Following LU ANN on. BILLY BOB WORTMAN is tall and lanky. He wears a white shirt, Levi's, boots, and a letter sweater. His crew-cut hair has been dyed green.)*

LU ANN: Ma! I'm home!

[CLAUDINE: *(Offstage.)* About time!]

LU ANN: Well, ah thought ah would die! Ah jest thought ah would curl up and die right there on the gym floor. When the coach introduced the basketball team and you-all come out there with your hair all dyed green. Well, sir, mah eyes liked to jumped plumb outta mah head! Why, Mary Beth Johnson jest hollered. That's right, jest hollered right out loud.

BILLY BOB: It was Pete Honeycutt's idea.

LU ANN: Why ever'one jest laughed and shouted and carried on so. Eveline Blair came runnin' over to me shoutin', "Look at the basketball boys, look at the basketball boys!"

BILLY BOB: It was Pete Honeycutt's idea.

LU ANN: *(Gestures to porch—they go out.)* After the assembly we cheerleaders all got together and decided we'd do somethin' funny too.

BILLY BOB: Aw, like what?

LU ANN: Now wouldn't you like to know? Mr. Green-headed Billy Bob Wortman.

BILLY BOB: Aw, come on, Lu Ann, what are you-all fixin' to do?

LU ANN: Oh, ah don't know, somethin', somethin' real neat.

BILLY BOB: You cain't dye you-all's hair. Pete Honeycutt already thought that one up.

LU ANN: Eveline Blair thought up different shoes.

BILLY BOB: Different shoes?

LU ANN: You know, come to school wearin' one high-heel shoe and one saddle shoe. Somethin' *neato* like that.

BILLY BOB: Yeah.

LU ANN: Ah don't know, though, it might be kinda tricky doin' the Locomotive in a high-heel shoe.

BILLY BOB: Might be at that.

LU ANN: But it might be fun.

BILLY BOB: Shore.

LU ANN: *(Sitting on swing.)* Maybe we can wear them out to the senior picnic.

BILLY BOB: *(Joins her.)* Shore!

LU ANN: We're still goin' in your daddy's Hudson, ain't we?

BILLY BOB: Well, uh, naw, we gotta use the pickup.

LU ANN: The pickup!

BILLY BOB: Yeah, my dad wants the car to go over to Big Spring.

LU ANN: But it's the senior picnic! Mah God, ah don't want to go to mah one and only senior picnic in a danged-old pickup.

BILLY BOB: Well, goshalmighty, Lu Ann, ah cain't help it.

LU ANN: What the heck good is it for your dad to have a bran'-new, step-down Hudson Hornet if we never get to use the danged old thing.

BILLY BOB: Seems like ever'thin' ah do is wrong.

LU ANN: Boy, that's the truth.

BILLY BOB: Gawlee, Ruthie Lee Lawell and Pete Honeycutt are goin' in his pickup.

LU ANN: So what.

BILLY BOB: Well, nuthin', ah jest mean that it don't seem to bother Ruthie Lee none.

LU ANN: Heck no, it don't bother Ruthie Lee none. Mah Gawd, she almost lives in Pete Honeycutt's pickup seat. I'll bet her bra spends more time on the danged gear shift than it spends on her.

BILLY BOB: *(Shocked.)* Lu Ann Hampton! You know that ain't true.

LU ANN: It is so, too. I seen 'em when they was parked out to the drive-in and she was danged near naked.

BILLY BOB: I never saw nuthin'.

LU ANN: 'Course you never saw nuthin'. You was too busy watchin' the movie. Mah Gawd, you was more worried about old Gary Cooper than Grace Kelly was.

BILLY BOB: Ah liked that movie.

LU ANN: Boy, you shore did.

BILLY BOB: Well, ah did.

LU ANN: No wonder Ruthie has so many chest colds in the wintertime.

BILLY BOB: If Pete and Ruthie Lee was actin' like the way you said, that jest means they don't have respect for each other.

LU ANN: Or for Gary Cooper.

BILLY BOB: Reverend Stone says that goin' on like that is a sinful sign of no respect.

LU ANN: Oh, brother.

BILLY BOB: People that behave thataway out to drive-ins and such-like is behavin' plumb un-Christian.

LU ANN: Well, at least they were sharin' somethin' more that a danged ol' box of popcorn.

BILLY BOB: A true Christian is pure in mind and body.

LU ANN: I wish you'd stop preachin', Billy Bob. Mah Gawd, ever' time we have somethin' important to discuss, you come up with a danged sermon.

BILLY BOB: What in the world are we discussin' that's important?

LU ANN: Your daddy's step-down Hudson Hornet, that's what!

BILLY BOB: My daddy's... For cryin' out loud, Lu Ann, sometimes you drive me absolutely nuts!

LU ANN: Well, you don't have to yell, Billy Bob.

BILLY BOB: Ah told you, an' told you, an' told you that we cain't have the Hudson.

LU ANN: Well, why not?

BILLY BOB: 'Cause my daddy's got to go over to Big Spring!

LU ANN: Well, it seems plumb funny to me that your daddy picked the very day of the senior picnic to go over to Big Spring. Ah mean, doesn't he know that the senior picnic is jest about the most important event in our whole schoolin' career?

BILLY BOB: Ah don't know if he does or not, he jest...

LU ANN: Don't hardly seem fair to look forward to somethin' all these years only to have your daddy come along and mess it up.

BILLY BOB: Daddy ain't messed up nothin', he jest...

LU ANN: He's only doin' it for spite, Billy Bob.

BILLY BOB: No, he ain't, he's jest...

LU ANN: And spite in my book is jest plain sinful and un-Christian. *(She turns to go.)* Good night, Billy Bob.

BILLY BOB: *(Grabbing her arm.)* Now wait a minute, Lu Ann. *(They are very close now.)* Oh, boy, uh, uh. Ah will talk to Dad tonight and ask for the car again, okay?

LU ANN: Swell, Billy Bob. *(She kisses him.)* Good night, now.

BILLY BOB: Good night. By gollies, Lu Ann, ah'm gonna make danged sure we git that car.

LU ANN: Fine.

BILLY BOB: Danged sure! *(He exits.)*

(LU ANN watches him for a moment and then enters the house.)

NICE PEOPLE DANCING TO GOOD COUNTRY MUSIC
by Lee Blessing
Jason (15) - Catherine (22)

The Play: It is a late afternoon in September in Houston, Texas. The title of the play is the name of a local bar—and an immediate indication of the kind of event Lee Blessing's play will detail. This playwright's plays are filled with unique people, richly drawn, and as much fun to play as to watch. This one-act play is a companion (forming the second part) to Mr. Blessing's *Toys for Men*, where some of the characters inhabit the same place. In *Nice People Dancing to Good Country Music*, we see the meeting of Eve Wilfong and her niece Catherine. Eve lives above the bar and is friends with many of its patrons. Catherine's problem is that she has just been expelled from the convent where she has been a novice nun. The circumstances are peculiar. Catherine was asked to leave the convent because she has an unsettling habit of blurting out inappropriate language (often off color) at inappropriate times. She is even given to making animal noises—and all of this without any intention of doing so. She can't control herself. Having been asked to leave the convent, she now has no direction in her life. Eve believes she just needs to settle down, meet someone nice, and get on with her life. In fact, Roy, one of the bar's patrons is real interested in her. However, before accepting his advances, Eve advises she learn about men from an expert, herself. Added to this mix, Eve's son, Jason, is visiting. Jason is on the brink of sexual awakening and this setting is full of the ingredients to make his visit a turning point in his manhood. The result is a delightful, often touching play. Mr. Blessing never provides a cliche, but rather offers a glimpse of an unusually universal microcosm of human relationships.

The Scene: Eve has gone donwstairs to head off Roy, who seems determined to court Catherine. Eve feels she's not yeat ready. Jason has been causing trouble in the bar—picking at the patrons. He's come to the roof deck to escape. Catherine is there still attempting to sort out where she should go now that she's been expelled from the convent.

NICE PEOPLE DANCING TO GOOD COUNTRY MUSIC

[(EVE exits. JASON regards CATHERINE)]
JASON: Hey, you look OK in real clothes for once. How come you're not wearing your nun stuff?
CATHERINE: I don't want to talk about it.
(A pause. They look out over the city. The bar door opens.. We hear Johnny Cash singing, "Life ain't easy for a boy named Sue... " and the door closes. JASON hurries over, looks down, returns)
JASON: False alarm.
(They look over the city)
CATHERINE: Don't you have something to do?
JASON: I think I'll just hang out.
(A pause)
CATHERINE: It's a nice view. You can see most of the city. Isn't it nice?
JASON: It sucks. This whole town sucks. Four billion people all talking like Gomer Pyle.
CATHERINE: Well, it's not Minnesota.
JASON: I'm going back tomorrow. About time.
CATHERINE: I suppose you'll be glad to see your Dad again.
JASON: Anything'd be better than here. Jim is nuts.
CATHERINE: Oh, I don't think he's...
JASON: What do you know? You only been here a few hours. I been here all summer. He's nuts. He makes me work in his crumby business. I'm on my vacation, and he makes me push beer cases around in the back room down there. He's a creepoid jerk.
CATHERINE: Well, I wouldn't say that...
JASON: 'Course not; you're a nun. Today he told me to move twenty cases of Schlitz from the front wall to the back wall and restack 'em. It's the same twenty cases I moved from the back wall to the front wall yesterday. He can't decide where they're "the most efficient." Efficient, my roaring butt. I'm going home tomorrow—what the hell do I care where they are?! *(A beat)* Does swearing bother you?
CATHERINE: I've, uh...I've heard worse.
JASON: So, anyway, I'm doing all this work for him, and when I'm done he comes in and looks at it, and says he liked it better the other

way. So I dumped three cases of Schlitz on his foot.

CATHERINE: You didn't.

JASON: I sure as hell did. He started screaming like crazy, and threw a bottle at my head. It missed by this much. He could've killed me, the stupid mother. Day before I go home.

CATHERINE: Maybe if you tried talking with him...

JASON: Advice for teens, huh? Actually, I didn't feel like waiting around to talk. There were three guys holding him down when I left. Besides, he's killed people. Did you know that?

CATHERINE: No.

JASON: He told me. Said he used to have a son by his first marriage, and the kid was always pissing him off, so he killed him.

CATHERINE: How?

JASON: With a Schlitz bottle.

CATHERINE: That's ridiculous.

JASON: How do you know? He said he did it.

CATHERINE: He was probably just trying to make you behave.

JASON: *(Picking up the flower pot, taking it to the edge of the deck just above the bar door, and sitting with it in his lap)* I behave. I'm a damn good kid. But he's pushed me too far this summer, that's all I can say. Working in the back room—how'm I supposed to meet any girls?

CATHERINE: *(After a pause)* What are you doing?

JASON: I'm going to wait for him to come out and drop this on his head.

CATHERINE: Jason!

JASON: Jay Bob.

CATHERINE: Jay Bob, you are not. That's absurd. Put that down.

JASON: You know, that's the only thing Jim ever did I liked. Started calling me Jay Bob. Jay Bob is just as stupid a name as Jason, but at least you can claim your folks didn't know any better.

CATHERINE: Look, um, Jay Bob—why do something like this? You're going home tomorrow. You'll be with your Dad again.

JASON: So what? He's not much better than Jim. Always talking to me about Latvia. He talks in a foreign language like eighty percent of the time. Nah, it doesn't matter where I am. I'm caught in a war between the generations.

CATHERINE: How about your mother? Don't you care about her?

JASON: She sleeps with Jim. Before that she slept with Dad. I mean, it's a pattern, you know? I know what side she's on. Go back and read your book. Don't mind me—I'll be all right.

CATHERINE: I'm going down and tell Eve.

JASON: You do, and I'll drop something on you.

CATHERINE: Jason, it's my duty to warn you that Roy Manual may be up here any minute.

JASON: Roy Manual? Why's he coming up?

CATHERINE: He wants to dance with me.

JASON: What do you want to dance with him for? He's the biggest dipstick in Houston.

CATHERINE: So I'm told.

JASON: Besides, you're a nun. You can't dance. There's a commandment about it or something.

CATHERINE: Well... I left the convent.

JASON: How come?

CATHERINE: It's a long story.

JASON: You're not a nun then, huh? You're just, like—what—like nobody, right?

CATHERINE: Pretty much.

JASON: *(Considers this, puts the flower pot aside, stands)* You wanna dance?

CATHERINE: What?

JASON: Come on, if you wanna dance, dance with me. I'm a lot better than Roy Manual.

CATHERINE: What happened to the war between the generations?

JASON: It'll wait.

CATHERINE: Jason...

JASON: Jay Bob. Come on—you're not a nun anymore. Hey—that's good; that's like an oldie. *(Dancing with her momentarily, singing part of the chant from "I want to be Bobby's girl")* "Your're not a nun any-more..."

NICE PEOPLE DANCING TO GOOD COUNTRY MUSIC

CATHERINE: *(Breaking away)* I'm your *cousin*, is what I am.

JASON: You're not that much older than me.

CATHERINE: Jay Bob. Listen to me. I—am—your—cousin.

JASON: So? There won't be all that getting-to-know-you crap. Come on, I've been trying to meet girls all summer. Everybody here talks like hicks. *(Approaching her again)* Come on, we'll do a close number. I'll sing. *(Softly)* "You're not a nun any-more..."

CATHERINE: *(Breaks aways)* No! I'm going to tell your mother.

JASON: You a virgin?

CATHERINE: Jay Bob!

JASON: I am. I'm not ashamed to admit it. I've been saving myself. I get a feeling you have, too. Is that true? If we want, we could do something about it.

CATHERINE: *You shut up! Right now! Shame on you! (She slaps him hard)*

JASON: *(Beginning to cry)* Why'd you hit me? Geez!

CATHERINE: Your are the most offensive teenager I've ever known!

JASON: *(Still in pain) Geez!*

CATHERINE: Well, don't cry...

JASON: I'm not crying! Damn grownup. Why's everybody always trying to hit me?

CATHERINE: Well, you were being so... aggressive.

JASON: I'm supposed to be aggressive. They said to be aggressive.

CATHERINE: Who? Who said?

JASON: The book I read.

CATHERINE: What book?

JASON: *(Pointing)* That book! *Sexual Advice for Teens*. Dating chapter. You just haven't gotten there yet.

CATHERINE: They said to be aggressive?

JASON: Well, kind of aggressive. I don't know. I never picked up a girl before. 'Course I'm not going to do it right the first time. *Geez!!*

CATHERINE: I'm sorry.

JASON: I'll be glad to get back to Latvia!

OUT OF GAS ON LOVERS LEAP
by Mark St. Germain
Myst (17) - Grouper (17)

The Play: Mark St. Germain's two character play is a shocking look at the desperation of youth to find a better tomorrow than the example given by their parents. The time is the present, the night of commencement of White Oaks Academy, an expensive boarding school for students with behavioral disorders. Eagle Point is the local "parking" spot. Here is where we find Myst and Grouper, two recent graduates of the Academy, and witness not only their romantic encounters but also a debate about life. Myst is the daughter of a once-successful rock singer and Grouper is the son of a narrow-minded U.S. Senator. Neither can grasp a future existence that follows the path of their parents. They also struggle for an alternative, one that seems reasonable, exciting, and more fulfilling than the parental example. The arguments are sharp, sophistocated, often humorous, and their needs and dreams are heartfelt. In the end, their disappointing sexual encounter and the inability to agree upon a future beyond tonight yields a dim glimpse of the future and the lovers leap.

The Scene: Myst and Grouper have been drinking beer and smoking pot. It is early in the evening after the graduation. Myst has been pressuring Grouper to make love, her "graduation" present, but he is avoiding the issue. Of the two, he is the virgin and extremely insecure with the status. Avoiding her advances, he wants to talk about the two of them living together for the summer at Seaside. Both are a bit high.

Special Note: Although both characters have just graduated from a special school for students with behavioral disorders, the actors should avoid overt protrayals of "crazy" people. The problems these two young people face are very real.

OUT OF GAS ON LOVERS LEAP

MYST: Grouper, you are a man after my own heart. *(Takes a joint.)*
GROUPER: *(With previously unseen sincerity.)* I am.
MYST: What?
GROUPER: After your heart.
MYST: *(Pause.)* You got it. *(Climbs on hood of car.)* How high up are we?
GROUPER: Me or you?
MYST: Us.
GROUPER: Very.
MYST: Isn't it dumb how they let cars park so close to the edge? Doesn't anyone ever drive off?
GROUPER: Are you kidding? People have respect for their cars. They park here and jump. You should have been here last Christmas—
MYST: *(Quickly, defensively.)* I couldn't be.
GROUPER: *(Pause.)* I know you couldn't.
MYST: *(Lightly.)* So you can lie as much as you want to.
GROUPER: *(Indicates over cliff.)* Guy in one of the houses down there had a fight with his wife over the Christmas tree, right? She said it didn't have enough tinsel on it or some fucking shit. The guys drags it from his living room, lights, decorations and all, throws it on top of his car and drives up here.
MYST: Want a beer?
GROUPER: Yeah. So the guy winds up to toss the tree over the side—guess he wanted to crash it thorugh his roof—just as he throws it over his leg gets caught in a string of lights.
MYST: *(Delighted, looking over cliff.)* Really?
GROUPER: I swear.
MYST: Right over? *(Grouper makes a diving motion.)* Wow!
GROUPER: It was a big goddamn tree.
MYST: Did he splatter?
GROUPER: Let me put it this way. There was a lot more hanging from that tree than tinsel.
MYST: *(Sings.)* "Oh Christmas tree, O CHRISTMAS TREE...
BOTH: "HOW LOVELY ARE THY BRANCHES."
GROUPER: So Myst—

OUT OF GAS ON LOVERS LEAP

MYST: So Group—

GROUPER: What do we do with the rest of our lives?

MYST: Number one, we finish these. *(They click beer bottles.)* My mother almost came tonight.

GROUPER: Jesus.

MYST: Her and Roger.

GROUPER: Captain Weave Job? The Man with the Plasticene Hair?

MYST: The one and only. They wanted to fly in from London; imagine that? Every asshole in the school would be hassling them.

GROUPER: Percy's lips would be in traction with all that ass kissing.

MYST: Damn right.

GROUPER: I used to think your mother was pretty hot when I was a kid.

MYST: So did I, until I grew up and she didn't. Barry Zenakus told me he used to have wet dreams about her. Did you?

GROUPER: Probably. I dreamed about anything female. My bed was a swamp.

MYST: Did you lock yourself in the bathroom with a copy of "Playboy"?

GROUPER: Nah. I'd leave it around the living room, especially if Mom and Dad were having company. They threatened to come up tonight, too.

MYST: My mom still looks good from a distance, but once you get up close, forget it. She's flopping all over the place. That's why she's always wearing leather, you know? Holds in the wobble. Really. She has no waist anymore. They build up her hips like Play Doh. I have a much better body. Wait 'till you see.

GROUPER: How did you talk her into not coming for graduation?

MYST: I didn't. I told her it was next week. She's coming Thursday.

GROUPER: I told my dad's secretary that if he or Mom showed up I'd phone in a bomb scare.

MYST: Cops wouldn't care. They probably get a dozen a day from this school. They're just hoping for the real thing. Could you believe how many people were taking pictures tonight?

GROUPER: The old fucks wanted proof that their kids graduated.

OUT OF GAS ON LOVERS LEAP

MYST: So many flash bulbs. When I walked in I thought we were getting nuked. I though, "Shit. I knew I wouldn't make it."

GROUPER: My father gets off on flash bulbs. Gives him a rush. I think when he and Mom do it they get the press corps in to shoot away and give him incentive?

MYST: They still do it, you think?

GROUPER: I guess. I'm not saying he takes off his suit, but they probably still do it. Doesn't your mother?

MYST: Oh, sure. But that's almost part of her job, you know?

GROUPER: The only person I wish could have been here is Matthew, but somebody would have had to bring him.

MYST: *(Pause; she changes the subject.)* I think the air is thinner up here, don't you?

GROUPER: How about letting my brother visit us once in awhile?

MYST: Sure. You remember our first date? When you stole the movie projector—

GROUPER: *(Cuts in.)* Borrowed. It's not stolen 'till they catch you.

MYST: *Borrowed* the copy of "Wizard of Oz," too, and we went up to the library tower roof and beamed it into the sky, drank a case of Moosehead and threw the empties over the side into the faculty parking lot? That was the most romantic night I ever had.

GROUPER: You know much about retarded kids?

MYST: Besides you?

GROUPER: *(Stiffens.)* I'm talking about my brother.

MYST: Oh.

GROUPER: You're going to like Matthew. A lot. He's always smiling, you know—but it's a real smile. Not a professional smile or a smart ass smile but a smile like he's really happy.

MYST: *(Casually.)* You really like kids, don't you?

GROUPER: *(Surprised.)* I guess. But he's not a kid.

MYST: You think we should go to Whorrie Laurie's party tonight?

GROUPER: You want to?

MYST: I don't know. It is our graduation.

GROUPER: That's right. Now we start real life.

MYST: You sound so nasty when you say that.

OUT OF GAS ON LOVERS LEAP

GROUPER: When do we leave for Seaside?

MYST: We don't necessarily have to go to Seaside just to live by the ocean, you know.

GROUPER: What do you mean?

MYST: I'm sure my mother would give us her house at Malibu—

GROUPER: Bite your tongue!

MYST: Why?

GROUPER: First of all, it's not even the same ocean. The Pacific Ocean's for pussies.

MYST: You're crazy.

GROUPER: It is *far* more mellow than the Atlantic.

MYST: Ocean is ocean.

GROUPER: Can you imagine *rides* on the beach ab Malibu? Can you picture roller coasters and whips and haunted houses—

MYST: Whips and haunted houses, maybe—

GROUPER: Does the Polar Bear club come out in sub-zero temperature in bathing suits to swim every New Year's Day at Malibu? Shit, if it ever got really cold out there they'd close the state. How can you even mention Seaside Heights and Malibu in the same breath? Seaside Heights is *real*. It's for real people, regular working people. The only thing you work for in Malibu is a tan—

MYST: *(Cutting him off.)* I was at the Malibu house this Christmas.

GROUPER: *(Stopped.)* So?

MYST: My mom, old Leather Stocking, had a Christmas party and invited everybody from the record company, and got stoned to oblivion because a couple of the biggies didn't show. She's not imaginative enough to think they might have families or people they actually liked who they'd rather see that day. Christ, I felt sorry for anybody who had to spend Christmas with us. She sat around petting my hair whenever I got close enough, saying to all these guys, "This is my little girl, would you believe it? This is Mystery." And meanwhile, these guys are eyeing the both of us trying to decide whose bones to jump—

GROUPER: I know whose I would—

MYST: Then jump.

OUT OF GAS ON LOVERS LEAP

GROUPER: I will.

MYST I'm waiting.

GROUPER: Have you ever done it in a ferris wheel? The largest ferris wheel on the east coast, on a pier right in the middle of the ocean? They'd stop the thing and look up and see the seat on the top rocking back and forth. That would be a first, even for you.

MYST: My mom bought me a doll for Christmas. One of these antique dolls that cost half a Porche—

GROUPER: Why do I get the impression I'm talking to myself?

MYST: She watched me unwrap it; she was jumping up and down like she was ten years old and I said, "Snow"—because God knows I can't call the woman "Mother" in front of company, "Snow, I think you need this more than I do."

GROUPER: *(Imitating radio transmission.)* This is Earth calling Angeleeds—Earth calling Angeleeds—come in please—

MYST: Funny—

GROUPER: *(Excited.)* I'm getting contact—a transmission from somewhere past Saturn—

MYST: Grouper!

GROUPER: *(Looking at her.)* Success! You *can* hear, you *can* listen. *(He grabs her.)* Then listen harder. *(Pause.)* I love you. More than I ever loved anybody. More than anybody's ever loved anybody. Because I'm totally sure we can be happy together 'till we both die. *(Pause.)* That's it, then. We live together, get married, or I jump off this cliff tonight. Your choice.

MYST: Don't your parents expect you home for the summer.

GROUPER: Probably. They always expect the worst. So?

MYST: *(Pause.)* My mom was talking about maybe going to France for awhile.

GROUPER: *(Pause.)* France?

MYST: Yeah; you know— Eiffel Tower and drinking on the street?

GROUPER: She's taking you?

MYST: I didn't say I'd go...

GROUPER: You'd rather spend the summer with her.

MYST: Of course not! *(Pause.)* But even you have to admit there's

71

a difference between Paris and Seaside Heights.

GROUPER: *(Ice cold.)* Get in the car.

MYST: Where are we going?

GROUPER: *We* are going nowhere, that's where we're going.

MYST: Grouper—are you driving over the edge?

GROUPER: You'll wish. I'm dropping you at Whorrie Laurie's party. *(Tries to start car, it won't turn over.)* Maybe you'll get lucky if somebody's looking for seconds.

MYST: Oh come on. Stop. This is our night.

GROUPER: Call your mother. Tell her to fly over early *if* you can reach her.

MYST: Did I say I'd go? I never said that.

GROUPER: You thought about it.

MYST: What if I did? What's wrong with that?

GROUPER: If you don't know there's nothing I can tell you.

THE RISE AND RISE OF DANIEL ROCKET
by Peter Parnell
Alice (13) - Richard (13)

The Play: Don't let the ages of these characters lead you astray. Peter Parnell's play is a play for all ages, as it deals with growing up and with what gets lost or destroyed when we become adults. The first act deals with a group of young people in a typical America community in the sixth-grade. In the second act, we return to the same people in the same community, twenty years later. The Daniel of the title is an exceptional boy, who believes that he can fly. For this belief others torture and ridicule him. No one believes the outrageous story. Alice has a crush on Richard, but Richard is oblivious. Daniel is in love with Alice, who eventually comes to care deeply for him when he stands up for himself in front of the others and "flies" off a cliff to the amazement of everyone. In a touching scene at the end of the first act, Daniel's conviction in what he believes leads him to everything he ever wanted: the ability to fly and the approval of others! However, the second act delivers the blow that cannot be survived. Daniel, now a celebrity—he flies!—returns to the community that caused him so much pain when growing up. The characters are older, but somehow they've not changed. Daniel is beginning to doubt himself, and those who knew him when he was younger are tired of hearing about him. The ridicule defeats him once more. In the end, Daniel crashes both emotionally and physically. The play has begun and ended with a hurtful destruction of someting beautiful.

The Scene: Alice longs for Richard to take interest in her. Richard seems involved with almost everything except noticing Alice's intentions. Finally, she catches up with him for a moment alone.

THIS RISE AND RISE OF DANIEL ROCKET

(Schoolyard. Richard alone, taking pictures of the clouds. Alice heard calling, off.)

ALICE: Richard? Richard? *(Alice enter.)* Hello, Richard.

RICHARD: Oh. Hi, Alice. Have you seen Snood?

ALICE: You mean Daniel?

RICHARD: Yes.

ALICE: I think he went off with the other boys.

RICHARD: But I told him to wait for me here.

ALICE: Do people always do what you tell them?

RICHARD: Snood's not people. Snood's my friend.

ALICE: Aren't Roger and Steven your friends?

RICHARD: Well, sure. But, it's not the same.

ALICE: Oh.

RICHARD: I mean, Snood and I are *close* friends.

ALICE: Mmn.

RICHARD: We've been friends since practically the first grade. And that's a long time. That's almost six years. Which is great, if you think about it. To have a friend like that.

ALICE: It is great.

RICHARD: I think so.

ALICE: I do, too. *(Pause.)* Penny and I used to be close friends.

RICHARD: You were?

ALICE: Yes.

RICHARD: That's right. You and Penny.

ALICE: Since before the first grade. Since almost even before kindergarten. We did everything together till this year.

RICHARD: Then what happened?

ALICE: We had a fight. Penny accused me of stealing one of her boyfriends.

RICHARD: Boyfriends!

ALICE: It was just a joke.

RICHARD: Who was it?

ALICE: Steven.

RICHARD: *(Laughs.)* You and Steven...

ALICE: No, Penny and Steven! Not me and Steven! I hate Steven!

RICHARD: Did Steven know about it?

74

THE RISE AND RISE OF DANIEL ROCKET

ALICE: Of course not, silly!

RICHARD: You and Steven...

ALICE: Penny and Steven! I told you I hate him!

RICHARD: Yeah, yeah.

ALICE: I hate him!

RICHARD: Why do you hate him?

ALICE: I just do! *(Pause.)* What are you looking at?

RICHARD: Clouds.

ALICE: Yes.

RICHARD: Nimbostratus.

ALICE: I thought nimbostratus are rain clouds.

RICHARD: They are.

ALICE: It doesn't look like it's going to rain.

RICHARD: Then maybe they're altocumulus lenticularis. *(Alice laughs.)* Very rare medium-level.

ALICE: You know, I think it's really bright of you to take pictures of clouds for your science project, Richard.

RICHARD: You do?

ALICE: Clouds are nice. I've always loved clouds. I would have chosen to do a cloud project if Mrs. Rice hadn't asked for somebody to do photosynthesis.

RICHARD: Photosynthesis will be fun, Alice.

ALICE: Not as much fun as clouds, Richard.

RICHARD: I guess not.

ALICE: I know not. *(Pause.)* You know, I was thinking. I'll be needing someone to take pictures of the plants, the ones that grow in the dark and the ones I keep in the light, and since I'm not any good with a camera...

RICHARD: Well, I don't know, Alice.

ALICE: It wouldn't take much time...

RICHARD: I'll be spending alot of time looking at the clouds...

ALICE: And I'd be happy to mention your name, which means you'd get double-credit, which I think could be pretty nice, don't you? (Pause.)

RICHARD: The thing is, I was sort of expecting to help Snood build his wings.

THE RISE AND RISE OF DANIEL ROCKET

ALICE: We could both help him.

RICHARD: He doesn't like to have too many people around when he works.

ALICE: You think he wouldn't trust me?

RICHARD: It's not that, Alice.

ALICE: He can trust me.

RICHARD: I'm sure he can.

ALICE: I'll tell him the next time I see him. Or you can tell him, if you want. *(Pause.)* Snood's strange, isn't he? *(Pause.)* Real strange. *(Pause.)* There's something mysterious about him.

RICHARD: Mysterious?

ALICE: This morning I walked in on him standing on top of Mrs. Rice's desk, waving his arms up and down.

RICHARD: You saw that, Alice?

ALICE: Yes.

RICHARD: I've seen him do that, too.

ALICE: It's as if he's got some sort of special power. The way he looks at me, with those eyes. It's scary, a little.

RICHARD: Sometimes I think so, too. *(Pause.)*

ALICE: Just give him another twenty years.

RICHARD: What does that mean?

ALICE: It's what my Mom always says.

RICHARD: What's twenty years?

ALICE: A long time.

RICHARD: A very long time.

ALICE: We'll see if he's still strange.

RICHARD: He will be.

ALICE: My mom says people change when they grow up.

RICHARD: Snood won't change.

ALICE: What if he does?

RICHARD: He won't!

ALICE: Yes, but, according to my mom...

RICHARD: Yeah, well, what if your Mom is wrong, Alice?

ALICE: She's not!

RICHARD: How do you know?!

ALICE: Because! I just do! *(Pause.)* If Snood wasn't your friend,

76

would he still be your friend?

RICHARD: Of course.

ALICE: Even though he's so strange?

RICHARD: He's not that strange.

ALICE: And everybody else hates him?

RICHARD: They don't hate him. They just don't understand him.

ALICE: Do you?

RICHARD: I'm trying.

ALICE: Do you understand me?

RICHARD: You, Alice?

ALICE: Yes.

RICHARD: I hadn't really thought about it.

ALICE: Well, think about it.

RICHARD: What? *(Pause.)*

ALICE: "Roses are red, violet are blue..."

RICHARD: You're acting a little strange yourself today, Alice.

ALICE: Am I, Richard?

RICHARD: Yes.

ALICE: Oh, really, oh am I really, really, really, Richard?

RICHARD: Alice...

ALICE: Well, what about you? *(Pause.)* "I love you, my Alice, I hope you love me, too."

RICHARD: What's that?

ALICE: "I love you, my Alice...!"

RICHARD: Alice, what are you talking about?

ALICE: "I hope you love me, too... !"

RICHARD: What are you saying?

ALICE: Don't you know, Richard?

RICHARD: Of course not!

ALICE: But I wrote you back an answer!

RICHARD: An answer?

ALICE: How can you be so cruel, Richard?

RICHARD: Me? I didn't do anything!

ALICE: You did, too!

RICHARD: What's happening? Stop crying, Alice. I didn't do anything. What did I do? *(Alice weeps.)*

STREET SCENE
by Elmer Rice
Rose (20) - Sam (21)

The Play: Elmer Rice was awarded the Pulitzer Prize in 1929 for this poignant look at life in a big city neighborhood. The play is set in "a mean quarter" of New York City, in the middle of a hot spell. The heat, in fact, contributes to flaring tempers and explosions of ideas and passions. The walk-up apartment house that serves as the backdrop for the action is inhabited by the Kaplan, Maurrant, Jones, Simpson, Hildebrand, Cushing, Buchanan and Fiorentino families, a diverse cross section of America, struggling through troubled times in cramped quarters. The interaction between the inhabitants is an interaction of cultures, beliefs, language, interests, and needs. The catalyst of the drama comes from the conflicts within the Maurrant family, when Mrs. Maurrant's husband catches her having an affair with the local milk collector and kills them both. Amidst the complex microcosm of this American composite is the romance of Rose Maurrant and Sam Kaplan, the young people of the story. Their perspective on life and the events of the play are unique in that they are attempting to sort out the destiny of their lives. As they see the mixture of life around them, conflicting beliefs and morals, they embrace an idealism for the future that is challenged not only by the heat of the city and the dramatic energy that rolls toward the murders, but equally by the search for a way to escape the hopelessness they see around them. When Sam asks Rose what else matters if they have each other, Rose answers, "...They [the adults] all start out loving each other and thinking that everything is going to be fine—and before you know it, they find out they haven't got anything and they wish they could do it all over again—only it's too late."

The Scene: Sam has just stood up to Vincent, who has been making unwanted advances toward Rose. Vincent, a bully who is bigger and older than Sam, has just pushed Sam to the pavement, shaming him in front of Rose. As the scene begins, Sam picks himself up and shouts at Vincent, who has just gone inside the building.

STREET SCENE

SAM *(hysterically, as he rushes to the foot of the stoop)*:   The dirty bum!   I'll kill him!

ROSE *(turning and going to him)*:   It's all right, Sam.   Never mind.

SAM *(sobbing)*:   I'll kill him!   *(He throws himself on the stoop and, burying his head in his arms, sobs hysterically.   ROSE sits beside him and puts her arm about him.)*

ROSE: It's all right, Sam.   Everything's all right.   Why should you pay any attention to a big tough like that?   *(SAM does not answer. ROSE caresses his hair and he grows calmer.)*   He's nothing but a loafer, you know that.   What do you care what he says?

SAM *(without raising his head)*:   I'm a coward.

ROSE: Why no, you're not, Sam.

SAM: Yes, I am.   I'm a coward.

ROSE: Why, he's not worth your little finger, Sam.   You wait and see.   Ten years from now, he'll still be driving a taxi and you—why, you'll be so far above him, you won't even remember he's alive.

SAM: I'll never be anything.

ROSE: Why, don't talk like that, Sam.   A boy with your brains and ability.   Graduating from college with honors and all that!   Why, if I were half as smart as you, I'd be just so proud of myself!

SAM: What's the good of having brains, if nobody ever looks at you—if nobody knows you exist?

ROSE *(gently)*:   I know you exist, Sam.

SAM: It wouldn't take much to make you forget me.

ROSE: I'm not so sure about that.   Why do you say that, Sam?

SAM: Because I know.   It's different with you.   You have beauty—people look at you—you have a place in the world—

ROSE: I don't know.   It's not always so easy, being a girl—I often wish I were a man.   It seems to me that when you're a man, it's so much easier to sort of—be yourself, to kind of be the way you feel.   But when you're a girl, it's different.   It doesn't seem to matter what you are, or what you're thinking or feeling—all that men seem to care about is just the one thing.   And when you're sort of trying to find out just where you're at, it makes it hard.   Do you see what I mean?   *(Hesitantly.)*   Sam, there's something I want to ask you—   *(She stops.)*

SAM *(turning to her)*: What is it, Rose?

ROSE: I wouldn't dream of asking anybody but you. *(With a great effort.)* Sam, do you think it's true—what they're saying about my mother?

(SAM averts his head, without answering.)

ROSE *(wretchedly)*: I guess it is, isn't it?

SAM *(agitatedly)*: They were talking here, before—I couldn't stand it any more! *(He clasps his head and, springing to his feet, goes to the right of the stoop.)* Oh, God, why do we go on living in this sewer?

ROSE *(appealingly)*: What can I do, Sam? *(SAM makes a helpless gesture.)* You see, my father means well enough, and all that, but he's always been sort of strict and—I don't know—sort of making you freeze up, when you really wanted to be nice and loving. That's the whole trouble, I guess; my mother never had anybody to really love her. She's sort of gay and happy-like—you know, she likes having a good time and all that. But my father is different. Only—the way things are now—everybody talking and making remarks, all the neighbors spying and whispering—it sort of makes me feel— *(She shudders.)* I don't know—!

SAM *(coming over to her again)*: I wish I could help you, Rose.

ROSE: You do help me, Sam—just by being nice and sympathetic and talking things over with me. There's so few people you can really talk to, do you know what I mean? Sometimes, I get the feeling that I'm all alone in the world and that—

(A scream of pain from MRS. BUCHANAN.)

ROSE *(springing to her feet)*: Oh, just listen to her!

SAM: Oh, God!

ROSE: The poor thing! She must be having terrible pains.

SAM: That's all there is in life—nothing but pain. From before we're born, until we die! Everywhere you look, oppression and cruelty! If it doesn't come from Nature, it comes from humanity—humanity trampling on itself and tearing at its own throat. The whole world is nothing but a blood-stained arena, filled with misery and suffering. It's too high a price to pay for life—life isn't worth it! *(He seats himself despairingly on the stoop.)*

STREET SCENE

ROSE (*putting her hand on his shoulder*): Oh, I don't know, Sam. I feel blue and discouraged sometimes, too. And I get a sort of feeling of, oh, what's the use. Like last night. I hardly slept all night, on account of the heat and on account of thinking about—well, all sorts of things. And this morning, when I got up, I felt so miserable. Well, all of a sudden, I decided I'd walk to the office. And when I got to the Park, everything looked so green and fresh, that I got a kind of feeling of, well, maybe it's not so bad, after all. And then; what do you think?—all of a sudden, I saw a big lilac-bush, with some flowers still on it. It made me think about the poem you said for me—remember?—the one about the lilacs.

SAM (*quoting*):

> "When lilacs last in the dooryard bloom'd
> And the great star early droop'd in the western
>   sky in the night,
> I mourn'd and yet shall mourn, with ever-
>   returning Spring."

(*He repeats the last line.*)

> I mourn'd and yet shall mourn, with ever-
>   returning Spring? Yes!

ROSE: No, not that part. I mean the part about the farmhouse. Say it for me, Sam. (*She sits at his feet.*)

SAM: "In the door-yard, fronting an old farm-house,
>   near the white-washed palings,
> Stands the lilac-bush, tall-growing, with
>   heart-shaped leaves of rich green,
> With many a pointed blossom, rising delicate,
>   with the perfume strong I love,
> With every leaf a miracle—and from this bush
>   in the door-yard,
> With delicate-color'd blossoms and heart-
>   shaped leaves of rich green,
> A sprig with its flower I break."

ROSE (*eagerly*): Yes, that's it! That's just what I felt like doing—breaking off a little bunch of the flowers. But then I thought, maybe a policeman or somebody would see me, and then I'd get into trouble; so I didn't. I'd better go up now, Sam.

SAM: Do you have to go to bed when you're told, like a child?

ROSE: I know, Sam, but there's so much wrangling goes on all the time, as it is, what's the use of having any more? Good night, Sam. There was something I wanted to talk to you about, but it will have to be another time.

(She holds out her hand. SAM takes it and holds it in his.)

SAM *(trembling and rising to his feet)*: Rose, will you kiss me?

ROSE *(simply)*: Why, of course I will, Sam.

(She offers him her lips. He clasps her in a fervent embrace, to which she submits but does not respond.)

ROSE *(freeing herself gently)*: Don't be discouraged about things, Sam. You wait and see—you're going to do big things some day. I've got lots of confidence in you.

SAM *(turning away his head)*: I wonder if you really have, Rose?

ROSE: Why, of course, I have! And don't forget it! Good night. I hope it won't be too hot to sleep.

SAM: Good night, Rose.

(He watches her, as she opens the door with her latchkey and goes into the house. Then he goes to the stoop and seating himself, falls into a reverie. A POLICEMAN appears at the right and strolls across, but SAM is oblivious to him. In the distance, a homecomer sings drunkenly. A light appears in the MAURRANT hall-bedroom, and a moment later ROSE comes to the wondow and leans out.)

ROSE *(calling softly)*: Hoo-hoo! Sam! *(SAM looks up, then rises.)* Good night, Sam.

(She wafts him a kiss.)

SAM *(with deep feeling)*: Good night, Rose dear.

(She smiles at him. Then she pulls down the shade. SAM looks up for a moment, then resumes his seat. A scream from MRS. BUCHANAN makes him shudder. A deep rhythmic snoring emanates from the Fiorentino apartment. A steamboat whistle is heard. The snoring in the Fiorentino apartment continues. SAM raises his clenched hands to heaven. A distant clock begins to strike twelve. SAM's arms and head drop forward.)

TRIBUTE
by Bernard Slade
Jud (20) - Sally (22)

The Play: Scottie Templeton, a former scriptwriter and occasional Broadway press agent, is a charming, elegant man who has managed to live his life without ever taking it too seriously, particularly love, marriage, and, unfortunately, fatherhood. While he has never been a great success at any one job, he has been a great success at making lasting friendships—even his ex-wife still adores him. In fact, everyone seems to like Scottie except his son, Jud, whom he has alienated through years of neglect. Now, at fifty-one, Scottie's life turns serious; he is terminally ill. There doesn't seem to be enough time to make up for all of his past sins, yet he is determined to win the love and respect of his son. Scottie sends for Jud, and the boy reluctantly comes for a visit. Father and son soon have a bitter, yet revealing and ultimately healing confrontation which brings about their reconciliation. Jud finally convinces Scottie to seek treatment for his illness, and then sets about organizing a major tribute for his father at a theater.

The Scene: Unbeknownst to Jud, who is somewhat awkward when it comes to girls, Scottie has arranged for his friend Sally (whom Jud has never met) to "pickup" his son while the boy is out visiting a museum (Jud is an intelligent young man who plans to attend UC/Berkeley for a Ph.D. in history). Jud has surprised himself by asking Sally back to his father's apartment. The two have decided to have an indoor picnic: Jud has just spread a blanket on the floor, and Sally is unpacking a shopping bag of food.

TRIBUTE

SALLY: You sure your father won't mind us turning his place into a picnic ground?

JUD: It'll probably make his day.

SALLY: *(Starting to put food on blanket)* There—this is going to work out just fine.

JUD: Well a lot better than your original idea. If it had rained we'd have been soaked.

SALLY: Your father must be pretty successful to afford a place like this.

JUD: Not really. *(She looks at him.)* His partner—his boss really—is an old friend of his. He owns the building. *(A somewhat awkward pause.)* I've always liked the name Sally.

SALLY: Yeah? I didn't but I finally came back to it.

JUD: You had other names?

SALLY: Dozens. *(She continues to set out food.)* My father was a construction engineer and we moved around a lot so I was always the new girl in town. *(She takes a bite from a pastrami sandwich.)* I was kind of a shy, scruffy-looking kid so it was tough making friends. *(She holds the sandwich for him as he takes a bite.)* Here, try this pastrami—it's terrific. Anyway, I hit on this dumb idea. I used to take the first name of the most popular girl from the last school. Believe it or not, for about three months, I was actually named Corky.

JUD: I can't imagine you ever being unattractive or shy.

SALLY: Well, I got over it.

JUD: How?

SALLY: *(Matter of factly.)* I grew tits.

JUD: *(Deadpan.)* Funny, that didn't work for me. *(She looks at him, notices him staring at her.)*

SALLY: What is it?

JUD: Oh, nothing. I just can't get over your being here.

SALLY: *(Puzzled.)* You invited me.

JUD: I know. It's just— *(Happily—blurting)* Well, you're my first pickup! *(She is too surprised to say anything. A slight pause.)* I guess this is a good time to tell you that my nickname is 'El Blurto.' *(Awkwardly)* I didn't mean to sound offensive. It's just that I've never

84

been very good at—meeting girls and I'm very pleased you're here.

SALLY: *(Amused.)* Yeah, well don't get too carried away. I practically had to tackle you around the knees to stop you leaving the Museum. *(She hands him a bottle of pickles to open.)* Why didn't you talk to me the first time I approached you?

JUD: I didn't know what to say.

SALLY: You have trouble talking to people?

JUD: I got out of practice.

SALLY: You were a monk?

JUD: I used to stutter. When that cleared up I had trouble—getting the hang of it again. *(Awkwardly.)* It's not as strange as it sounds.

SALLY: *(Grinning.)* Wanta bet? *(They smile at one another.)* You see how well this is working out? You're holding up your end of the conversation beautifully.

JUD: You want to hear something hysterical? Well, interesting maybe. *(He tries to open the bottle without success.)* My father's very—you know—glib. No—socially adept. Very gregarious—you'd like him—everybody does. He's not at all like me. *(He gives up on the bottle.)* Anyway, during the winter, I used to carry around this exercise book so I could jot down amusing things to say when I saw him in the summer. I tried it a couple of times but then I gave up.

SALLY: Why?

JUD: A certain look of panic comes into people's eyes when they're confronted by a fourteen-year-old Henny Youngman. *(He turns the jar top the opposite way and it unscrews easily.)* Why'd you want to meet me anyway?

SALLY: Oh, I'm always attracted to eccentrics. *(Sitting back.)* Do you visit your father every summer?

JUD: No, I used to but I haven't seen him for a couple of years.

SALLY: Why not?

JUD: *(Shrugs.)* I had summer jobs—one thing and another—you know.

SALLY: What made you decide to see him this summer?

JUD: *(Evasively.)* Oh, a lot of reasons.

SALLY: You don't like to talk about anything personal, do you?

JUD: *(Half kidding)* Yeah—well, I don't know you very well. Here—

(He gives her a cushion for her back. She looks at him for a moment.)

SALLY: Thanks. Can I have a bite of your pickle?

JUD: *(Indicating.)* There's one right here.

SALLY: No, I want a bite of yours.

JUD: *(Offering it.)* Here, have a whole pickle.

SALLY: No, just a bite. *(She takes a fairly large bite.)* There—now we've shared a pickle.

JUD: I noticed that.

SALLY: So now we know each other a lot better and you can tell me anything.

(He looks at her for a moment.)

JUD: Okay—I wanted to tie up some loose ends. *(She doesn't understand.)* I realized my father and I were both getting older and that this was probably the last chance we'd have to—reach some understanding.

SALLY: See, was that so hard? *(She leans over and kisses him lightly. They gaze at one another.)* You really hated me taking a bite of your pickle, didn't you?

JUD: *(Earnestly)* It was nothing personal. I don't like *anybody* touching my food.

SALLY: *(Teasing.)* And you don't think *that's* weird?

(He looks at her for a moment and then impulsively kisses her. [The front door opens and Scottie enters. He looks at them and fakes outrage.)]

WHAT I DID LAST SUMMER
by A.R. Gurney, Jr.
Ted (16) - Bonny (14)

The Play: Set during summer vacation, 1945, on the Canadian shores
of Lake Erie near Buffalo, New York, this warm-hearted memory play
is the coming of age story of fourteen-year-old Charlie Higgins. World
War II is just winding down, and Charlie Higgins and his mother and
sister are attempting to carry on with their lives as best they can while
Mr. Higgins is serving in the Pacific. Charlie's mother, Grace, has
been finding it increasingly difficult to make Charlie behave, so she has
decided to send him to boarding school in the fall. But Charlie rebels;
he takes a part-time job to earn spending money rather than tutor Latin.
He approaches Anna Trumbull, a Tuscarora Indian know in the area as
the "pig woman." Anna is a bohemian spirit devoted to organic living
and self expression. She finds a kindred and impressionable spirit in
Charlie, whose mother, it turns out, was once one of Anna's prize
students. Much to Grace's consternation, Anna stretches Charlie's mind
and soul by teaching him painting and sculpture, and filling him with
radical ideas about life which eventually cause him to reject the
conservative values of his family. This crisis results in a showdown
between Grace and Anna in which the conflicting values of Materialism
and Idealism are brought into sharp focus. At the end of the summer,
Charlie leaves the tutelage of Anna Trumbull with a new sense of
himself and his purpose in life.

The Scene: Charlie and his friend Ted have been vying for the
attentions of Bonny. Bonny has opted for the more experienced and
older Ted, however, despite the disapproval of her mother and father.
Bonny is at the beach serving as lifeguard to some younger girls when
Ted arrives with news about their date for that night.

WHAT I DID LAST SUMMER

BONNY: *(Bonny spreads the towel, as if she were on a beach. She speaks quietly to the audience.)* Sometimes I think this play is secretly about me. That's what I secretly think. Because, for me, this is a crucial summer. All sorts of important things are beginning to happen. My father's letting me skipper the boat occasionally. And my mother says I can smoke, as long as it's in front of her. And I've got a paid baby-sitting job three times a week. *(She calls out.)* It's not cold, Susie. Just go in slowly. Bit by bit. And it'll be fine. *(To audience.)* And tonight, one of the most crucial things of all might happen. Tonight we might be riding this roller coaster. It's called The Cyclone, and on a calm night you can hear it roar, even though the amusement park is over five miles away! Oh it's the scariest thing! It's built right out over the lake, all rickety and shakey, and they say when you climb to the top, you can see all the way to town. And when you start down, it's so basically terrifying that *women* have thrown their *babies* over the *side!* It costs five tickets per person per ride, and there's a big sign right at the gate saying you have to be at least sixteen before you can ride it. But Ted knows the Canadian boys who take tickets, and right now he's seeing if they can sneak us on. *(Calls out.)* Nobody goes out beyond the sandbar, please! Stay in the shallow water where I can see you! *(Ted comes on eagerly, from U.L.)*

TED: Everything's copasetic.

BONNY: They'll let us on.

TED: No problem.

BONNY: Oh I'm shaking like a leaf. Did you tell Charlie?

TED: How could I tell Charle? He's over at the Pig Woman's again.

BONNY: We'll have to wait and see if he can come too.

TED: Why Charlie?

BONNY: Because last summer we all promised to ride it together.

TED: They won't let him on. He's too young.

BONNY: He's my age.

TED: That's different. I told them you were my girl.

BONNY: Your *girl*?

TED: So they'd let you through.

BONNY: You mean you didn't mention Charlie?

WHAT I DID LAST SUMMER

TED: I said I was bringing my girl.

BONNY: Oh. *(She calls out.)* Stay together, everybody! Everybody stay close together! *(Pause.)*

TED: So what do you say?

BONNY: How would we get there?

TED: How do you think? By car.

BONNY: With you driving? Or your father?

TED: I got my license, remember?

BONNY: I can't then.

TED: How come?

BONNY: My mother doesn't want me to go out alone at night in cars with older boys. She was even mad I took you sailing with me.

TED: That wasn't a car. And it wasn't at night.

BONNY: Well I don't know. She thinks you're too old for me.

TED: She didn't think that last summer.

BONNY: Well maybe you weren't last summer. *(Calling out.)* Yes I saw, Susie! I saw you do that somersault! That was very good, Susie.

TED: Don't tell her then.

BONNY: Don't *tell* her?

TED: Just meet me out by the main road.

BONNY: Without Charlie?

TED: Look, Charlie's going his way, why can't we go ours? Come on. I'll fix it so we ride in the front row. And I'll take you to the Frozen Custard place afterwards. And introduce you to my whole gang from high school.

BONNY: Gosh...

TED: *(Touching her arm.)* Sure. It'll be like a date. A real date.

BONNY: You're distracting me, Ted. I'm supposed to be watching these... *(She looks out at the lake.)* ... kids. *(She jumps to her feet.)* Uh-oh.

TED: What?

BONNY: How many heads do you see out there?

TED: *(Counting quickly.)* One...two...three...four...

BONNY: There's supposed to be five!

WHAT I DID LAST SUMMER

TED: *(Pointing.)* And five, over there!

BONNY: Thank God! *(Calling out angrily.)* Susie, when you decide to swim underwater, would you *tell* people, please?

TED: Close call, huh?

BONNY: That wouldn't have happened if I had used the buddy system.

TED: I hate the buddy system.

BONNY: Well at least it's safe. *(Clapping her hands.)* Everyone out of the water, please. I'm instigating a new rule! *(She starts Off U.R.)*

TED: What about our date?

BONNY: Tell you what: I'll ask my father.

TED: He'll say no.

BONNY: He might not. He lets me do more than my mother. *(She goes Off U.R.)* New rule, everybody! New rule! We're going to have the buddy system! *(She goes Off.)*

TED: *(Calling after her.)* Your father will say no! *(To audience.)* Sure he'll say no. Lookit, someday somebody ought to write a play about a Canadian kid who hangs around Americans while his dad takes care of their summer homes. Here's the story: First, he's friends with those kids, trading comics with them, playing tennis, horsing around on the raft. Everything's hunky-dory. Then he starts growing hair on his nuts, and what do you know? The plot thickens. Suddenly when he shows up at the tennis courts, he gets the fish-eye from Mrs. Putnam for even sitting down and watching, for Christ sake. And soon he feels creepy even going down to the beach, like now it's out of bounds, or something. And then suppose he wants to take out an American girl. My God, suddenly it's like he wants to French kiss her, and bang her, and carry her off to Saskatchewan, all on the first date! I dunno. All I know is somebody ought to write about it sometime.

WOMEN AND WALLACE
by Jonathan Marc Sherman
Wallace (16) - Sarah (16)

The Play: Jonathan Marc Sherman wrote this unique coming of age play at the age of eighteen. In flashback, we see a young man in various relationships with the women in his life, including his grandmother, a first love, and a psychiatrist who helps him unravel his complicated life. The play opens with eighteen-year-old Wallace pelting a young lady with a ripe tomato and declaring his love. We then see Mother and six-year-old Wallace as she sends him off to school, followed by the shocking discovery of her suicide. The play builds momentum as it unemotionally addresses Wallace's journey toward manhood, encountering women at various points along the way. Seen through Wallace's eyes, the play presents a series of troubled, funny, and insightful life moments. Although faced with unique circumstances, his delights, problems, desires, and needs reflect a universal picture of growing up that is informed by the basic relationship between all men and women. Here Wallace's gender and age are far less significant than the life-struggle to understand and to grow as a human interacting with the opposite sex. Clever and sparse in its style, the play is an excellent example of how the theater is a place to reflect and articulate all life experiences, particularly those of young people.

The Scene: The scene takes place in Wallace's bedroom. Wallace and Sarah are high school friends. However, this is the first attempt to date each other.

Special Note: A careful examination of the entire play will yield other scenes worth studying, and two fine speeches by Wallace suitable for solo work.

WOMEN AND WALLACE

(Wallace's bedroom. Wallace and Sarah are sitting on the bed. Sarah is reading something on a piece of paper.)

SARAH: Oh, I *really* like it.

WALLACE: *Really?*

SARAH: *Really.* It's very good.

WALLACE: *Why?*

SARAH: Well, it's funny, but it's also *sad.* It's really *sad.* And it's so *true.* I mean, there's so much of *you* in there. I mean, if I didn't know you, I'd *know* you after I read this. You know what I mean? I think it's really talented work. What's it for?

WALLACE: *For?*

SARAH: I mean, is it for English class or something?

WALLACE: No, I just sort of *wrote* it. Not really *for* anything. For me, I guess.

SARAH: You should submit it to the school newspaper. I bet they'd publish it.

WALLACE: I don't think I want the whole school reading this.

SARAH: Why not? I mean, you shouldn't be *ashamed* or anything—

WALLACE: I'm not *ashamed.* It just seems a little *sensationalist,* you know?

SARAH: I don't know. I guess so.

WALLACE: *So. (Pause.)* What do you want to do?

SARAH: Oh, I don't know.

WALLACE: We could go see a movie.

SARAH: Sure.

WALLACE: Or we could stay here.

SARAH: Sure.

WALLACE: Well, which one?

SARAH: Whichever.

WALLACE: Come on, I'm horrible with decisions.

SARAH: So am I.

WALLACE: Sarah, you're the valedictorian of our *class,* for Chrissakes. If you can't make a decision, who can?

SARAH: Umm, do you want to...stay *here*?

WALLACE: Yes.

WOMEN AND WALLACE

SARAH: Okay. Let's stay here, then.

WALLACE: Settled. Do you want something to drink?

SARAH: Umm, sure.

WALLACE: What do you want? Some wine? A screwdriver?

SARAH: Oh, you mean something to *drink*. I don't drink.

WALLACE: Oh. *(Pause.)* Do you mind if I drink something?

SARAH: Oh, no, don't let me stand in your way.

WALLACE: I'll be right back.

SARAH: Okay. *(Wallace walks out. Sarah looks around the room. She looks at a photograph in a frame by the bed. Wallace walks in, sipping a glass of wine.)*

WALLACE: *In vino veritas.*

SARAH: Who's this?

WALLACE: It's my mother.

SARAH: She was beautiful.

WALLACE: She was okay. I'm going to light a candle, okay?

SARAH: Sure. *(Wallace get a candle. He takes a lighter from his pocket.)*

WALLACE: My great-grandfather was lighting a pipe with this lighter when he died. It's a Zippo. Pretty sharp, huh?

SARAH: It's very nice. *(Wallace tries to light the lighter. It won't light.)*

WALLACE: I think it has to warm up. *(Pause. Wallace tries to light the lighter a few more times. It won't light.)* Uhh, I guess my great-grandfather forgot to refill it before he died. It's just as well. I hate candles. They're so *cliched*. *(Pause.)* You want to listen to some music?

SARAH: Sure.

WALLACE: What do you like?

SARAH: Oh, *anything*.

WALLACE: You like James Taylor?

SARAH: Sure.

WALLACE: Let me just find the tape. *(Wallace looks for the tape.)* I don't know where I put it. Maybe it's out in the car. I can go check—

SARAH: That's okay. We don't *need* music. Do we?

WALLACE: Uhh, *no*, I guess *not*. *(Pause.) Well.*

SARAH: What was your mother like, Wallace?

WALLACE: What was she *like*?

SARAH: Yeah.

WALLACE: She was like Sylvia Plath without a Fulbright scholarship.

SARAH: What do you mean?

WALLACE: I mean—I don't know what I mean. I'm *sixteen*. *(Wallace drinks his glass of wine.)* Would you mind if I kissed you?

SARAH: The wine works fast.

WALLACE: No, *I* do. Can I?

SARAH: Umm, can't we *talk* for a while—

WALLACE: I don't *want* to talk, I want to *kiss*. Can I kiss you?

SARAH: I'd really feel better if we just—

WALLACE: Oh, come *on*— *(Wallace kisses Sarah, long and hard.)*

SARAH: Maybe I should go.

WALLACE: What? Oh, come on—

SARAH: No, I mean, maybe this wasn't such a good idea.

WALLACE: Don't you *like* me?

SARAH: Very much, Wallace. But I don't want this to be just—I don't know, a lot of *stupidity*. Just kissing and nothing else. I wanted to *talk* to you, you know?

WALLACE: Yeah, whatever.

SARAH: Oh, Wallace, don't do that—

WALLACE: Just go, please.

SARAH: What?

WALLACE: You said maybe you should leave, so leave. I don't want to—I just don't want to *deal* with this, okay?

SARAH: But—

WALLACE: But *nothing*. Just, please, go, okay?

SARAH: I—*fine*. Bye, Wallace.

WALLACE: Yeah, yeah, see you—

SARAH: I'm sorry this didn't work out. *(Pause.)* I'll see you in school on Monday. Okay? *(Pause.)* Okay, bye. *(Sarah walks out.)*

Note: The actors may wish to stop the scene here or go on to scenes 11 and 12.

WOMEN AND WALLACE

SCENE ELEVEN

(Wallace's bedroom. Wallace is sitting on his bed, talking on the phone.)

WALLACE: Yeah, I wanted to see if I could make a song request and a dedication... Umm, "Something In The Way She Moves"... By James Taylor... You *don't*? I mean, it's on "Greatest Hits". You see I'm trying to right a wrong, as they say.... I don't know, it's an expression.... Umm, do you have any, I don't know, like, Cat Stevens or something, somebody *close* to James Taylor? You know, one man and a guitar, that sort of thing... Only top forty?...Who's in the top forty? Anybody named James?... No, that's not really appropriate.... Umm, could I just make a dedication, then?... Well, I *know* it's supposed to be for a song, but you don't seem to have the song I *need*, so if I could just maybe make the dedication and then you could maybe not play anything for about three minutes in *place* of the song I need and that way—*hello*? *(Pause.)* Shit. *(Wallace hangs up the phone.)*

SCENE TWELVE

(Sarah's front door. Sarah inside, Wallace outside.)

SARAH: Wallace.

WALLACE: Sarah.

SARAH: What are you doing here?

WALLACE: I wanted—umm, I wanted to *apologize*.

SARAH: You don't *have* to—

WALLACE: Yeah, I do.

SARAH: Okay. *(Pause.)* So?

WALLACE: You know, I just—it's funny, you know, sometimes I just wish I were a little kid again, when sorry *was* okay, you know?

SARAH: Yeah, well, we're not little kids, Wallace.

WALLACE: We're *not*? Umm, no, no, we're *not*. We're *certainly* not. Umm—*okay*. *Well*, I was acting *really* stupid before, I mean, just very—*stupid*. It was—I was being, umm—

SARAH: Stupid.

WALLACE: *Yeah*. And it was *wrong*, and it was—you know, it made you—it was *unfair*. And I *apologize*.

SARAH: Okay—

95

WOMEN AND WALLACE

WALLACE: And I thought maybe we could try *again*.

SARAH: Again?

WALLACE: Yeah, you know, maybe I could come *in*—

SARAH: My parents are sleeping.

WALLACE: Oh. *(Pause.)* I could try to be quiet.

SARAH: It's kind of *late*.

WALLACE: Umm, well, you know, maybe you could come back over to my house and we could start from the *beginning*.

SARAH: *Wallace*—

WALLACE: I mean, I know it *sounds* like a stupid idea, but trust me, I'll behave this time, I know what to do. We can *talk*. We can have a *conversation*. We don't even have to kiss, we'll just *talk* and then you can go. *(Pause.)* Or we can just sit in *silence* for a while. We don't *have* to talk.

SARAH: I don't think that's a very good *idea*, Wallace.

WALLACE: All I'm *asking* for is another chance, Sarah. Don't make me beg.

SARAH: There's no need to *beg*, Wallace, I just don't think—

WALLACE: Okay. I'll beg. *(Wallace drops to his knees.)* I'm *begging*, Sarah give me another shot.

SARAH: Wallace—

WALLACE: I'll be *good*.

SARAH: *Wallace*—

WALLACE: Look at the moon, Sarah. It's *full*. It's *romantic*.

SARAH: Wallace, get off your knees.

WALLACE: *(Pause.)* That's okay. I kind of like it down here. *(Pause.)* I was going to bring a guitar and maybe *serenade* you, Romantic Thoughts, though.

SARAH: That's very sweet, Wallace. *(Pause.)* I really should go back *inside*—

WALLACE: Yeah, I understand. You know, I tried to dedicate a song to you on the radio, you know, something by James Taylor, and they didn't *have* any James Taylor. Can you *believe* that?

SARAH: That's pretty funny.

WALLACE: Yeah. Pretty Funny World.

SARAH: Sure is.

WALLACE: So, umm, you wouldn't want to maybe try again, say *next* weekend? A movie or—

SARAH: *Wallace.*

WALLACE: No, I understand. Okay.

SARAH: I'm *sorry*, Wallace.

WALLACE: Yeah, no, *I'm* sorry.

SARAH: *(Pause.)* Are you going to *stay* down there?

WALLACE: For a little while, yeah. If you don't mind.

SARAH: No, I don't mind.

WALLACE: Thanks.

SARAH: Yeah, well, okay. Goodnight, Wallace.

WALLACE: 'Night.

SARAH: Bye.

WALLACE: Bye. *(Sarah walks out, closing the door behind her. Pause. Wallace looks up at the moon.)* Thanks a lot, Moon. You really came through for me.

ANTIGONE
by Jean Anouilh
translated by Alexander Szogyi
Antigone (18) - Ismene (17)

The Play: Jean Anouilh's retelling of Sophocles' *Antigone* (the second tragedy in the Oedipus Cycle) was motivated by the Nazi occupation of Paris during World War II. The parallels between the tyranny of Hitler's rule and that of Creon's Thebes are at once evident. Eteocles and Polyneices, the sons of the late Theban King Oedipus, and the brothers of Antigone and Ismene, have recently killed one another in a civil war to gain control of Thebes. Their uncle Creon has become King. Creon has decreed that Polyneices, whom he believes provoked the war, be left unburied—his spirit left to roam eternally. Antigone considers this edict a sacrilege and defies her uncle by covering her brother's body with earth. When Creon learns of the deed, he is unyielding, and condemns his niece to be buried alive. This act brings about the suicide of Creon's son, Hemon (Antigone's fiance), and Creon's wife, Eurydice. Creon is left to face the tribulations of life alone. Ultimately *Antigone* explores questions concerning human responsibility to family, government and personal honor.

The Scene: Antigone has risen early and gone to bury her brother. She has now returned to her rooms, where she is confronted by her sister, Ismene.

Special Note: A comparison of Alex Szogyi's translation of Anouilh's *Antigone* with Lewis Galantiere's version and Sophocles' Oedipus Cycle may prove helpful to a full exploration of the text.

ANTIGONE

(Enter Ismene.)

ISMENE: You're up already? I was just in your room.

ANTIGONE: Yes, I'm up already.

ISMENE: Are you sick?

ANTIGONE: It's nothing. A little fatigue. *(She smiles.)* It's because I got up too early.

ISMENE: I couldn't sleep either.

ANTIGONE *(still smiling)*: You must sleep. You'll be less beautiful tomorrow.

ISMENE: Don't make fun of me.

ANTIGONE: I'm not. It reassures me this morning that you're beautiful. When I was little, I was so unhappy, you remember? I got you all full of dirt, I put worms on your neck. Once, I tied you to a tree and I cut your hair, your beautiful hair... *(She caresses ISMENE's hair.)* How easy it must be not to think up mischief when you have such beautiful smooth hair, so beautifully arranged around your head!

ISMENE *(suddenly)*: Why have you changed the subject?

ANTIGONE *(softly, without ceasing to caress her hair)*: I haven't changed the subject...

ISMENE: You know, I've been thinking, Antigone.

ANTIGONE: Yes.

ISMENE: I've been thinking all night. You're crazy.

ANTIGONE: Yes.

ISMENE: We can't do it.

ANTIGONE *(after a silence, with her small voice)*: Why?

ISMENE: They would have us put to death.

ANTIGONE: Of course they would. To each his own role. *He* must put us to death and *we* must go and bury our brother. That's how the roles have been distributed. What can we do about it?

ISMENE: I don't want to die.

ANTIGONE *(sweetly)*: I, too, don't want to die.

ISMENE: Listen, I was thinking all night. I'm the older one. I think more than you do. You always give yourself up to the first thought to cross your mind, and so what if it's foolish. I'm more level-headed. I reflect.

ANTIGONE

ANTIGONE: There are times when one musn't reflect too much.

ISMENE: Yes, Antigone. It's horrible, of course, and I have pity for my brother, but I think I understand our Uncle a little.

ANTIGONE: I don't wish to understand a little.

ISMENE: He is the King. He must set the example.

ANTIGONE: But I am not the King. And I don't have to set an example... The things that go on in that head of hers, little Antigone, such a dirty thing, such a stubborn girl, such a bad girl, you have to put her in a corner or down a hole. And that's all she deserves: All that was expected of her was not to disobey!

ISMENE: Now, come on! You're frowning, you're staring right into space and you're launched without listening to anybody. Listen to me. I'm right more often then you are.

ANTIGONE: I don't want to be right.

ISMENE: At least try to understand.

ANTIGONE: Understand... That's the only word you have in your mouth, all of you, ever since I was a little girl. You had to understand that you can't touch the water, the beautiful cold and fleeting water because it gets the flagstones wet, can't touch the earth because that stains dresses. You had to understand that you musn't eat everything at once, nor give everything in your pockets to the beggar you encounter, nor run, with the wind until you fall to the ground, nor drink when you're warm nor bathe either too early or too late, but just exactly when you don't want to! Understand. Always understand. I don't want to understand. I will understand when I am old. *(She finishes softly.)* If I become old. Not now.

ISMENE: He's stronger than we are, Antigone. He's the king. And the whole city thinks as he does. There are thousands and thousands around us, swarming through the streets of Thebes.

ANTIGONE: I'm not listening to you.

ISMENE: They will jeer at us. They'll seize us with their thousand arms, jeer at us with their thousand faces congealed into a single gaze. They will spit into our face. And in our open cart we'll have to move ahead surrounded by their hate, their zeal and their cruel laughter stalking us to our death. And there will be the guards with their imbecilic faces, looking congested over their stiff collars, their huge scrubbed hands, their cattle-like gaze—so that you think you can keep shouting forever, trying to make them understand, but they're like slaves and they will always do as they are told, scrupulously, without knowing whether it's for good or evil... Suffer? We'll have to suffer, feeling the pain mount, until it gets to the point when one can't bear it anymore; it will eventually have to stop, and yet it will continue and even increase, like a piercing scream... Oh I cannot, I cannot bear it...

ANTIGONE: How well you've thought everything out.

ISMENE: All night. Didn't you?

ANTIGONE: Yes, of course.

ISMENE: I'm not very brave, you know.

ANTIGONE *(softly)*: Nor I. But what does it matter?

(A silence. ISMENE asks suddenly.)

ISMENE: Don't you have any desire to live?

ANTIGONE *(a murmur)*: No desire to live... *(and softer yet, if that were possible)* Who got up first, in the morning, if only to feel the cold air on her skin? Who went to bed last, and only when she was so exhausted with fatigue, just to live a little more at night? Who cried when she was very young, thinking there were so many little animals, so many blades of grass in the meadow knowing you can't touch them all?

ISMENE *(with a sudden movement toward her)*: My little sister...

ANTIGONE *(pulls back and cries out)*: Oh no! Leave me alone! Let's not whine together now. You've thought it all out, you say? You think that the entire city howling at you, the pain and the fear of death are enough?

ISMENE *(lowers her head)*: Yes.

ANTIGONE: Take advantage of these pretexts.

ISMENE *(throwing herself at her)*: Antigone! I beg of you! It's for men to believe in ideas and to die for them. You are a girl.

ANTIGONE *(her teeth clenched)*: A girl, yes. Haven't I wept enough for being a girl!

ISMENE: Your happiness is right there ahead of you and you have only to take it. You are engaged, you're young, you're beautiful.

ANTIGONE

ANTIGONE *(hollow sound)*: No, I am not beautiful.

ISMENE: Not beautiful as we are, but in another way. You know perfectly well that it's you that all the little boys stare at in the street; that it's you the girls look at when you pass by, suddenly mute without being able to take their eyes off you until you've turned the corner.

ANTIGONE *(with a barely perceptible smile)*: Little boys, little girls...

ISMENE *(after a moment)*: And Hemon, Antigone?

ANTIGONE *(inaccessible)*: I shall speak to Hemon in a little while: Hemon will be a settled matter in a little while.

ISMENE: You're mad.

ANTIGONE *(smiles)*: You always told me I was mad, in everything, ever since I can remember. Go back to bed, Ismene... It's daylight now, you see, and, anyway, I can't do anything about it. My dead brother is now surrounded by guards exactly as if he had succeeded in becoming king. Go back to bed. You're still pale with fatigue.

ISMENE: And you?

ANTIGONE: I have no desire for sleep... But I promise you I won't move from here until you return. Nurse will bring me something to eat. Go and sleep some more. The sun is just rising. Your eyes are heavy with sleep. Go...

ISMENE: You will let me convince you, won't you? You'll let me talk to you again?

ANTIGONE *(a little tired)*: I will let you speak to me, yes. I will let you all speak to me. Now go and sleep, please, or you'll be less beautiful tomorrow. *(She watches her leave with a sad little smile, then suddenly weary, she falls into a chair.)* Poor Ismene!...

ASCENSION DAY
by Timothy Mason
Faith (18) - Charity (16)

The Play: Life often takes a turn when we are young that affects us forever. This theme is explored with an edge in Timothy Mason's short play set in a Lutheran Bible camp in Wisconsin, late in May, 1947. The story centers around nine teenagers spending a week at camp, strengthening their faith through testimonials, enriching the quality of their lives by study (everything from "nature tips" to lifesaving), and having time to spend with each other, sharing life experiences. If all of this seems expected church camp business, what is underneath this engrossing drama certainly isn't. In this seemingly tranquil environment, on the shores of a beautiful lake, loon song abounding, a series of moments compose a score that will not only change many lives, but will allow us the opportunity to reflect on the path our lives have taken. Written with economy, the issues are significant, the characters crystalline. The week is seen through the eyes of the young people. In fact, the adults at camp never appear—but are always a threatening presence. Specifically we follow the story of two sisters, Faith and Charity. Faith, the older of the two, is returning to camp—this year as a junior counselor. Last year at camp, her life began to change. Having been brought up in a strict home, overseen by a demanding, single-minded father, Faith found her experiences at camp exciting but disturbing. She met a boy, a boy who has returned this year. Faith struggles to handle the feelings in her heart, while at the same time, striving for perfection in the eyes of her parents, her sister, and herself. Her rigid instincts for right and wrong (influenced by her father) have driven away the boys and, during the course of the play, will sever the close bond that for years has held her and Charity together. Charity wants the freedom to explore a new-found excitement away from the watchful eye of her parents and resists Faith's firm governance. Perhaps seeing her own choices in Charity's actions, Faith drifts further away until the desperation demands action. A rekindled spark with Wesley, last year's boyfriend, ends in disaster. Those around her seem shallow, mindlessly content for the same kind of life that their parents live. Faith somehow demands more from life.

103

ASCENSION DAY

As the loons cry on the lake, Faith shatters inside, unable to maintain her fragile facade. Her final fateful move brings the play to its startling climax, and forever changes the course of her life.

The Scene: This is the first evening of camp. There has been a general assembly earlier in the evening where Pastor Tollefson called on the young people to give testimonials. Faith and Charity are assigned to the same cabin—with Faith the counselor in charge. For Charity this entire camp experience is new. For Faith, returning to camp brings a mixture of feelings.

ASCENSION DAY

(Charity and Faith are sitting on Faith's bed. Faith is brushing Charity's hair.)

CHARITY: I don't think I could ever do that, how am I ever going to do that?

FAITH: Charity, nobody gets out of here without giving a testimony.

CHARITY: Imagine talking in front of everybody about your complexion problems.

FAITH: Judging from his skin, we're still waiting for the miracle.

CHARITY: Oh, did you think? I thought he was adorable.

FAITH: With you, Charity, this is a broad category.

CHARITY: Strange, but cute as a bug. What was his name? Randy?

FAITH: Oh! Listen. Those loons again...

(They listen to the wailing of loons across the lake.)

CHARITY: I'm glad you're our junior counselor.

FAITH: So am I.

CHARITY: It's just... Well, I'm sorry, Faith, but just please try to remember that in some ways it's not easy, having the person in charge of your whole cabin be your sister.

FAITH: You're afraid I'll embarrass you.

CHARITY: Well you know what I mean.

FAITH: Oh, I do. I'll cut back on the chewing tobacco and I'll only spit on the floor after the lights are out.

CHARITY: You get it from Mother, you're so sarcastic, both of you. *(Beat.)* If you could just, you know, be a little more... I don't know... Easy-going.

FAITH: What does that mean?

CHARITY: Like, if a boy smiles at you, you don't have to turn to stone or anything.

FAITH: What on earth...?

CHARITY: You just don't act like the other girls and that makes them, I don't know...

FAITH: *(Overlapping.)* I certainly hope I'm not like the other girls...

CHARITY: ...uncomfortable.

FAITH: ...for one thing, I'm older than the other girls...

CHARITY: Only a year and a half...

ASCENSION DAY

FAITH: ...I'm not a giggling sixteen-year-old.

CHARITY: There, that's just the sort of thing I mean. We're not supposed to giggle or laugh, we're not supposed to goof around or have a good time or...

FAITH: Charity, of course I want you to have a good time, I don't know what you're talking about. *(Beat.)* I want you to have a good time. This is a very special place, this camp meant so much to me last year, I want it to be the same for you, I really do. *(Beat.)* Listen, it's simple. I'll just ask Pastor Tollefson to assign me to another cabin, it doesn't matter to me.

CHARITY: No, Faith, I'm sorry...

FAITH: Really it doesn't .

CHARITY: No, really.

FAITH: June can take the Naomi cabin, I'll take the Ruth cabin, it's no trouble at all.

CHARITY: No, please...

FAITH: I think I'd be better with the younger girls anyway.

CHARITY: I wish I hadn't said a thing, I really do.

FAITH: I'm not just saying this...

CHARITY: Faith, no! Please. I think I'm just nervous, is all, it's the first day, I just want...you know, people to like me. *(Beat.)* You met somebody here last year, didn't you, that's why it was so special.

FAITH: I met lots of people.

CHARITY: A boy, I mean.

FAITH: And I accepted our Lord as my personal Savior.

CHARITY: Is he here again this year? Wesley? *(Faith stops brushing Charity's hair.)* You wrote his name on the inside back cover of one of your notebooks. About a dozen times. *(The cries of the loons rise again, demented, maniacal.)*

FAITH: There they go again.

CHARITY: They're going crazy out there.

FAITH: It's so mournful, it's so lonely and despairing.
(They listen.)

CHARITY: *(Finally.)* Can you imagine being that horny?

FAITH: Honest to goodness, Charity, why do you insist on reducing

106

everything to...

CHARITY: To what?

FAITH: To the lowest common denominator, that's what.

CHARITY: You can't even say it, you can't even say the word.

FAITH: Anyway, you don't know a thing about loons.

CHARITY: And nothing's beautiful to you unless it's *mournful* and *awful* and *sad* and...*touching*.

FAITH: They have half a dozen different cries and each one has a different purpose.

CHARITY: I'm just so frightened you'll turn into a spinster.

FAITH: There's one for alarm, there's a feeding call, and yes, of course, there's mating, obviously.

CHARITY: My sister, the spinster Sunday School teacher.

FAITH: There's one particular cry for when they're lost, for when they've become separated and can't find each other. It's a terrible cry, I've heard it, it's so terribly desperate.

CHARITY: Just please...I need you. I'd be twice as scared if you weren't here.

COURTSHIP
by Horton Foote
Elizabeth (early 20's) - Laura (late teens)

The Play: *Courtship* is the fifth of nine plays that comprise the Orphans' Home Cycle by one of America's most prolific playwrights, Horton Foote. Mr. Foote is the recipient of two Academy Awards, one for his film *Tender Mercies* and one for the screen adaptation of Harper Lee's *To Kill a Mockingbird*.   Set in Texas, Foote's nine-play cycle deals with the life journey of Horace Robedaux beginning in 1902, when at the age of twelve his father dies, to 1928, when his twelve-year-old son (Horace, Jr.) must deal with the death of his maternal grandfather. The characters are rich and the language often poetic but always true to the heart.   The courtship of the title is in part the courthship between Horace Robedaux and Elizabeth Vaughn (who by the beginning of *Valentine's Day*, the next play in the cycle, has become Horace's wife.) However, we are not to see as much of their courtship as we are to be treated to a front porch discussion of dating, marriage, infidelity, and youthful rebellion. The play opens and closes with sisters Elizabeth (the older of the two) and Laura Vaughn. Laura has been away at school and is just home in time for a local dance—a dance that they have been forbidden to attend.   Elizabeth, having finished two years of music study, teaches piano in Harrison and still lives at home, under the watchful eye of the strict Mr. Vaughn. Secretly, Elizabeth has been seeing Horace Robedaux. Mr. and Mrs. Vaughn don't approve of Horace. In fact, they don't approve of the girls dating at all. If Mr. Vaughn could, he would see to it that they never marry. Struggling with this restriction in their lives, the sisters discuss their futures. It seems like every relationship presented them is troubled. During the play, a young contemporary of the sisters dies in childbirth on the same day that she marries the baby's father. The Vaughn family tree is also laced with reminders of failed love and unhappy marriage. It's no wonder Laura and Elizabeth spend so much time worrying that they won't find happiness. In the end, we realize that the painful examples in life will never replace the passion that governs the heart. Parents will try to protect their children and children will act as they must to find the destiny of their lives.   Elizabeth,

COURTSHIP

already secretly engaged to Horace, declares to her sister at the end of the play that she WILL marry Horace Robedaux when he asks.

The Scene: Elizabeth and Laura are on the front gallery of the Vaughn Home listening to the music from the dance. It's 1915. They've just heard that Sybil Thomas has died in childbirth, on this her wedding day.

Special Note: We urge the actors to explore the entire nine-play Orphan's Home Cycle as it provides wonderful insights into the history and relationships of the characters in the Horace Robedaux story.

COURTSHIP

LAURA: How old was Sybyl Thomas?

ELIZABETH: Twenty-one. She was one year older than I am.

LAURA: She wasn't in your crowd though.

ELIZABETH: Sometimes.

LAURA: Did you like her?

ELIZABETH: She was always jolly and had a very sweet disposition.

LAURA: I thought she was pretty. Didn't you?

ELIZABETH: Yes, I did.

LAURA: I think you're very pretty, Elizabeth.

ELIZABETH: Thank you.

LAURA: I love the way you do your hair and the way you dress.

ELIZABETH: Thank you.

LAURA; Do you think I'm going to be pretty?

ELIZABETH: I think you're lovely now.

LAURA: If it wasn't for the scar on my throat.

ELIZABETH: I don't even notice it.

LAURA: I do. I'm very conscious of it.

ELIZABETH: You're lucky to be alive.

LAURA: Yes, I am. I guess they thought I would die. Do you remember it at all when I drank the carbolic acid?

ELIZABETH: Of course, I do.

LAURA: I was two, wasn't I?

ELIZABETH: Yes. I remember hearing Mama scream when she discovered it. I remember Mama and Papa both yelling at the nurse for being so careless and letting you near the bottle of acid and I remember Mama sitting by your bed, night and day nursing you. I remember Papa saying she would kill herself if she didn't get some rest.

LAURA: I try to forget the whole thing and just when I think I have, Mrs. Jordan will say to me, "We didn't expect you to live, Honey. We thought for sure we were all going to your funeral." *(A pause.)* Do you ever think about dying?

ELIZABETH: Sometimes.

LAURA: I wonder why did the two little girls die and not us? Why are they out in the graveyard and we are here?

ELIZABETH: I don't know.

COURTSHIP

LAURA: You're not half listening to me. What are you thinking about?

ELIZABETH: I don't know.

LAURA: I bet I know what you're thinking about.

ELIZABETH: What?

LAURA: Horace Robedaux.

ELIZABETH: Maybe. *(A pause.)* I'm in love with him.

LAURA: How can you know that?

ELIZABETH: I know.

LAURA: How can you be sure of that?

ELIZABETH: I'm sure.

LAURA: I hope someday I can be sure of something like that.

ELIZABETH: You will be.

LAURA: Be careful though, Elizabeth. You were sure about Syd, but then you changed your mind. You could change your mind again. *(A pause.)* Ruth Amos said if Miss Agnes Sweet didn't stop singing so loud in the choir she was going to quit.

ELIZABETH: Ruth Amos is the most sensitive human being I've ever heard of. She's always getting her feelings hurt about something and walking out of the choir.

LAURA; Mrs. Cookenboo said she only joined the methodist Church so she could sing solos in the choir. *(A pause.)* Do you smell the honeysuckle?

ELIZABETH: Yes.

LAURA: I think my favorite smell is chinaberry blossoms in the Spring. *(A pause.)* It's been a dry Fall. I hope we make a good cotton crop. Papa says he needs a good cotton crop to get me to school in Virginia. I wish I weren't going quite so far away. I'm afraid I'll get lonesome. *(A pause.)* Do you think I'll get lonesome?

ELIZABETH: If you do, you'll get over it.

LAURA: Were you lonesome off at school?

ELIZABETH: At first.

LAURA: How long were you lonesome?

ELIZABETH: Not long.

LAURA: The dance music has stopped.

111

COURTSHIP

ELIZABETH: It stopped quite a while ago.

LAURA: I wonder why it stopped so early?

ELIZABETH: Maybe they heard about Sibyl Thomas.

LAURA: Maybe they did.

ELIZABETH: Why did you ask Mama about Mrs. Borden?

LAURA: I don't know. Wasn't I supposed to?

ELIZABETH: When I tell you secrets I like to feel you won't repeat them.

LAURA: I didn't know that was a secret.

ELIZABETH: It was a secret, my knowing anything about it. My being in love with Horace Robedaux is a secret.

LAURA: I know that. I would never tell that. *(A pause.)* Does Horace know how you feel?

ELIZABETH: I don't know.

LAURA: Do you think he feels that way about you?

ELIZABETH: I don't know.

LAURA: Are you going to tell him how you feel?

ELIZABETH: Certainly not!

LAURA: What if he tells you first he feels that way about you? Would you tell him then?

ELIZABETH: I don't know.

LAURA: Would you marry him if he asked you?

ELIZABETH: I don't know.

LAURA: You'd have to be engaged first, I suppose. Do you think Mama would let you be engaged to him?

ELIZABETH: I don't know.

LAURA: What do you think?

ELIZABETH: I think Mama might, but Papa wouldn't.

LAURA: Do you think you would have to elope to marry him?

ELIZABETH: Yes.

LAURA: Would you?

ELIZABETH: Yes.

LAURA: Even if it meant Mama and Papa never would forgive you?

ELIZABETH: Yes.

LAURA: Don't say that.

COURTSHIP

ELIZABETH: I mean it.

LAURA: Fifer Ecker's Mama and Papa never forgave her for eloping and her husband deserted her and she died all alone, in New Orleans. What if that happened to you?

ELIZABETH: I don't think it will happen to me. Not if I marry Horace. I don't think Horace would ever desert me. I think we will live together a long time and that we will be very happy all our married life.

LAURA: How can you be sure?

ELIZABETH: Because I am sure.

LAURA: Suppose he doesn't love you and is just infatuated and he meets someone out on the road while he's travelling around that he likes much better than you and he never asks you to marry him? What will you do then?

ELIZABETH: I don't know. I wouldn't know what I would do about that unless it happened.

LAURA: Would you ever marry someone older than you like Aunt Evy and Aunt Lucy did? Just because it was the sensible thing to do?

ELIZABETH: No.

LAURA: What if...what if no one you like ever asks you to marry them? And you get to be thirty or thirty-five like Aunt Sarah? And you met a nice older man, a widower say, and you didn't love him, but you respected him and he was kind and thoughtful, would you marry him or go on being an old maid?

ELIZABETH: I don't know.

LAURA: I worry about that so much. Don't you worry about things like that at all?

ELIZABETH: No. The other night when I was out riding with Horace he said he was not going to take out any other girls while he was away travelling this time. And I said I would not see any other young men. I said I would write to him at least three times a week, but I asked him not to write me but every ten days or so, because I didn't want Mama and Papa nagging me about it.

LAURA: If you're not seeing anyone else and he's not seeing anyone else does that mean you're engaged?

COURTSHIP

ELIZABETH: In a way. *(She reaches into her dress and pulls out a ring that is on a chain around her neck. She shows it to her.)* Look here.

LAURA: What's that?

ELIZABETH: It's a ring he gave me. I keep it hidden so Mama and Papa won't ask any questions.

LAURA: Is that an engagement ring?

ELIZABETH: I consider it so.

LAURA: And he must consider it so. I bet that's why he didn't take a date to the dance tonight and why he didn't dance when he got there. Because he thinks you're engaged. Can I tell Annie Gayle?

ELIZABETH: You can't tell a living soul. *(Laura cries.)* Why are you crying?

LAURA: I think it's terrible we have to deceive and slip around this way. Why can't we be like other girls and have our beaux come to the house and receive presents and go to the dances? I think we should just defy Papa and Mama and tell them right out.

ELIZABETH: I did that with Syd and it does no good. It just means constant fighting. The boys won't come here because no one wants to be insulted.

LAURA: Of course, with Syd it was a good thing they opposed your marrying him, because you didn't really love him.

ELIZABETH: No.

LAURA: Oh, my God! That worries me so. Suppose I think I'm in love with a man and I marry him and it turns out I'm not in love with him. *(A pause.)* What does being in love mean?

ELIZABETH: Oh, Laura, you'll go crazy if you always think of the bad things that can happen. I don't think of that.

LAURA: What do you think of?

ELIZABETH: I don't think.

LAURA: I wish to heaven I didn't. Everything bad that happens to a girl I begin to worry it will happen to me. All night I've been worrying. Part of the time I've been worrying that I'd end an old maid like Aunt Sarah, and part of the time I worry that I'll fall in love with someone like Syd and defy Papa and run off with him and then realize

I made a mistake and part of the time I worry... *(A pause.)* that what happened to Sibyl Thomas will happen to me and... *(A pause.)* could what happened to Sibyl Thomas ever happen to you? I don't mean the dying part. I know we all have to die. I mean the other part...having a baby before she was married. How do you think it happened to her? Do you think he loved her? Do you think it was the only time she did? You know... *(A pause.)* Old, common, Anna Landry said in the girls room at school, she did it whenever she wanted to, with whomever she wanted to and nothing ever happened to her. And if it did whe would get rid of it. How do women do that?

ELIZABETH: Do what?

LAURA: Not have children if they don't want them?

ELIZABETH: I don't know.

LAURA: I guess we'll never know. I don't trust Anna Landry and I don't know who else to ask. Can you imagine the expression on Mama's face, or Aunt Lucy's of Mrs. Cookenboo's if I asked them something like that? *(A pause.)* Anyway, even if I knew I would be afraid to do something like that before I got married for fear God would strike me dead. *(A pause.)* Aunt Sarah said that Sibyl's baby dying was God's punishment of her sin. Aunt Lucy said if God punished sinners that way there would be a lot of dead babies.

LA DISPUTE
by Pierre Carlet de Chamblain de Marivaux
translated by Timberlake Wertenbaker
Egle (18) - Adine (18)

The Play: Marivaux has long been considered the fourth most popular playwright at the *Comédie-Française* (after Moliere, Corneille, and Racine). In a recent volume, playwright Timberlake Wertenbaker has made available an exciting English translation of Marivaux's enchanting *La Dispute*. The "dispute" is over whether it was man or woman who was the first to be unfaithful in love. Some eighteen years ago this dispute took place at the court of the King, a man of science who decided to recreate an environment that would be like the beginning of the world when man and woman first encountered each other. The experiment consisted of selecting four new born babies (two girls and two boys), placing them in four separate homes in the forest, with each raised by guardians Mesrou and his sister Carise (both black, unlike the four babies). This very day is the first opportunity each of the four children, now eighteen, are permitted out of their respective environments, thus allowing the FIRST meeting to take place between man and woman. The play first introduces each boy to each girl, provides encounters between the two girls, and the two boys, and ultimately all four together. What begins as a delightful discovery, soon turns to selfishness and jealousy. In the end, *La Dispute* remains unresolved.

The Scene: Egle has met and fallen in love with Azor. Adine has met and fallen in love with Mesrin. Both are thrilled with their discovery of love and are feeling very special with the attentions from their new-found boyfriends. In this scene (the ninth in the play), the girls meet each other for the first time. It is, in fact, the first time they have seen another female other than Carise.

Special Note: The editors have selected this scene for advanced students and encourage in-depth examination into period and style.

116

LA DISPUTE

ADINE: What's this?

EGLE: Oh. This seems to be yet another person.

ADINE: A new object. I'll get closer and have a look.

EGLE: The person's studying me with care, but it doesn't seem to feel admiration for me. This is not another Azor. *(She looks at herself in the mirror.)* Nor is it an Eglé, no, definitely not. And yet, it seems to be making comparisons.

ADINE; I don't know what to think of that face. It lacks something; it's rather insipid.

EGLE: There's something about this person I don't like.

ADINE: Does it have a language? Let's see. Hm, hm. Are you a person?

EGLE: Yes, I am very much a person.

ADINE: Well? *(Pause)* Have you nothing to say to me?

EGLE: No. People are usually eager to speak to me.

ADINE: But aren't you delighted by me?

EGLE: By you? I am the one who delights others.

ADINE: What? You're not overjoyed to see me?

EGLE: Neither overjoyed not particularly displeased. Why should I care whether I see you or not?

ADINE: This is very strange. I show myself to you, you look at me. And yet you feel nothing. You must be looking somewhere else by mistake. Gaze upon me with a little more care. Now. How do you find me?

EGLE: You, you, you. Who cares about you? I've already told you that I'm the one who is gazed upon. I'm the one who's spoken to and told about the impression I've made. That's how it is. How can you ask me to look at you when I myself am here?

ADINE: Surely it's the one who is the more beautiful who waits for others to notice her and gaze upon her in astonishment.

EGLE: Then what are you waiting for? Be astonished.

ADINE: Didn't you hear me? I said it was the more beautiful one who waits for the admiration of others.

EGLE: And I've told you the more beautiful one is waiting.

ADINE; If I am not that one, then where is she? There are three

117

people in this world and they are all lost in admiration of me.

EGLE; I know nothing about these people of yours, but there are three who are enchanted with me and who treat me as I deserve to be treated.

ADINE: I know that I am beautiful, so beautiful I delight myself every time I look at myself. You see how things are.

EGLE; What is this tale you're telling me? I who am speaking to you can never look at myself without becoming totally enraptured.

ADINE: Enraptured? I admit you're quite passable, even rather pleasant. You see that I'm not like you and that I'm making an effort to be fair.

EGLE: *(Aside)* I'd like to beat her with her fairness.

ADINE: You're not seriously thinking of entering into a dispute with me over who is the more beautiful, are you? Why, one need only look.

EGLE: But it's by looking that I find you rather ugly.

ADINE: That's because you can't help finding me beautiful and you're jealous.

EGLE: The only thing that prevents me from finding you beautiful is your face.

ADINE: My face? Oh, you can't vex me that way. I've seen my face. Go and ask the waters of the stream about my face. Ask Mesrin who adores me.

EGLE: The waters of the stream are making fun of you and they've already told me that there is nothing more beautiful than my own face. I know nothing about this Mesrin of yours but he will need only catch a glimpse of my face to stop looking at you. Furthermore I have an Azor who's worth much more than your Mesrin, an Azor I love and who is almost as enchanting as I am. And he says I am his life. You're nobody's life. *And* I have a mirror which confirms everything the stream and Azor have already told me. Can anything beat that?

ADINE: *(Laughing)* A mirror? You have a mirror as well? What can a mirror do for you except make you look at yourself. Hahaha.

EGLE: Hahaha. I knew I wouldn't like her.

ADINE: Here. Take a look at this mirror which tells the truth. Learn to know yourself better and to keep quiet.

EGLE: Why don't you take this one and look at yourself in there. It will teach you how mediocre you are and to adopt a tone of modesty when speaking to me.

ADINE: Go away. I have no use for you if you will persist in your refusal to admire me. I'm turning my back on you. There.

EGLE: As for me, I don't even know you're here.

ADINE: What a madwoman.

EGLE: She's deluded. What world can such a person have come from? There's Carise, I'll ask her.

LEMON SKY
by Lanford Wilson
Ronnie (mid-thirties) - Carol (18)

The Play: Based in part on the playwright's own life experiences, *Lemon Sky* is the story of Alan, a young man separated in early life from his father when his parents divorced. At age seventeen, Alan spent time with his father, attempting to repair the damage done to their relationship caused by the distance of years and miles. Dad remarried, had two children by the new wife, Ronnie, and two foster daughters, Carol and Penny. Alan felt that he was never there for him during all of those years he was being raised by his mother. The uniqueness of the this play is the manner in which Mr. Wilson presents the drama. We see the attempted reconciliation between Alan and Doug (his father)—not when it happened, but after a few years have passed. The device allows the characters to reconstruct the events, while at the same time commenting on how they felt at the time. In this way, Alan tells us at the beginning of the play, he hopes to finally recover from what became a devastating conclusion to the attempted reconciliation. Although the story begins from Alan's point of view, before the evening is over, all the characters have the opportunity to voice their view on how it happened. It is an insightful process, filled with much humor, pain as the style is not only unique but provocative. In the end, Alan has been able to see the events, hear it all again—with insight—and speak his mind once and for all. We aren't left with any assurances that all will be repaired, however. Alan has experienced a classic catharsis which changes his life. In the process, we have been urged to examine the very texture of our own familial relationships.

The Scene: Ronnie, Alan's stepmother, has greeted Alan on arrival. They've had a long talk and started to get to know each other. Doug, Alan's father, went to work before Alan arrived. It is very late. Although Alan has gone to bed, Ronnie stayed up to wait for Carol, one of the two foster children in her charge. Carol has a history of trouble, and Ronnie can't rest until she's home.

LEMON SKY

CAROL: *(Entering. Carol is nearly 18, tall, very thin and smashingly attractive and quite a wreck.)* I know, it's late, I wasn't watching. Where's Alan, did he come?

RONNIE: Yes, he came.

CAROL: Doug here?

RONNIE: He went on to work.

CAROL: Went to *work*? Well, of course, he went to work, Carol, what'd you think, he stayed here with his son? How's Alan?

RONNIE; Very nice. But that isn't the subject.

CAROL: Oh, Christ, Ronnie, don't start!

RONNIE; It's two o'clock.

CAROL: *(Looks at her watch, puts it to her ear, shakes her arm during speech.)* It isn't any—well, my watch's stopped. Damn.

RONNIE: You know I don't care, but they ask.

CAROL: We've been sitting out in front for over an hour, didn't you hear us drive up, I thought I saw you at the window.

RONNIE: Carol, I don't care.

CAROL: Well, neither do I. He was so sweet.

RONNIE: I like Sonny.

CAROL: We talked— *(Partly to audience)* Sonny's dad has a ranch in Texas—over twenty thousand acres, which he says is small— That's probably larger than Rhode Island. And they raise Herefords and houses and oil and have about half the money in the country and investments everywhere. His mom and dad are paralyzed over what's going on in Cuba, apparently they own it.

RONNIE; Anyway, be that as it may, I've a vivid imagination but it fails me when I try to conjure up what you do until—

CAROL: *(Cutting in violently.)* Oh, Ronnie, would you stop it! Just stop it, already! No he doesn't lay me, no, never, not once, look at my hands for God's sake! You think I can stand it? *(Exposing her hands, which are bloody on the palms.)*

RONNIE: Good god, what's wrong with—

CAROL: —Well, it isn't stigmata, you can count on that. Sonny is Catholic with a vengeance and I've never thought I could be in love with anyone. There it is! *(Rather to the audience.)* Carol's problem,

121

never thought she could cut it and I am—very much in love with a Rich Texan Catholic and he has land, lots of land and principles that I never even knew were principles. And I used to take "downs," but pills are wrong, of course, so I promised him I wouldn't take them any more. No, we no longer live in a yellow submarine, we live on a Red Perch. And he makes out so damn beautifully and I can't ask him and I can't be "bad," his word, not mine, and I can't calm down with the pills and I claw my hands, the palms of my hands apart. *(Totally breaking off—disgusted with herself.)* Well, shit, Carol, there's no sense in causing a war about it, I cut them down yesterday, I'll cut them off tonight. But that won't help, because I'll bite my lip or something else if I can't get a hold of something to take to calm my damned, frazzled—

RONNIE: Carol, I'm very lenient and I know you can wrap me around your little finger; I know you've had to do that in order to get anything—

CAROL: —Don't make excuses for me for God's—

RONNIE: —Carol, I want to say something. I know you want to stay here for the next eight or whatever months until you're eighteen, and I want you here, but if I see one pill, one of your tranquilizers, I'll report it. It's something I can't tolerate. I have two young sons here and I can't risk them taking something by mistake...

CAROL: *(Overlapping.)* You don't have to tell me that. Do you think Sonny would stand for it? He's a lot better police dog than—a LOT better police dog than you, believe me—

RONNIE: There've been two different cases in the last year of kids being poisoned by taking their mother's barbiturates or someone's who had left them around the house. If I know you're taking them I'll feel obliged to tell Sonny as well as the welfare...

CAROL: *(Screaming.)* You don't have to tell anybody any goddamned thing! Because I PROMISED him, you know what that MEANS? *(Regains her control, holding her hands.)* That I didn't need them.

RONNIE: Does your hand hurt?

CAROL: Yes, they hurt like fire.

RONNIE: Let me put something—

CAROL: Oh, I'll do it; you're supposed to be bawling me out. You *can't* Ronnie. I can get out of anything, I'm a master.

RONNIE: You're also a mess.

CAROL: You're telling me.

RONNIE: Let me put something on them.

CAROL: *(Hotly.)* No, dammit; you're not going to stain me up with iodine, thanks.

RONNIE: I'll put some salve on them, not iodine.

CAROL: They're not that bad, really. I'll do it. Are you waiting up for Doug?

RONNIE: No. He'll be in.

CAROL: Alan's in my room?

RONNIE; For tonight. We'll arrange something.

CAROL: Just let me flop somewhere.

RONNIE: Put something on your hands, that salve.

CAROL: Okay. Goodnight.

RONNIE: Carol. Don't. *(Pause.)* Don't stay out this late. They want you in by twelve.

CAROL: I won't, Ronnie. You're great. I'm sorry, I won't. *(Kisses her on the cheek.)*

RONNIE: *(To the audience.)* She will, and I can't blame her, of course. He's the only thing she's got—Sonny. She's on probation with the state and us and Sonny too.

CAROL: So, I'm used to it. Don't make me out a martyr. I hate it. Besides I can do better. I haven't even got started on my mom and dad and poor upbringing and what a rotten life I've had. Besides I'm a nymphomaniac—coupled with a for-all-practical-purposes—eunuch—in the shape of a Greek God.

RONNIE; Which isn't necessary with you but it doesn't hurt anything.

CAROL: It hurts. It hurts. Everything. All over. Goodnight.

(She goes off to the girls' bedroom. Ronnie stands a moment, then goes off to the girls' bedroom.)

LYDIE BREEZE
by John Guare
Lydie (15) - Gussie (22)

The Play: The time is 1895. The place is a dilapidated beach house on Nantucket Island, Massachusetts that once served as the center for an idealistic commune (such as those popular with the Transcendentalists during the middle of the 19th century). A scandal of adultery, murder and suicide shattered the noble dreams of this Utopia in years past, however. Patriarch of the commune, Joshua Hickman, killed his wife's lover and was sent to prison. Now pardoned, he has returned to his home in an attempt to unravel the twisted tragedy of his life. Among the other players in this web of corruption: Lydie, his younger daughter (the namesake of her mother, who committed suicide); Gussie, his older daughter (secretary-mistress of a U.S. Senator); and Jeremiah Grady, the long-lost son of the murdered lover. As the mystery is unraveled, we not only discover much about the Idealism that runs deep in the American character, we also learn about the frailty of that character.

The Scene: Gussie has just arrived, dressed in very elegant yachting clothes. Lydie, her plainer sister, has just confronted her about being a whore.

Special Note: The actors may wish to read John Guare's *Gardenia*, which depicts the early years of many of these same characters.

LYDIE BREEZE

GUSSIE: I dress as good as any girl can! *(To Lydie.)* Feel my dress. Can you feel the silk?

LYDIE: I never felt silk.

GUSSIE: Well, that's English silk, goddamit. And these are my beautiful English shoes. And these are beautiful English hairpins. I am doing so fine!

LYDIE: You went to England?

GUSSIE; Those English make me so mad. Can you imagine— We tell England to frig off in 1776. Not till 1894 does England finally decide to open an embassy in Washington. But Amos says I must forgive. So Amos and I had to return the honor and go over there.

LYDIE: Did you meet the Queen? Is everything gold?

GUSSIE: I've been in Buckingham Palace. Saw Prince Edward. The Prince of Wales. He's Queen Victoria's son. The next King. We talked.

LYDIE: You talked to the next King of Wales?

GUSSIE: England! England! Are you an idiot? We were talking back and forth. If I ever get to England, I wouldn't mind looking him up. Buckingham Palace.

LYDIE: What did you talk about?

GUSSIE: Most of our chat revolved around the theatre. When you meet people of that royal ilk, you have to have cultural things to talk about.

LYDIE: The theatre?

GUSSIE: We saw *Frankenstein*. It was worth sailing an ocean for.

LYDIE: *Frankenstein*?

GUSSIE; Frankenstein is this wonderful scientist who cuts up old corpses...

LYDIE: Right on stage?

GUSSIE: He makes this monster who's controlled by all the dreams of the parts he's made out of. Other people's dreams. Other people's nightmares. It scares the bejesus out of you. To hear all those tight-lipped English tiaras and white ties in the audience screaming like residents of Bedlam.

LYDIE BREEZE

LYDIE: Is he hideous? Is he ghastly?

GUSSIE: No... Dr. Frankenstein must've got hold of the best-looking parts of all the corpses because the monster is...truly attractive. He pulls you toward him.

LYDIE: I don't want to go near him.

GUSSIE: In the last scene, the doctor goes up to the North Pole where he's chased the monster!

LYDIE: They have the North Pole right on stage!

GUSSIE: And they walk across the ice! And it's quiet... It's very still... *(Gussie spins Lydie around.)* And you hear the wind swirling... And you know the monster is out there somewhere... Woooo... Woooo...! *(Gussie hides.)*

LYDIE: Gussie? Gussie, don't scare me! *(Gussie sneaks up from behind Lydie.)*

GUSSIE: And the monster leaps up... *(Gussie grabs Lydie. Lydie screams with pleasure.)* And he grabs Dr. Frankenstein and pulls him down, down under the ice. *(Lydie and Gussie fall to the floor.)*

LYDIE: No!!

GUSSIE: And the monster looks out into the audience in the dark theatre. "Come, my enemies, we have yet to wrestle for our lives. My reign is not yet over." Every evil ugly thing that ever happened woke up inside me. Ma killing herself. Pa going to prison. I got asthma worse than ever.

LYDIE: *(Hugging Gussie.)* I hate the evil ugly things inside of me.

GUSSIE: You're a goddamn little saint. You never did anything bad.

LYDIE: Ma killed herself. Maybe over something I did.

GUSSIE: You were just a baby. Ma killed herself because she was still in love with the other man.

LYDIE: Dan Grady. I know the name of Dan Grady.

GUSSIE; Pa killed Dan Grady and Pa went to prison. And then Pa came home and then Ma died. It was all for love. All for love.

LYDIE: Gussie, were you ever afraid of Pa?

GUSSIE: Yes, I was afraid of Pa. After he came home from jail, I could never sleep at night. If I was a bad girl, I was sure Pa would come in and kill me the same as he did to Dan Grady.

LYDIE BREEZE

LYDIE: Is that why you left home?

GUSSIE: *(Rise.)* I dream all the time I'm going to be killed. I'd rather be killed by a stranger than have Pa be the one.

LYDIE: Don't say that about Pa. *(Gussie takes a comb from her purse and goes to the mirror to adjust her hairdo.)*

GUSSIE; Sometimes I wish they had left Pa in that Charlestown prison. What'd he ever do for any of us? Look at you. What's he doing for you? You can't read.

LYDIE: I can. A bit.

GUSSIE: You get decent grades in school?

LYDIE: I don't go to school.

GUSSIE: Do you know your ABC's?

LYDIE: Beaty teaches me.

GUSSIE: Those letters you write to me.

LYDIE: They're love letters.

GUSSIE: I can't read your letters. Zulus in Darkest Africa send out better love letters.

LYDIE: It's very hot in here.

GUSSIE: *(Taking Lydie's arm.)* How're you going to learn shorthand if you don't even have any longhand?

LYDIE: *(Pulling away.)* I don't want to learn shorthand.

GUSSIE: Don't you care about your life?

LYDIE: I care! I'm fine!

GUSSIE: Don't Pa care?

LYDIE: Pa cares.

GUSSIE: Some people even say Pa is not your real father. Amos Mason says Dan Grady is your father. If he is, I envy you.

LYDIE: You never come home. You never answer my letters.

GUSSIE: Baby, maybe I have kind of ignored the family the past few years. But I come back—see this—I think Ma'd like you travelling with me.

LYDIE: But Ma is here. I hear Ma's voice everyday.

GUSSIE: I only hear my own voice. And my own voice is saying that I want to learn shorthand so bad. That's the ticket. When I went down to Washington, I just showed up at the Capitol building. Amos could've thrown me out with a gold piece. But he didn't. He took me in and he's taught me to read and recognize the good things. *(She strokes Lydie's face.)*

LYDIE: Your hand feels so nice.

GUSSIE: Oh, baby, I'd love you to meet Amos. You'd score a bull's eye, Lydie. A pretty young girl in Washington. And you could keep me company.

LYDIE: But I have to stay here with Pa...

GUSSIE: Pa!? Pa lost Ma. Pa lost me. Pa lost Amos as a friend. Pa won't even notice you're gone. Baby, electricity's been invented. I'm introducing you to power. You got a bag? I'm packing you up and taking you away.

LYDIE: I don't want to be like you. I don't want to go into bed with everybody.

GUSSIE: What do you know about going into bed.

LYDIE: Beaty tells me about going into bed.

GUSSIE: Beaty don't know nothing! Hills of beans have flags in them announcing what Beaty knows!

MY SISTER IN THIS HOUSE
by Wendy Kesselman
Christine (early 20's) - Lea (late teens)

The Play: Christine and Lea are sisters, who are employed by the
Danzards (mother and daughter) as maids. Having been raised in
convents because their mother, also a maid, could not keep the girls
with her, they have come to rely on one another. While growing up,
they were frequently moved from one convent to another by the mother.
When Christine became old enough, the mother insisted on placing her
in a household to earn money. Young Lea has recently come of age
and finally gotten placed in the same household as her beloved sister.
What begins as the happiest of arrangements—for Christine and Lea are
finally together again—turns into a chilling psychological thriller.
Playwright Kesselman based her drama on a famous murder which took
place in Le Mans, France, in 1933. It is the same case that so
fascinated Jean Genet and lead to his important play, *The Maids*. In
Kesselman's play, not only do we see the contrast in social class
structure (the rich and cruel Danzards against the poor young maids
who only dream of a better life), but we also see a contrast in
relationships (mother-daughter, sisters, employer-employee). The
closeness the sisters share leads to an exclusive relationship that is
complicated by sexual confusion. Psychologically tormented by the
Danzards, the girls become alarmingly desperate in their situation and
are driven more and more to one another. Finally, at the powerful and
intense climax of the play, Christine and Lea strike back.

The Scene: This scene (the third in the play) takes place shortly after
Lea's arrival at the Danzard home. It has been years since the sisters
lived together and they are just now beginning to feel a bonding that
will fuse their relationship. It is early morning.

Special Note: An examination of Jean Genet's *The Maids* would be a
helpful exploration for this scene.

(Early morning. CHRISTINE and LEA'S room is almost dark. They are asleep. The alarm clock rings. CHRISTINE turns is off. She reaches out to touch LEA, curled up beside her. Gently she touches her shoulder, strokes her hair.)

LEA: *(Turning towar CHRISTINE.)* Is it time?

CHRISTINE: Sleep, turtle. Go back in your shell.

LEA: But—

CHRISTINE: Sleep. There's time. I'll wake you. *(LEA turns over again. She is holding the small blanket their Mother has made. CHRISTINE covers LEA'S shoulder with the blanket. Shivering, she gets out of bed, stands on the cold floor. She puts on her shoes.)* Lea...it's almost six.

LEA: Mmmm. Another minute, Christine. Just one more.

CHRISTINE: Just one—all right. *(At the sink, she washes her face and hands. She shivers from the cold water, fixes her hair in the mirror. She removes her long white nightgown and puts on her maids's uniform. She goes over to the bed. Tickling LEA'S feet.)* Come on now. Come on. *(She pulls the blanket off LEA.)*

LEA: *(Sitting up.)* It's freezing here. Is it always like this?

CHRISTINE: *(Laying out LEA'S uniform on the bed.)* Always.

LEA: Everywhere you've been?

CHRISTINE: Everywhere.

LEA: *(Putting on her shoes.)* I polished the banister yesterday. Did you notice how it shines?

CHRISTINE: I noticed. *(To herself.)* I thought it would be easier with two of us.

LEA: You're disappointed, aren't you? You're unhappy with me here. Tell me.

CHRISTINE: Don't be silly.

LEA: I can't seem to do anything right. I can't seem to please you.

CHRISTINE: You please me, turtle. You please me more than anything.

LEA: You're so quick. You get things done in a minute.

CHRISTINE: You're fine the way you are.

LEA: *(Struggling with her nightgown.)* Maybe this was a mistake. I slow you down.

CHRISTINE: Stop it, Lea.

LEA: *(Still struggling.)* Sister Veronica always said I was too slow. She said I'd never be as quick as you.

CHRISTINE: What did she know?

LEA: *(Helping LEA take off her nightgown.)* That was a long time ago. I've gotten over all that now.

LEA: You were famous at the convent. Your sewing! They still have that dress you made for the Virgin Mary. She's still wearing it.

CHRISTINE: And yet I remember, when I was at Saint Mary's, I could never go down the stairs like the others. One, two, one, two. I could never take a step with my left foot. It was always my right, my right, my right. I used to envy them running down the stairs when it took me forever.

LEA: Tell me a story, Christine. Just one—before we go down.

CHRISTINE: Which one?

LEA: When I was little.

CHRISTINE: You're still little.

LEA: No, I mean really little—you know—the story with the horse.

CHRISTINE: Again? Don't you ever get tired of it.

LEA: No—tell me.

CHRISTINE: *(Making the bed.)* When you were just a tiny thing, Maman sent me out one day to get bread. You came with me, the way you always did. And as we were walking, you let go of my hand and ran into the street to pick something up.

LEA: Tell it slower. You're telling it too fast.

CHRISTINE: It was a *long* narrow street—you remember—on a hill. At the top of the street a horse and carriage loaded with bottles was coming down and galloping right toward you. I ran into the street and pulled you across and pushed you down into the gutter with me. *(Falling down on the bed with LEA.)* What a noise when the horse galloped by! Everyone was screaming. Maman said the horse had gone mad. And when we stood up, we were both bleeding. But it was the same wound. It started on my arm and went down across your wrist. Look—*(She lines up her arm with LEA'S.)* We have it still.

131

LEA: And Maman—what did she say?

CHRISTINE: Oh Maman. Maman was terrified. You know how her face gets. She screamed at us.

LEA: And then—then what happened?

CHRISTINE: Then there was the gypsy—Mad Flower they used to call her.

LEA: And what did she say?

CHRISTINE: She said—oh you—you know it so well.

LEA: But tell me again, Christine. Tell me again.

CHRISTINE; They're bound for life. Mad Flower said. Bound in blood. *(A bell rings.)*

THE RIMERS OF ELDRITCH
by Lanford Wilson
Patsy (mid-teens) - Lena (mid-teens)

The Play: The Middle Western Town of Eldritch is the scene of a murder. But who is the murdered man, and what are the circumstances surrounding his death? To solve this mystery, we learn much about the relationships of the inhabitants of the little town, among them: Cora Groves and her lover, Walter, a young man who works at her café; Nelly Winrod, a strong-willed woman who mistreats her aged, retarded mother; Eva Jackson, a dreamy crippled girl, and Robert Conklin, the boy who cares for her. Poetic in spirit, *The Rimers of Eldritch* ultimately depicts the bigotry and hypocrisy of small-town life.

The Scene: Patsy tells her friend Lena about her soon-to-be wedding.

(Cast enters, with Patsy and Lena going to C. When all are in place lights up on Patsy and Lena.)

PATSY: *(To Lena.)* It wasn't really sudden. I knew he wanted to, he'd let on, you know, in little ways. He said would I mind not being in school; he'll graduate, of course, 'cause this is his last year—and I said would I *mind*?

LENA: That's just incredible; when's it going to be?

PATSY: We aren't messing around; he said two weeks from this Saturday. He didn't want to have a church wedding at first—you know how he is, and I said, Chuck Melton, if you think I'm going to just run off to a preacher and practically elope you got another think coming. So it'll be the First Presberterian of Centerville, but I want it to be just simple. I said I wanted a street length dress—I know but that's what I want and I'll have a veil, a little pill-box hat, I love those, and a veil and probably roses, if it's not too early for roses.

[MARY: *(On top platform. Over.)* Bonnie? Here girl. Bonnie? Here kitty, kitty.]

LENA: I'm just so surprised.

PATSY: Well, it wasn't really sudden, I knew he wanted to, he'd let on. I love the First Presberterian.

[PREACHER: *(Light on Preacher. Over.)* Now you know I'm aware we all want to get this settled and go home and forget about it. *(Light out on Preacher.)*]

PATSY: I only hope the trial and all is quieted down. That could just ruin it all.

LENA: Oh, it will be.

PATSY: It's a beautiful church.

LENA: I really love it; it's just beautiful.

PATSY: And my aunt's gonna give the bride's breakfast.

LENA: Aren't you excited?

PATSY: I imagine we'll live in Centerville. You know, till we have enough money to get a place or maybe move somewhere. Probably right in town; there's a wonderful place over the barbershop, the Reganson one on the corner with windows on both sides that's been empty for weeks. I only hope someone doesn't beat us to it. I want to tell Chuck to put some money down on it. I don't want to live with his folks. I just can't stand them and I don't think they think too much of me either. They're so square and old-fashioned. They really are. They don't even smoke or believe in make-up or anything.

LENA: Chuck is wonderful, he really is. I'm just so surprised.

PATSY: *(Beginning to cry gently.)* He was so cute; he said would I mind not being in school next year, junior year and I said of course I'll miss my friends, but would I *mind*?

LENA: It's so beautiful. It's a beautiful church for a wedding.

PATSY: Isn't it?

LENA; Aren't you excited? What's wrong?

PATSY: Well, of course I am, silly.

LENA: I don't think Josh and me want to get married though until after I'm out of school.

PATSY: Oh, my god, you don't want to marry Josh. My Lord, I can't imagine it. You're not serious about him. Lord, he's so childish.

LENA: He isn't. He's six years older than you are. He's worked for two years.

PATSY: Well, I know, but you don't want to marry him. Age doesn't have anything to do with it. He's all right and he's sweet and all, but I mean to go to the show with and hold hands. I don't know how you can bear to ride into town in that garage tow-truck, though.

LENA; I drive it sometimes; it's not bad.

PATSY: Well, I know, but Josh! Lord, Lena, I've got so many things to do yet. You know the thing I think I like most about Chuck is that he's so clean and neat and all. The way he takes care of his Mercury. It's always like spanking new.

SENIORITY
by Eric Ziegenhagen
Debbie (17) - Fiona (15)

The Play: *Seniority* was first produced at the Playwrights Horizons in New York City after being selected as one of the winners from the 1988 Young Playwrights Festival. Eric Ziegenhagen was sixteen when he wrote this short one-act play about two sisters who confront each other. Debbie seems to be a self-assured young woman. She is intelligent and very focused in what she wants. After graduation she's spending the summer in Europe, and then going to college in the fall. Her confidence is shaken, however, when she learns that her younger sister, Fiona (a freshman), has been dating Ian, a senior she, herself, had wanted to date at one time. Suddenly, all of Debbie's careful planning for the future doesn't seem to matter. Her insecurity about dating and Fiona's apparent success with boys leaves Debbie feeling lonely and confused. Ian's arrival on the scene complicates the situation. Ultimately, *Seniority* raises the question that troubles us all: "What's to become of me?"

The Scene: Midnight in the living room of a suburban home. Debbie has waited up for her younger sister, who has been out on a date.

SENIORITY

(DEBBIE is paging through a pamphlet. Offstage, a teakettle blows. DEBBIE exits to kitchen and comes back with a cup in her hands. A car is heard outside. DEBBIE exits to kitchen again. The car idles and then pulls away. DEBBIE reenters carrying another cup and the kettle. As FIONA enters, DEBBIE pours two cups of tea.)

FIONA: Hi.

DEBBIE: 'Morning.

FIONA: You're still up. It's late, isn't it?

DEBBIE: Midnight.

FIONA: Oh. I didn't wear my watch.

DEBBIE: I made you some tea.

FIONA: Thank you.

DEBBIE: Just was making some and figured you'd be back soon, so I made a little extra.

FIONA: Thank you.

DEBBIE: Dawn called for you tonight.

FIONA: What did you tell her?

DEBBIE: I said that you were going to be out late.

FIONA: She didn't ask where I was?

DEBBIE: She just wanted to know if you wanted to do something tomorrow.

FIONA: Did she ask where I was?

DEBBIE: No. I told her you were out.

FIONA: Good.

DEBBIE: So how was it?

FIONA: Fun. Really fun. What happened in here?

DEBBIE: What?

FIONA: All this mess.

DEBBIE: Bridge game. Grandmother Jessica's staying here. There's a bridge tournament at the Holiday Inn.

FIONA: Then why is this stuff here?

DEBBIE: She had some of her friends over.

FIONA: Why don't they just play over at the Holiday Inn if she's staying over there?

DEBBIE: The tournament's there, but she's staying upstairs. She's sleeping in the TV room. Don't worry about it, anyway, you won't

137

have to clean it up. I'll take care of it.

FIONA *(noticing pamphlets)*: What are these?

DEBBIE: Pamphlets I picked up today. European exchanges. Two weeks in Holland, two weeks in England. Room and board at universities in London and Amsterdam. Seventeen hundred dollars including everything except extra spending. There's time to study and time to tour. Four weeks to get away. Exactly the sort of thing I'm looking for.

FIONA: You were thinking of doing this alone?

DEBBIE: No. With a study group. Well, "alone" meaning not being with anyone I know, yeah, I guess.

FIONA: And you think Mom will let you do that?

DEBBIE: Yes, I do.

FIONA: I beg to differ.

DEBBIE: Oh. We'll see. If I'm going to be going away to college next year, I don't see why she wouldn't let me spend a few weeks by myself in Europe.

FIONA: Because it's dangerous, Debbie. Dangerous. I mean, Amsterdam...it's, it's heroin and hookers...guys in ugly trench coats who want to feed you sourdough bread with poison in it...get your purse stolen, bad rates on money exchange...

DEBBIE: I'd be careful. I'd know where not to walk.

FIONA: It's too dangerous, Debbie. She'll never let you go.

DEBBIE: Then where could I go that wouldn't be dangerous? Omaha? I could be an exchange student in Omaha, and then it would be okay?

FIONA: I didn't mean to start an argument, Debbie.

DEBBIE: It won't hurt to bring it up with Mom.

FIONA: True.

DEBBIE: I'm responsible and careful enough for it.

(Pause.)

DEBBIE: Does Mom know that you went out tonight?

FIONA: She knew that I went out...

DEBBIE: ...but not with a guy.

FIONA: Right. You didn't say anything, did you?

DEBBIE: No, but didn't he come in when he picked you up?

FIONA: No.

SENIORITY

DEBBIE: You just went out there and met him?

FIONA: Yeah. Is there something wrong—

DEBBIE: No, no, it's just whenever I've gone out on dates, it's always kind of cute and romantic to meet the parents. You know, he would always go in and shake hands with Mom or whatever when he picked me up.

FIONA: Why should a guy have to go through that trouble when Mom probably won't like him anyway?

DEBBIE: It's kind of a custom.

FIONA: And that's what you've done on dates.

DEBBIE: Yeah, I've done that. Once we even went into the house after going out to a movie and, well, all right, we didn't expect his parents to be home, but his mom made some cocoa, and we all stayed up late just talking. The three of us. It wasn't bad at all.

FIONA: When was this?

DEBBIE: Last year.

FIONA: When did you go out?

DEBBIE: I went to prom, Fiona, remember? I also went out a few times this summer.

FIONA: I don't remember that.

DEBBIE: It was while you were out in Phoenix visiting Dad, that's why.

FIONA: Oh, I see.

DEBBIE: So where did you go?

FIONA: We just went out to the mall and walked around and ate some dinner.

DEBBIE: You ate in the mall?

FIONA: That fifties place over by the movie theater. It has those pink neon...

DEBBIE *(overlapping)*: Yeah, I know what you're talking about.

FIONA: ...lights in the window and an old Wurlitzer jukebox. The kind with little water bubbles going up the sides in different colors.

DEBBIE: Yeah.

FIONA: Real cute.

DEBBIE: Yeah.

FIONA: And then after that we went to a movie.

SENIORITY

DEBBIE: At the mall?

FIONA: Yeah, where else would you go?

DEBBIE: What did you see?

FIONA: What?

DEBBIE: What was the movie?

FIONA: Boring. Something real boring. Some horror movie. Didn't watch it much.

DEBBIE: Oh.

FIONA: So that's about it.

DEBBIE: That leaves about three hours to spare.

FIONA: You don't have to clock my every moment, Debbie.

DEBBIE: Just curious, that's all.

FIONA: We drove around a little. Went out around the outskirts of town. You know, you can't see many stars around here, but way out on Highway Nineteen, past the suburbs and into the country, there were so many stars, I couldn't believe it. Not just the Big Dipper. Ones you can't see from here. And it's such a beautiful night out. Not too chilly. A thin, cool wind. Crickets. We just laid in some field by the side of the road, breathing the air and watching the stars. It was romantic and fun. What else is a date supposed to be?

DEBBIE: You did it, didn't you?

FIONA: We just went out, Debbie. A date.

DEBBIE: I knew I could see something even when you came in here. You're light.

FIONA: I can't be happy?

DEBBIE: You're more than happy...

FIONA: Sure we kissed, but—

DEBBIE: More than that. I can see it, Fiona. You're transparent.

FIONA: You're wrong.

DEBBIE: Right through you.

FIONA: Debbie.

(Long pause.)

FIONA: And so what if I did? So what if I "did it"? What then? You're just jealous, Debbie. You wish that you were in my place. Not with him, maybe, but with anyone. Anyone under the stars.

DEBBIE: That's not true!

140

SENIORITY

FIONA: Anyone that would offer it!

DEBBIE: I've had the—

FIONA: But no one asks you, so you just wait and wait and wait, and now you're jealous. I can read you, too. You envy me because I had a chance that you never did.

DEBBIE: I've had the opportunity, Fiona. I just didn't take it. It wasn't like he was so sure about it either.

FIONA *(overlapping)*: Who?

DEBBIE: He asked if it would seem right and I said that it wouldn't.

FIONA *(overlapping)*: Who?

DEBBIE: And it didn't seem right. It was that simple. And he understood. He gave me a choice.

FIONA: I didn't do it against my will...

DEBBIE: I know.

FIONA: ... we wanted to and we did.

DEBBIE: And when you miss your period next month and end up with a little embryo inside of you, you'll know something about taking chances.

FIONA: We were careful.

DEBBIE: But let's say something went wrong and something happened to sneak inside you and you get pregnant. Then you'll be a mommy. And our mother will be a grandma. And this man, this *guy*, this guy whose middle name you probably don't even know, will be the father. And you'll both have to take care...

FIONA *(overlapping)*: We were careful.

DEBBIE: ...of it for the next eighteen years.

FIONA: There would always be abortion or adoption or something. Anyway, I'm not pregnant.

DEBBIE: How can you be sure?

FIONA: We were careful.

DEBBIE: The point is... Fiona, the point is *responsibility*. I don't think you're responsible enough—

FIONA: We were responsible enough to be careful, so I don't care how you feel about it. It's none of your business.

141

WHO WILL CARRY THE WORD?
by Charlotte Delbo
translated by Cynthia Haft
Claire (early 20's) - Francoise (early 20's)

The Play: "Why should you believe those stories of ghosts...ghosts who came back and who are not able to explain how?" This is the last line in Charlotte Delbo's startling and touching play set in the 1940's in a Nazi death camp where thousands of women are confined. Among the greatest of human atrocities, the Holocaust of World War II continues to haunt the globe, somehow never to be forgotten or understood. In Ms. Delbo's stirring account of one camp, a camp with women of many nationalities, the issues addressed are of survival, friendship and the maintaining of personal values in the face of the horrible cruelty of the Holocaust concentration camp experience. The particular focus is a group of French women, some in their teens, some in their twenties. The characters are constantly barraged with choices—minute to minute they must decide which move to make in order to survive. It is as if they are living on a chess board. Ultimately, the decision becomes whether or not to survive in a world turned upside down by Nazi terror. Is it worth it? What price does one put on survival? When does one "give up?" To some, perhaps death is preferable to a tortured existance. For others, resistance, pride, anger, and a need to survive and make sure that this atrocity never again happens, becomes the breathe of life. The internal struggle between those who have lost faith in this life and those who will never give in or become the victims is the passionate argument that drives this drama. The play opens with a haunting prologue, poetic and challenging, and closes with the question, "Why should you believe..." In a stark series of scenes, we are placed in the middle of this human dilemma, forced by the hand of mankind at its worst. Ultimately the decision to survive become fueled by the burning need to "carry the word" and tell the world what has happened to those who were consigned to the camps.

The Scene: This is the first scene in the play (following the Prologue). The setting is the barracks. Claire and Francoise, who knew each other prior to consignment to the camp, set forth the argument that drives the

WHO WILL CARRY THE WORD?

play.

Special Note: The editors have selected this scene for advanced students. The playwright insists that no make-up be used and that the costumes be simple smocks or tunics with no stripes. In addition, we remind the actors that any thorough work on this scene must include an exploration of the Holocaust.

WHO WILL CARRY THE WORD?

(In the barracks. In an aisle between the boxes which serve as beds, that is to say, in front of the inclined plane, in the foreground. Some groups chat. On one side, a group composed of FRANCOISE, MOUNETTE, YVONNE, GINA, MADELEINE. Coming from another group, CLAIRE, who will be followed by RÉINE. Some standing up, the others lying down. It is late afternoon in winter. Hazy light inside. Outside, the light is hard and cutting on the snow.)

CLAIRE: Come here. I want to talk to you.

FRANCOISE: Who, me?

CLAIRE: Yes, you.

FRANCOISE: And who are you?

CLAIRE: Claire. Don't you recognize me?

FRANCOISE: Now I recognize your voice. Voices are difficult to recognize. Even the voices have changed. Are they muffled or is it my ears? And what did you want with me, Claire?

CLAIRE: Come over here.

FRANCOISE: Talk. Here, we think out loud.

CLAIRE: What have I heard?

FRANCOISE: What have you heard?

CLAIRE: That you wanted to commit suicide.

FRANCOISE: Yes, so what?

CLAIRE: You have no right to.

FRANCOISE: Oh, that'll do, Claire. Forget your formulas; here they aren't worth anything. It's the only right I have left, the only choice. The last free act.

CLAIRE: There are no free acts here. No choices like that.

FRANCOISE: Oh yes. I have a choice. I have a choice, between becoming a cadaver which will have suffered for only eight days, which will still be clean enough to look at, and one which will have suffered fifteen days, which will be horrible to look at.

CLAIRE: You have nothing left. No such choices, nothing. You are not free to do it. You don't have the right to take your life.

FRANCOISE: And why don't I have the right?

CLAIRE: A fighter doesn't commit suicide.

FRANCOISE: Claire, please. Forget your affirmations, forget your

144

certitudes. None of them fit here. Don't you see that truth has changed, that truth is no longer the same?

CLAIRE: I am asking you why you decided to commit suicide.

FRANCOISE: You ask me!... Ask those who are lying rigid in the snow; ask their faces which are no longer faces; ask the sockets of their eyes which the rats have widened; ask their limbs which resemble dead wood; ask their skin which is a color no one has ever seen before. Don't you know all that a human being can withstand before dying? Don't you believe that to become so scrawny, so ugly, so convulsed, so trapped in what remains of skin and flesh, you have to have suffered to the limit, a limit which no one reached before us? I don't want to suffer to that limit.

CLAIRE: Can't you see further than yourself and your own death? Can't you see...

FRANCOISE: I see. I am lucid. I am logical. I've never been more reasonable.

CLAIRE: You don't want to fight.

FRANCOISE: I'm willing to fight, to try, but with a chance, even a little one, however small, but a chance. And I don't see any. No one will survive. If it's to be death for death's sake, then better right away, before having suffered that suffering you see written on the dead there in the snow, over there on the pile where the ravens and the rats get together, those naked dead bodies, entangled in a pile, even on top of those still alive, who arrived a week before us. I prefer to die before becoming a corpse as ugly as those.

CLAIRE: Coquetry is out of place here.

FRANCOISE: I have no gift for lost courage.

CLAIRE: Will you listen to me?

FRANCOISE: You must wait until my eyes do not see what they see, for my ears to listen to you.

CLAIRE: My eyes see as well as yours. You're afraid. You're a coward.

FRANCOISE: Afraid to suffer, yes. A coward—another word that is meaningless here.

CLAIRE: I'll tell you again that you don't have the right to take your

145

WHO WILL CARRY THE WORD?

life. You don't have the right because you're not alone. There are the others. And above all, there are the little ones, Mounette, Denise, and her sister, Rosette, big Hélène and little Hélène. Aurore, Rosie who isn't even sixteen, all the little ones whom you taught to recite poetry, whom you had perform in plays before we left, when we invented pastimes while we waited for the departure. They admired you because you were grown up. They listen to you, they follow you. If you commit suicide, they may imitate you. Suppose that among them, there is one who has a chance to come back, just one, and that because of you, she loses that chance. Even if you were to die in fifteen days and become as tortured a cadaver as those, you have to stand it.

FRANCOISE: What good will it do? None of us has a chance. No one knows we're here. We're fighters off the battlefield, useless. If we fight to get out, it's no use to anyone, not even to ourselves. We are cut off from everything, cut off from ourselves.

CLAIRE: There must be one who returns, you or another, it doesn't matter. Each of us expects to die here. She is ready. She knows her life doesn't matter any more. Every one of us looks to the others. There must be one who comes back, one who will tell. Would you want millions of people to have been destroyed here and all those cadavers to remain mute for all eternity, all those lives to have been sacrificed for nothing?

FRANCOISE: It's exactly that. For nothing. To die here, in this place, whose name we don't even know—perhaps it has no name?

CLAIRE: There must be one who comes back, who will give it its name.

FRANCOISE: Here, at the frontiers of the inhabited world, yes, it's to die for nothing. It's already as if we were dead.

CLAIRE: If the world never knows anything about it. But there will be one who will return and who will talk and who will tell, and who will make known, because it is no longer we who are at stake, it's history—and people want to know their history. Haven't you heard them, the dying, who all say, "If you return, you'll tell"? Why do they say that? They say that because none of us is alone and each must render an account to all the others.

146

WHO WILL CARRY THE WORD?

FRANCOISE: The others... Other people in other places. To us, here, *they* have lost their reality. Everything has lost its shape, its depth, its sense, its color. All that is left is the amount of time we must suffer before dying.

CLAIRE: Yes, the others, the people you know, your friends—this one or that particular one—have lost their reality. But I speak of men, of the men of the whole world, those who are now and those who will come afterwards. To them you must render an account.

FRANCOISE: Why me? One more, one less... Choose someone else for your mission.

CLAIRE: We arrived two hundred, 200 women from all the provinces, from all classes, who were thrown here into this population of 15,000 women. 15,000 women who are never the same. They die by the hundreds each day, they arrive by the hundreds each day. Of these 15,000 women from all countries of all the languages of Europe, how many will survive? 15,000 women more or less, 200 women more or less, what difference does it make? You, me; it doesn't matter who—no one matters. They will only matter if there is one who returns.

FRANCOISE: It won't be me.

CLAIRE: Don't you really want to understand anything? Even if you hold out for only fifteen days...

FRANCOISE: I won't hold out for fifteen days because I don't want to, because I don't believe it matters, because I prefer to finish it off right away and skip those fifteen days.

CLAIRE: Suppose you hold out fifteen days during which you will have helped others to hold out? Even if you give up then, fifteen days will have been gained. Another will take your place, then another, then another, so that there will be one who makes it until the end.

FRANCOISE: Until the end... When do you see it arriving?

CLAIRE: I don't see it any more than you. Even if there is no hope, even if all is lost, you still have to try.

A YOUNG LADY OF PROPERTY
by Horton Foote
Wilma (15) - Arabella (15)

The Play: As with most of Horton Foote's plays, *A Young Lady of Property* is set in the fictitious town of Harrison, Texas. The year is 1925. The young lady of the title is Miss Wilma Thompson, a strong girl with vision and a zest for life. Since the death of her mother, Wilma has had to live with her Aunt Gertrude. Wilma's father is unable to be responsible for his own life, let alone raise a daughter. Before dying, Wilma's mother saw to it that the house and the property would go to her daughter. When she comes of age, this will all be hers; in the meantime she must live with Aunt Gert. The loneliness she feels comes from the loss of her mother at an early age and her troubled relationship with her father. Life has made unexpected turns, and the only constant in this life, which has turned complicated and painful, is her property. At one point, Wilma decides to seek an appointment with a Hollywood director for a screen test. If she can become a "star" perhaps her life can be exciting and have meaning. But in her heart, Wilma really wants a traditional life with a loving husband and family. When her father threatens to sell the house and property, marry Mrs. Leighton (whom Wilma despises), and move to Houston, Wilma becomes desperate and does everything she can to prevent this from happening. If the property goes, so does everything Wilma treasures. In the end, Wilma's father is stopped by Mrs. Leighton, who turns out to be on Wilma's side after all. Wilma is now able to reconcile her problems with her father, and has remained not only "a young lady of property" but has discovered the true destiny of her life.

The Scene: Wilma's best friend is Arabella Cookenboo. Foote describes Arabella as, "...Wilma's shadow and obviously her adoring slave." As the scene begins, Wilma is sitting in the swing on the front porch of her vacant house. She has been awaiting a letter of response to her request for a screen test. Arabella enters, concealing letters to both girls granting them the screen test. Arabella is terrified about the prospects of leaving Harrison, and equally fearful that she might lose her best friend.

148

A YOUNG LADY OF PROPERTY

WILMA: Heh, Arabella. Come sit and swing.

ARABELLA: All right. Your letter came.

WILMA: Whoopee. Where is it?

ARABELLA: Here. *(She gives it to her. Wilma tears it open. She reads.)*

WILMA: *(Reading)* Dear Miss Thompson: Mr. Delafonte will be glad to see you any time next week about your contemplated screen test. We suggest you call the office when you arrive in the city and we will set an exact time. Yours truly, Adele Murray. Well... Did you get yours?

ARABELLA: Yes.

WILMA: What did it say?

ARABELLA: The same.

WILMA: Exactly the same?

ARABELLA: Yes.

WILMA: Well, let's pack out bags. Hollywood, here we come.

ARBELLA: Wilma...

WILMA: Yes?

ARABELLA: I have to tell you something... Well... I...

WILMA: What is it?

ARABELLA: Well...promise me you won't hate me, or stop being my friend. I never had a friend, Wilma, until you began being nice to me, and I couldn't stand it if you weren't my friend any longer...

WILMA: Oh, my cow. Stop talking like that. I'll never stop being your friend. What do you want to tell me?

ARABELLA: Well...I don't want to go to see Mr. Delafonte, Wilma...

WILMA: You don't?

ARABELLA: No. I don't want to be a movie star. I don't want to leave Harrison or my mother or father... I just want to stay here the rest of my life and get married and settle down and have children.

WILMA: Arabella...

ARABELLA: I just pretended like I wanted to go to Hollywood because I knew you wanted me to, and I wanted you to like me...

WILMA: Oh, Arabella...

ARABELLA: Don't hate me, Wilma. You see, I'd be afraid... I'd die if I had to go to see Mr. Delafonte. Why, I even get faint when I

149

have to recite before the class. I'm not like you. You're not scared of anything.

WILMA: Why do you say that?

ARABELLA: Because you're not. I know.

WILMA: Oh, yes, I am. I'm scared of lots of things.

ARABELLA: What?

WILMA: Getting lost in a city. Being bitten by dogs. Old lady Leighton taking my daddy away... *(A pause.)*

ARABELLA: Will you still be my friend?

WILMA: Sure. I'll always be your friend.

ARABELLA: I'm glad. Oh, I almost forgot. Your Aunt Gert said for you to come on home.

WILMA: I'll go in a little. I love to swing in my front yard. Aunt Gert has a swing in her front yard, but it's not the same. Mama and I used to come out here and swing together. Some nights when Daddy was out all night gambling, I used to wake up and hear her out here swinging away. Sometimes she'd let me come and sit beside her. We'd swing until three or four in the morning. *(A pause. She looks out into the yard.)* The pear tree looks sickly, doesn't it? The fig trees are doing nicely though. I was out in back and the weeds are near knee high, but fig trees just seem to thrive in the weeds. The freeze must have killed off the banana trees... *(A pause. Wilma stops swinging—she walks around the yard.)* Maybe I won't leave either. Maybe I won't go to Hollywood after all.

ARABELLA: You won't?

WILMA: No. Maybe I shouldn't. That just comes to me now. You know sometimes my old house looks so lonesome it tears at my heart. I used to think it looks lonesome just whenever it had no tenants, but now it comes to me it has looked lonesome ever since Mama died and we moved away, and it will look lonesome until some of us move back here. Of course, Mama can't, and Daddy won't. So it's up to me.

ARABELLA: Are you gonna live here all by yourself?

WILMA: No. I talk big about living here by myself, but I'm too much of a coward to do that. But maybe I'll finish school and live with Aunt Gert and keep on renting the house until I meet some nice boy with good habits and steady ways, and marry him. Then we'll move here and have children and I bet this old house won't be lonely any more. I'll get Mama's old croquet set and put it out under the pecan trees and play croquet with my children, or sit in this yard and swing and wave to people as they pass by.

ARABELLA: Oh, I wish you would. Mama says that's a normal life for a girl, marrying and having children. She says being an actress is all right, but the other's better.

WILMA: Maybe I've come to agree with your mama. Maybe I was going to Hollywood out of pure lonesomeness. I felt so alone with Mrs. Leighton getting my daddy and my mama having left the world. Daddy could have taken away my lonesomeness, but he didn't want to or couldn't. Aunt Gert says nobody is lonesome with a house full of children, so maybe that's what I just ought to stay here and have...

ARABELLA: Have you decided on a husband yet?

WILMA: No.

AREBELLA: Mama says that's the bad feature of being a girl, you have to wait for the boy to ask you and just pray that the one you want wants you. Tommy Murray is nice, isn't he?

WILMA: I think so.

ARABELLA: Jay Godfrey told me once he wanted to ask you for a date, but he didn't dare because he was afraid you'd turn him down.

WILMA: Why did he think that?

ARABELLA: He said the way you talked he didn't think you would go out with anything less than a movie star.

WILMA: Maybe you'd tell him different...

ARABELLA: All right. I think Jay Godfrey is very nice. Don't you?

WILMA: Yes, I think he's very nice and Tommy is nice...

ARABELLA: Maybe we could double-date sometimes.

WILMA: That might be fun.

ARABELLA: Oh, Wilma. Don't go to Hollywood. Stay here in Harrison and let's be friends forever....

WILMA: All right. I will.

ARABELLA: You will?

WILMA: Sure, why not? I'll stay here. I'll stay and marry and live in my house.

ARABELLA: Oh, Wilma. I'm so glad. I'm so very glad.

ALBUM
by David Rimmer
Billy (16) - Boo (16)

The Play: A comedy about growing up and coming of age in the turbulent sixties, *Album* spans three-and-a-half years from October 1963 to June 1965, and chronicles the adventures and misadventures of two teenaged couples, Peggy and Billy, and Trish and Boo. The action takes them from playing strip poker in Trish's bedroom to summer camp and graduation day. Along the way there is a wonderful counterpoint of the popular music of the day—The Beatles, The Doors, The Rolling Stones, and Bob Dylan—underscoring their hopes and dreams, and their fears and insecurities. *Album* is a sometimes frank yet poignantly humorous look at those last carefree years of youth.

The Scene: "Ain't It Just Like the Night": November 1965 in Billy and Boo's dorm room at boarding school. Bob Dylan's "Positively 4th Street" is playing on the record player. Boo, always full of energy, is moving with the music and singing along. Billy, more cool and together, is a bit bored; he is idly playing with a football.

Special Note: This edition incorporates changes in dialogue specified by the author in the acting edition.

ALBUM

BOO: See? What'd I tell ya? Greatest song of all time.

BILLY: *(Holding back.)* It's all right.

BOO: It's all right? That's the greatest song I ever heard in my life. It's all right. *(Dylan voice.)* Such an incredible drag for me to see you. He's greater than the Beatles.

BILLY: How can he be greater than the Beatles? They're four guys. That's stupid.

BOO: *(Dylan voice.)* Got some kinda nerve sayin' you're my friend.

BILLY: *(Acting tough.)* Oh yeah? Who said I was?

BOO: You. *(Beat.)* 'Bout time this song came out up here. Takes everything ten years to get here. *(Dylan.)* This place's so slow, it's invisible. —I can't believe you didn't like that song.

BILLY: What song?

BOO: Aarrhh! I'm gonna kill you!

BILLY: *(Jumps off the bed; fists up.)* Put up your dukes.

BOO: *(Beginning to laugh.)* Wh—? Put up my dukes?... That's stupid— *(Both of them jockeying around each other like fighters in the ring, giggling.)*

BILLY: What's stupid?

BOO: You're stupid—

BILLY: —Oh yeah?—

BOO: You're brain-damaged—

BILLY: Where ya think I got it from? Hangin' around spastics like you—

BOO: Whoa...vicious...

BILLY: Whoa... *(Viciously sarastic.)* Awww...

BOO: *(Yelling; overlapping.)* How much time before dinner, dinkweed?

BILLY: HEY, MORONS!! *(Ducks; Boo dives under the bed.)* The clock onna Science Building says twenty to six.

BOO: Twenty minutes! I wanted to hear *Highway 61* and the first side... *(Billy fakes yawning, going to sleep.)* of *Bringing It All Back Home.* There's never enough time to do anything in this stupid place! I hate this school—

BILLY: Big deal, who doesn't?

153

BOO: Every minute you hafta *do* somethin'. Can't stay up late, can't smoke cigerettes, hafta wear ties. It's always *daytime* here.

BILLY: *(Shrugs.)* Stay up all night.

BOO: Sure. They'd kick me right outta here. *(Sudden rage, frustration.) God, ya can't even stay up at night!* Aaaaaaaaaaaarrrrrhh!! *(Bitter chant.)* Give us this day our daily hate... —Bet Dylan never gets up during the daytime.

BILLY: He's a vampire.

BOO: Be cool to be a vampire. Cooler than this. Get to be invisible.

BILLY: See a lotta free movies.

BOO: Hey...I just remembered this dream I had last night.

BILLY: *(Scornful.)* What dream?

BOO: I was at this big posh party in London, at this really rich house. It was really high up, and there were these big picture windows, you could see the river and all the lights of the town. I was with a girl—you know who it was? Trish.

BILLY: That weirdo? What happened, she letcha go all the way or somethin'?

BOO: Nah, we were just lookin' out the window... And all these rich little old ladies started runnin' around all over the place, all excited, sayin' Mick Jagger's coming, isn't that wonderful, Mick Jagger's coming. They came up to us and they told us be careful cause the latest thing in London now was sadism, and Mick was really into it. Then they flitted away, laughin' and eatin' *hors d'oeuvres* and stuff, and everybody was just waitin' for Mick to show up. Finally he did, he just walked right in, Marianne Faithfull was with him—she had purple hair. And this whole crowd of little old ladies swarmed all around him. They introduced me to him, and he was incredibly scary-looking, his face, he really made me scared just lookin' at him. He had lipstick on and make-up and he was dressed like a woman, but it was more like he really *was* a woman, a woman and a man at the same time. All of a sudden he started pullin' my hair, really vicious, and he had these bracelets on that were made outta spikes, they jabbed into me, I saw drops of blood drippin' off 'em like a horror movie. I screamed or somethin', I just ran away I was so scared. I ended up in this room

154

away from the party, nobody around, and I saw this guy sittin' on a couch, just sittin' there by himself, really quiet, watchin' TV. I sat down and watched the TV for a couple of minutes, then I turned and looked at the guy... and it was Dylan.

BILLY: Wow... I never get anybody like that in mine. All I ever get is all my aunts and uncles and cousins givin' me grief all the time. Always at these big family reunions...gross.

BOO: Hey, you wanna stay up all night tonight? It'll be cool, we can take No-Doz..

BILLY: Nah...

BOO: Nah... You never want to do anything. *(Muttering; pacing.)* Aahh... Gotta do somethin'... *(Suddenly excited.)* Hey! Did I tell you about that song?

BILLY: *(Mocking.)* Oh that song that song!

BOO: Yeah—

BILLY: *(Abrupt.)* What song?

BOO: That song. I told ya. The greatest song I ever heard—

BILLY: —Yeah yeah, there's about thirty of those—

BOO: —Remember? At the concert? Dylan. I told you—

BILLY: —sure sure—

BOO: —Your brain is like Swiss Cheese. —Oh right, I told my roommate.

BILLY: Think I'm brain-damaged...

BOO: Friend, roommate, what's the difference—? *(Billy slams a football into Boo's gut, then sings the Beatles' "You've Got to Hide Your Love Away." Boo, overlapping.)* —I heard it at the concert I went to at the end of the summer— Whaddayou doin'? *(Yelling over Billy's singing.)* Shut up! He played this new song, it was the first time he ever played it— *Hey!*

BILLY: *(Belting it like Dylan.)* Hey! Gotta hide your love away!

BOO: See? Even the Beatles imitate Dylan.

BILLY: The Beatles don't need to imitate nobody, specially Dylan.

BOO: Everybody needs to imitate Dylan.

BILLY: Yeah, you do it enough.

BOO: Whoa...vicious... *(Dylan voice.)* Got some kinda nerve—

ALBUM

BILLY: —sayin' I'm your friend?

BOO: You just got a lotta nerve, buddy. It's called "Visions of Johanna," it's not on an album yet, but it's greater than anything he ever did—

BILLY: So let's hear it, world's greatest Bob Dylan fan.

BOO: I don't have it, ya jerk, it isn't out yet.

BILLY: So play somethin' else.

BOO: *(Can't believe his ears.)* What? I'm gonna die. *You* wanna hear Dylan?

BILLY: *(Muttered.)* ...Anything to get you to shut up... —Yeah sure, I like Dylan.

BOO: Bull.

BILLY: I do. I just like givin' you grief, that's all.

BOO: *(Dubious.)* Okay. How about the flip side of "4th Street"?

BILLY: *(Could care less.)* Sure.

BOO: You're really crackin' up. *(Puts the record on, holding his hands up, signalling for silence, announcing.)* All right: "From a Buick 6." Produced by Bob Johnston, Al Kooper on organ, Michael Bloomfield on guitar.

BILLY: Just play the record— *("From a Buick 6" starts, volume way up. Billy shakes his head in disgust. Boo smiles, listens, closes his eyes, bops around.)* Hey! HEY!

BOO: WHAT?

BILLY: TURN IT DOWN!

BOO: WH—? NAH!

BILLY: IT'S TOO LOUD!

BOO: I LIKE IT LOUD!

BILLY: I DON'T CARE, TURN IT DOWN!

BOO: BITE THE HAIRY WAZOO! *(Billy goes to the record player, reaches for the volume. Suddenly the lights in the room flicker and go out, and the record player goes off. All the elctricity is off. They're totally in the dark.)*

BILLY: Hey! What is this—

BOO: Aw jeez. The lights go out right in the middle of Dylan.

BILLY: Think it's just your room or the whole dorm?

ALBUM

BOO: *(Amused.)* Hey, this is cool.

BILLY: Whaddaya think it is?

BOO: I dunno, but we need two things.

BILLY: What?

BOO: Candles and a portable record player.

BILLY: Whaddayou talkin' about?

BOO: I got one over here. Used to be my sister's. Y'wanna hear the song, don'tcha? There's candles in the drawer—

BILLY: Candles? Whaddaya have candles for ?

BOO: Just get 'em. I'll get the record player.

BILLY: Candles, portable record player... What else ya got, a fallout shelter? *(Gets up cautiously, makes his way across the room, muttering.)* Can't see anything... *(Bangs into the bed.)* Ow! Why am I doing this?

BOO: It's okay, just get your eyes used to it.

BILLY: Yeah, great.

BOO: *(Dylan.)* Don't get hung up on your eyelids.

BILLY: *(Billy reaches the desk, opens the drawer and takes out the candles and matches. Boo finds the portable record player.)* Candles...weird...

BOO: Hey. Billy.

BILLY: What is it now?

BOO: If I can make it over there without touching anything, everything'll be all right for the rest of our lives. Okay?

BILLY: Okay. *(Boo begins moving slowly forward. But Billy lights the candle—)*

BOO: Hey! —Okay, I'll close my eyes. *(He continues across the room, which is a little lighter now. Billy notices something out the window.)*

BILLY: Hey.

BOO: What?

BILLY: C'mere, look at this.

BOO: I gotta do this—

BILLY: Put the record player down, Marston, look at this.

BOO: *What? (He opens his eyes, puts it down on the desk, looks out the window with Billy.)*

BILLY: The lights in the Dining Hall aren't on. See? And the Science Building... The clock stopped. See? And the Gym...

BOO: It's great. Look at that star.

BILLY: Look— All the lights in town are off!

BOO: It's so dark you can see everything.

BILLY: Huh?

BOO: *(Dylan voice.)* Dark into nighttime...makin' daytime black...

BILLY: Cut it out willya. Whadda we gonna do?

BOO: *(Dreamy.)* Do?

BILLY: Whadda we gonna do?

BOO: Whaddaya mean?

BILLY: *(Half-kidding.)* It's gotta be the Russians, right?, or the Martians, or whoever it's supposed to be on those Conelrad things.

BOO: Nah, it's the Transylvanians, y'never hear about them any more, they're prob'ly still mad about Dracula.

BILLY: Shut up. Whaddaya think it is?

BOO: End of the world.

BILLY: Get your radio.

BOO: The transistor?

BILLY: Yeah.

BOO: It's not mine, it's my roommate's, I just borrow it after lights-out.

BILLY: I don't care whose it is, just get it.

BOO: Whaddaya want?

BILLY: *Just get the radio, okay?*

BOO: Okay.

BILLY: If we get a station, then we'll know it's just a local thing, okay? *(Boo crosses to his bed and gets the radio from under the pillow. They sit on the bed, the radio in Boo's lap. He fakes turning it on, goes into a Dylan voice.)*

BOO: HOW DOES IT FEEL? *(Billy doesn't laugh, his face set like stone. He grabs the radio from Boo and turns it on. No sound comes out. He turns the dial slowly around, getting nothing. Gets up, paces nervously.)*

ALBUM

BILLY: All the radio stations are off!

BOO: This radio isn't very strong—

BILLY: —The batteries in?—

BOO: —Yeah it's got—

BILLY: —The whole country— It *is* somebody. It's the Russians, for God's sake.

BOO: Russians don't believe in God.

BILLY: What—? Don't be funny—

BOO: Why not—?

BILLY: —World War III— *(He turns suddenly and heads for the window, pokes his head out.)* What're those kids doin'? They're chasin' that kid! Hey! WHAT'S GOIN' ON? HEY! YOU GUYS! This place's goin' crazy—

BOO: Take it easy, whaddaya tryin' to do, scare the pants offa me?

BILLY: *(Heads for the door.)* I'm goin' out. I gotta find out what's happenin'—

BOO: *(Stopping him.)* Whaddaya nuts? Whaddaya doin'? Don't go out there.

BILLY: Why not?

BOO: I don't know. Just don't. It's stupid.

BILLY: Yeah...okay...uh... What time is it?

BOO: Who cares what time it is? All the clocks stopped.

BILLY: *Hey!* Watch it! I'm tellin' you—

BOO: I'm sorry. Look, the best thing is just stay here, see what happens. Really. C'mon. This is fun.

BILLY: Yeah...maybe...

BOO: Least we got a record player here. Times like this ya need Dylan. *(He takes "Positively 4th Sreet" off the electric record player. Billy just watches him, dumb-struck.)* You don't think I'm gonna let myself get blown up without—

BILLY: —You're crazy—

BOO: —a little Dylan.

BILLY: I don't believe this. The world's gonna blow up and you're—

BOO: —Let's play "4th Street" again—

BILLY: —Maybe not the whole world. Just certain parts of America.

Like right here. *(Boo opens the portable, puts on the record.)* You can't play that now.

BOO: Why not? *(BIlly throws up his hands in disgust, giving up. "Positively 4th Street" starts. Boo turns the volume way up.)*

BILLY: *(Shouting over the sound.)* You really can't just sit here—

BOO: Sit down, have a good time—

BILLY: We gotta *do* somethin', find out what's goin' on—

BOO: So, Billy, I'll tell ya 'bout that song, that concert—

BILLY: *(Pacing madly.)* Where is everybody?

BOO: It was just him the first half, playin' guitar, had his harmonica 'round his neck—

BILLY: *(Holding his ears.)* —so *loud!*— *(Turns the volume down.)*

BOO: —played "Love Minus Zero," "Mr. Tambourine Man," stuff like that—

BILLY: *Whaddayou talkin' about?*

BOO: —then he brought out the guys in the band— *(Whips the volume back up high.)* —and a few kids booed, not too many, he looked kinda happy about that—

BILLY: *Shut up!*—

BOO: —I hate all those folk music jerks, music's so much cooler when everything's plugged in—

BILLY: WILL YOU SHUT UP!!

BOO: HEY!

(Billy yanks the record off. Boo shoves him. Billy shoves him back. Boo lunges for him. They scuffle madly, grappling, arms pumping, flailing wildly. After a minute, they pull away, ready like wrestlers, crouching, feinting.)

BOO: Leave my records alone!

BILLY: I'm so sick of Dylan—

BOO: I'm so sick of you— *(Boo jumps at him, yelling. They fight each other insanely, in close contact, bashing into furniture, pushing each other all over the room, finally falling on the floor. Billy easily takes Boo, getting him in a vise-like half-nelson, then pushes him away. Boo stays on the floor, Billy gets to his feet.)*

BILLY: Now cut it out! You're really outta your mind!

BOO: *(Bitterly sarcastic.)* Put up your dukes...

BILLY: Shut up! Dylan. Whaddaya in love with him? All you ever say—

BOO: *(scornful, nasty.)* I thought you *liked* him.

BILLY: I just said that to get you to shut up. Every minute— You're like a girl. *(Boo rises to his feet, singing the last verse of "Positively 4th Street" as loud as he can, screaming lines like "I wish that for just one time you could stand inside my shoes" and "You'd know what a drag it is to see you" to show his crazed anger. Billy screams to be heard over him, shoving him, belting his shoulder.)* SHUT UP! *SHUT UP!!!!* —What's good about him? He isn't cool, he can't sing. His songs're stupid, they don't make any sense. His voice stinks— *(They're facing each other, screaming simultaneously at the top of their lungs.)*

BILLY: IT STINKS!	BOO: BRAIN-DAMAGED!
STINKS!	YOU STINK!
HE STINKS!	SHUT UP!!
SHUT UP!!	

(Billy reaches the breaking point and hurls Boo head first into the door. A loud bang, and Boo crumples onto the floor, holding his face in pain. Billy backs away, shaking.)

BILLY: I hate Dylan.

BOO: I hate you.

BILLY: *(Pacing, muttering.)* I can't take this.

BOO: You can't take anything. You're always so worried about everything—

BILLY: Don't gimme that—

BOO: You don't like anything— *(An involuntary cry pain escapes from Boo. He stifles it right away, hiding his face from Billy, who comes over to him.)*

BILLY: *(Scared.)* Are you okay?

BOO: *(Muttered bitterly.)* Put up your dukes...

BILLY: There's really somethin' wrong with you, Marston, I swear—

BOO: There's nothin' wrong with you...

BILLY: I never know what you're talkin' about—

BOO: *(Spiteful Dylan voice.)* Your ears're in your back pocket, your eyes're on the ground.

BILLY: *(Gets mad again.)* See? *(Makes a move toward Boo, but stops himself in time. Stalks around the room, muttering, trying to figure things out. Boo stays where he is on the floor, not reacting to him at all, not moving. Stops, takes a long look at Boo.)* We just beat each other up over Bob Dylan. *(No response from Boo. Beat. Billy softens a little.)* Hey Boo, I— *(Doesn't know what to say. Takes out a piece of gum, about to offer it to Boo. Doesn't; tosses it aside.)* You wanna try and find out what's goin' on?

BOO: No.

BILLY: *(Voice of reason.)* Don'tcha wanna see what everybody's doin', find out about the lights?

BOO: I like it the way it is.

BILLY: Uh... okay. I'm gonna go. You be all right?

BOO: Yeh.

BILLY: I'll try and find somebody, see what's goin' on. Then maybe I'll—come back— Maybe the lights'll go back on.

BOO: Hope not.

BILLY: Okay, guess I'll...

BOO: Know what?

BILLY: What?

BOO: I'm the one that's brain-damaged.

BILLY: Take it easy...

BOO: I wanted that to happen. I planned it. *(They look at each other a second, look away. Beat.)* I didn't tell you about the song. The guys in the band came out, started playin' electric, really loud, and he was singin'. Never said anything, just stood up there, these blue lights on him, this halo around his hair, it looked like those fires on the edge of the sun.

BILLY: Hey, I'm gonna go—

BOO: Go ahead. *(Billy takes a candle, leaving one on the floor next to Boo. He crosses to the door, opens it.)*

BILLY: Bye. *(Boo doesn't look at him. Billy silently slips away, glancing down the corridor with the light from the candle. Exits.)*

ALBUM

BOO: *(Dylan voice: soft, hoarse.)* You're invisible now. *(Beat.)* See, he wasn't sayin' anything before the songs. But this time he did. He said the next song was a new song, he never did it in front of anybody before, he hoped we liked it. *(Dylan voice: soft, far away.)* Hope ya like it. —And in the song he keeps seein' these visions of Johanna. He's in this motel room with Louise, but these visions keep comin' in. He tries to stop 'em, but they're everyplace he looks, and then his conscience explodes, and the visions take his place, and he just fades away, right in the song, this amazing song, and there's nothin' left 'cept these visions... All these visions... *(Stops, looks around the room. Looks out the window. Softly sings the opening of "Visons of Johanna," beginning "Ain't it just like the night..." After a couple of lines, he calms down a bit. Picks up the candle.)* Ain't never gonna get light again. *(Blows the candle out.)*

ANOTHER COUNTRY
by Julian Mitchell
Guy Bennett (17) - Tommy Judd (17)

The Play: Julian Mitchell's drama is set in 1930 in an English Public school for boys. Guy Bennett and Tommy Judd are destined, by heritage, to become members of the ruling class in England. They have in common a resistance to assuming their respective roles in that ruling class. Bennett feels he cannot fit into a society that is unwilling to accept his homosexuality—something he has struggled to come to grips with in himself. His love of another boy leads him to ridicule and physical punishment. Judd, a sophistocated intellectual, refuses to accept the political climate in England, preferring to commit his energies to the Marxist movement. His unmoving political convictions isolate him from the other students. Alike in their rebellious natures, Bennett and Judd become friends, providing support to each other as they struggle to resist conformity in an unyielding structure at school. Finally, each boy seeks "another country," one that is more suitable to the essence of their beings.

The Scene: Bennett has been caught passing a note to James, a young man at school whom he cares for deeply. The note, a frank declaration of his love, has lead to a final showdown (late in the play) between Bennett and the boys who head the house—his fellow students. In previous disagreements, Bennett has been successful by blackmailing his way out of trouble, therefore allowing him to stay true to his beliefs. This has not worked this time. As the scene begins, Bennett has just returned from having been caned (a beating) by the heads of the house.

Special Note: The editors have selected this scene for advanced students and encourage in-depth examination into period and style.

(It is evening.   JUDD is working.   The door is flung open and BENNETT rushes in, throws himself on the window-seat and hides his face. JUDD gets quietly up and shuts the door, then goes back to the table. Pause.)

JUDD: Didn't the blackmail work this time?

BENNETT: *(muffled)* I couldn't use it.

JUDD: I don't see why not.

BENNETT: *(still hiding his face) Because. (Pause.)*

JUDD: Because what?

BENNETT: *(turning his tear-stained face)* Because James has two more years here! And if I'd gone to Farcical they'd have reported him too!

JUDD: So what?

BENNETT: I couldn't do that! I *love* him!

JUDD: Guy—

BENNETT: *(sitting up)* You still don't believe me, do you?

JUDD: I think you may *think* you're in love with him.

BENNETT: Look—I'm not going to pretend any more. I'm sick of pretending. I'm—*(He can't find a suitable word.)*—I'm never going to love women.

JUDD: Don't be rediculous.

(Pause.)

BENNETT: It's why Martineau killed himself. He'd known since he was ten, he told me. I didn't know. Well—I wasn't sure. Till James.

JUDD: You can't possibly know a thing like that at ten. Or now.

BENNETT: Oh, yes you can. *(Pause.)* It doesn't come as any great revelation. It's more like admitting to yourself—what you've always known. Owning up to yourself. It's a great relief. In some ways. *(Pause.)* All this acting it up—making a joke of it even to myself—it was only a way of trying to pretend it wasn't true. But it is.

JUDD: Of course it's not.

BENNETT: Tommy, when you come down to it, it's as simple as knowing whether or not you like spinach.

JUDD: I can never make up my mind about spinach.

BENNETT: Then perhaps you're ambidextrous.

JUDD: No, I am *not*!

BENNETT: You see? You know.

(Pause.)

JUDD: You can't trust intuitions like that.

BENNETT: What else is there? Are you a communist because you read Karl Marx? No. You read Karl Marx because you know you're a communist.

(Pause.)

JUDD: Well—I'm very sorry.

BENNETT: Thanks! If that's how friends react—

JUDD: What do you want me to do? Get a horsewhip?

BENNETT: *(standing and feeling himself)* Not after Delahay, thanks.

JUDD: Why Delahay?

BENNETT: Barclay's lost his nerve. And Delahay has a very whippy wrist.

(Pause.)

JUDD: I apologise. You're quite right. It was patronising and unforgivable.

BENNETT: But you couldn't help it, could you? In your heart of hearts, like Barclay and Delahay and Menzies and Sanderson—in spite of your talk about equality and fraternity—you really believe that some people are better than others because of the way they make love.

JUDD: There's complete sexual freedom in Russia.

BENNETT: That's not a lot of comfort at the moment, actually. *(Pause.)* Martineau killed himself because he simply couldn't face a lifetime of *that*.

JUDD: But you said it was a great relief, knowing.

BENNETT: Oh, don't you ever listen? I said, in some ways. It's also a life sentence. *(Pause.)* Poor Martineau! He was just the sort of pathetic dope who'd've got caught the whole time. Spent his life in prison, being sent down every few months by magistrates called Barclay and Delahay.

(Pause.)

JUDD: I'm sorry, but I don't see how you can be so sure about it.

BENNETT: Because I *love* him!

ANOTHER COUNTRY

JUDD: Come on!

BENNETT: You've never been in love. You don't understand. *(Pause.)* Everything seems different. Everything seems possible. You can really believe life could be—it's so obvious! It's madness what we have now. Strikes and beating and Twenty Two and—how many unemployed are there?

JUDD: Three million, seven hundred and fifty thousand.

BENNETT: God, are there really?

JUDD: Yes.

BENNETT: Well—there must be a better way to run things. And when you're in love, it all seems so easy. *(JUDD looks disapproving.)* Don't cluck at me, Tommy. You don't know what I'm talking about. *(Pause.)* We've been meeting every night. In Gridley Field pavilion. We don't just—actually we don't more often than we do. We just—hold each other. And talk. Or not talk. Till dawn last night. *(Pause.)* Maintaining ecstasy.

JUDD: Is he getting beaten, too?

BENNETT: No, no. He never got the note. They couldn't pin anything on him. And after Martineau and Robbins—Barclay doesn't want anyone in Longford's even suspecting. *(Pause.)* I understand all about Martineau now. He was in love with Robbins, but Robbins wasn't with him.

JUDD: Don't let your imagination run away with you.

BENNETT: For Robbins it was just a game. Assignation—excitement—hands fumbling with buttons in the dark—all perfectly normal! School practice! But then poor Martineau—he went and told him. And Robbins was revolted—disgusted! He shoved him away. *That's* not what he'd come for! And Martineau knocked something over and Nickers came in to see what was happening and—

JUDD: Yes.

BENNETT: Robbins furiously buttoning. Martineau—sobbing and sobbing with his trousers down. *(Pause.)* Think of that for a lifetime. *(Pause.)* Think of the names. Pansy. Nancy. Fairy. Fruit. *(Pause.)* Brown nose.

(Pause.)

JUDD: Do I detect just a touch of self-pity?

BENNETT: Probably.

JUDD: Fight it. Every time someone calls you a name—thump him.

BENNETT: Thanks! And spend my whole life locked up?

JUDD: The suffragettes didn't get the vote by whining.

BENNETT: Suffragettes!

JUDD: You have to change the fundamental social attitudes, Guy. You have to make people *see*. It always comes down to that.

BENNETT: It does with you.

BLUE DENIM
by James Leo Herlihy and William Noble
Arthur (15) - Ernie (15)

The Play: First produced on Broadway in 1958, *Blue Denim* is a compassionate drama concerning the communication problem between the younger and older generations. The plot centers around Arthur Bartley, son of a retired Army Major, his mother, sister, friend Ernie, and his girl friend, Janet, and concerns the crisis that develops when Arthur finds out that he and Janet are about to become parents. Arthur is scared and alone; he can't turn to his parents for help, they just don't seem to speak the same language. When Arthur and Janet decide that an abortion is the only answer to the problem, Arthur turns to his friend Ernie for advice on how to handle the situation. Ernie advises against such action and urges Arthur to talk to his parents. The boy tries to do so, but is unable to make himself understood; his parents seem unwilling to truly listen. Ultimately, the play depicts the insecurity of youth and the failure of many parents to ever really come to know their children.

The Scene: Arthur and Ernie are in the basement of Arthur's house. Arthur has asked Ernie over to talk to him about a "serious" problem. Ernie is playing solitaire and Arthur has just picked up a wad of bed sheets that his sister has hurled down the stairs.

Special Note: While the issues and concerns of *Blue Denim* remain timely, the language is that of the late 1950's when the play was written. Because of this, the play may be best served when set during this period.

BLUE DENIM

(ARTHUR picks up the sheets, wraps them around his neck thought-lessly, then drapes them over his head)

ERNIE: Well, you going to turn it off or aren't you?

ARTHUR: *(From under the sheets)* Shut up. *(ARTHUR sits on the day bed, listlessly places his hands over his sheet-covered face)*

ERNIE: I'm on your side, y'know. But if you *don't* turn the tank off the whole house'll blow up and they'll blame it all on you. I can just see the fire engines screaming up Seven Mile Road—and your old man standing out front in his nightshirt with a row o' World War ribbons across his chest.

ARTHUR: My old man wears pajamas.

ERNIE: Pajamas, then. And Lillian and your ma with their hair up in curlers bawling hell out of you 'cause you wouldn't turn off the hot-water tank.

(ARTHUR rips the sheets from his face and takes them to the far corner of the basement, where he deposits them in a laundry basket. Then he opens the door under the stairway and turns off the tank)

ARTHUR: You know something, Ernie? You're getting on my nerves lately. You're always talking. You don't know how to just plain shut up. Sorry, but that's one o' your faults. Maybe you don't even realize it even.

ERNIE: I don't get it. Invite me over to talk about something serious—and when I get here all I get is a big lecture about how nervous I make you. *(Gathering cards together)* Oh, well, this isn't coming out right, anyhow.

ARTHUR: Sit down.

ERNIE: Nah, I think I'll go home and give your nerves a rest.

ARTHUR: *(Pushing him back into the chair)* Sit down, I said. I do want to talk to you. Only...

ERNIE: Yeah?

ARTHUR: I just hadn't got around to it yet— You know what you said once about a doctor that does operations on girls?

ERNIE: On girls?

ARTHUR: Don't act square!

ERNIE: I'm not acting square. What doctor?

ARTHUR: You said, Clifford Truckston came to you when his girl

170

was in trouble.

ERNIE: Art, so help me—

ARTHUR: *(Standing over him)* You know what I'm talking about. Don't act square, I said!

ERNIE: Okay, I remember.

ARTHUR: Well, I met a guy the other day wants to get hold of that doctor.

ERNIE: *What* guy?

ARTHUR: I can't say; I swore I wouldn't tell a soul.

ERNIE: Well, you better not tell *me*, then.

ARTHUR: He's a real nice guy. He really is. A friend of the family, you know, kind of like a cousin, only he's *not* my cousin.

ERNIE: Where's he live?

ARTHUR: Hazel Park.

ERNIE: How come you never mentioned him before?

ARTHUR: I said, he's a friend of the family. *(When ERNIE does not answer)* I promised him and he's counting on me, Ernie. I told him all about you, and—how you know everything.

ERNIE: *(A little sickly)* Yeah?

ARTHUR: Yeah. I told him what a swell guy you are and—he said he'd like to meet you sometime.

ERNIE: Look, Art, I'd like to help this bird, but you don't want to get mixed up in it. I mean, hell, you could get thrown in jail so fast it'd make your teeth chatter. Abortion's a crime. It's murder.

ARTHUR: *(Intensely)* The hell it is! *(ARTHUR grips ERNIE's wrist tightly)* Always yakkin'! Always running off at the mouth!

ERNIE: Hey, leggo, Art.

ARTHUR: *(Not letting go)* Tell me!

ERNIE: Tell you what?

ARTHUR: The doctor!

ERNIE: *(Trying to rise)* You're awful hard to get along with lately, Art. Pretty soon you won't have any friends left if you keep on—

(ARTHUR pushes the card table out of the way and grips ERNIE's head in the crook of one arm; with the other he restrains ERNIE's resistance)

ARTHUR: Who is he? Where's he live?

ERNIE: You're chokin' me!

BLUE DENIM

ARTHUR: *(Applying greater pressure)* You gonna tell?

ERNIE: Leggo, you stupid sonofabitch!

(ARTHUR forces ERNIE to the floor, straddles him with one knee on his chest, his hands clenched around his throat)

ARTHUR: *(Hysterical)* You're not stupid, are you, Ernie! Know all the answers! Know everything! Just ask Ernie! *(Then, in a hoarse whisper, inclining his head toward ERNIE until their faces almost touch)* That's baby's getting bigger and bigger every minute!

ERNIE: Art, if you kill me they'll put you in jail!

ARTHUR: Tell me!

ERNIE: I can't! I was lying!

(ARTHUR releases his grip on ERNIE. He slumps into a chair and stares at the floor)

ARTHUR: *(Dully)* You were lying? Why?

ERNIE: I dunno, Art. I just thought of saying it—and out it came.

ARTHUR: Yeah.

ERNIE: Don't be mad, Art. *(A small nervous laugh)* Maybe I got a big-shot complex or something. 'Cause I'm little—and kinda skinny—and...

ARTHUR: *(Quietly)* Ernie, what am I gonna do?

ARNIE: *(Rising to a sitting position)* What're...*you* gonna do? *(Staring reverently at ARTHUR)* I'll find out for you, Art.

(Throwing his right arm into the air) I swear to God may my father be struck dead! Who's the g—girl? Never mind, you don't have to tell me. *(A pause)* That was all true about Truckston. Only he didn't come to me. I just heard about it.

ARTHUR: *(Quietly pleading)* Where, Ernie? Where'd you hear about it?

ERNIE: At the drugstore. You know that kid with the funny arm? Well, he knows, 'cause the doctor is his uncle or something.

ARTHUR: You sure?

ERNIE: I'm not sure it's his uncle. But I can find out because that kid knows all about it.

ARHTUR: How come you're holding your neck?

ERNIE: No reason.

ARTHUR: I'm sorry, Ernie. I don't know my own strength

172

sometimes.

ERNIE: Good crap, forget it. You got *real* problems. Say I find out about the doctor, where you going to get the money?

ARTHUR: Don't worry, I'll get it. I'll get it if I have to steal it!

ERNIE: That much?

ARTHUR; How much's it cost?

ERNIE: I think a hundred and twenty-five.

ARTHUR: *(Breathing it)* Brother!

ERNIE: You got any dough at all?

ARTHUR: I got a war bond. The ten years was up on my birthday.

ERNIE: How much?

ARTHUR: Only twenty-five. *You* got any dough?

ERNIE: Not a cent.

ARTHUR: How much could I get for my air rifle? And my bike—I mean if I fixed the tires?

ERNIE: A couple of bucks, maybe. That's just junk. *(Carefully)* Maybe Janet's got some.

ARTHUR: *(Vehemently)* Who said anything about *Janet*?

(ERNIE moves quickly away, holding his neck protectively)

ERNIE: Hey, not again!

ARTHUR: Don't tell anybody, Ernie. *(Raising his right hand)* Swear!

ERNIE: Hell, no, I won't swear. What you got a buddy for if you can't trust him?

ARTHUR: It's just—well, you're always talkin'. It could slip out.

ERNIE: Relax!

ARTHUR: Anyway, Janet's only got eight dollars.

ERNIE: How far along is she?

ARTHUR: I don't know exactly. What's eight and twenty-five? Thirty-three dollars. How much's that leave?

ERNIE: Ninety-two. *If* the price is still a hundred an' a quarter.

ARTHUR: It wouldn't go up, would it?

(There is a pause)

ERNIE: Art.

ARTHUR: Yeah?

ERNIE: I suppose you and Janet talked plenty about this?

ARTHUR: O' course we did. Ever since—we found out.

173

BLUE DENIM

ERNIE: How's she feel about it?

ARTHUR: Just like me. Trapped.

ERNIE: I mean about the operation.

ARTHUR: Janet says she'll do whatever I want.

ERNIE: Sounds like she really loves you.

ARTHUR: Yeah. She does.

ERNIE: But you don't really love her, is that it?

ARTHUR: Sure I do.

ERNIE: Then why don't you get married? If you—

ARTHUR: *(Interrupting angrily)* We're too young! Listen Ernie. You're the one's always talking about being realistic. Where'd we live? And what *on*?

ERNIE: Maybe you could move in with her dad.

ARTHUR; Nah! He's—he cries.

ERNIE: Maybe here then, with your folks.

ARTHUR: *(Groaning)* Aw, Ernie!... Sometimes you talk like you didn't even know the facts of life.

ERNIE: You talk like your folks didn't.

ARTHUR: *(Seriously)* Maybe they don't.

ERNIE: You got born, didn't you?

ARTHUR: *(Doubtfully)* Yeah, but... Ernie, answer me something serious. Can you picture my mom and dad in bed together?

ERNIE: *(After careful consideration, shakes his head)* Hunhunh.

ARTHUR; Neither can I.

ERNIE: Look, Art, I can stand around and be your stooge. Or I can be your friend and tell you what I really think.

ARTHUR; You are my friend!

ERNIE: Yeah, but will you keep your goddam hands off my throat?

ARTHUR: I said I was sorry! I just got excited, is all. Tell me what you think.

ERNIE: If it was me, I'd give up this abortion idea. No kidding, Art.

ARTHUR: How can we? I can't just go upstairs and—*tell* 'em! My mom'd start to shake. When she gets upset, she starts to breathe funny. And my old man just goes up in smoke! A thing like this could *kill* 'em even!

ERNIE: Look, I'm not trying to scare hell out of you or anything,

174

but... Well—like I said before—it's murder.

ARTHUR: Don't keep saying that! We didn't mean it to be a baby. It was just her and me, Ernie, we didn't think!... Besides, it hasn't even got a heart or a name yet. It's just—trouble. Not a person.

ERNIE: It's *alive*, isn't it? Listen, Art, these operations are dangerous. I mean, the doctors that do it aren't so hot sometimes. That's why they got kicked out of the profession, 'cause they weren't very ethical to start with.

(ARTHUR moves away. ERNIE follows)

ARTHUR: I don't want to talk about it! It'll turn out all right, it's got to!

ERNIE: Yeah? Say he uses a dirty knife or something and Janet got blood poisoning?

ARTHUR: Shut up!

ERNIE: Or he slipped up some way and killed her, even?

ARTHUR: *(Hysterically)* Will you shut up!

(ARTHUR throws himself face-down on the bed, grabs the pillow and tries to shut out ERNIE's voice)

ERNIE; They'd blame it on you, Art; and then what'd you do? Tell 'em you did it 'cause you were scared of your old man? Scared your mother might faint or something? *(ARTHUR groans into the pillow)* I think you'd better face it, Art. Maybe start off by telling 'em you're going to get married, no matter what they say. Then lead into the baby part—casually.

ARTHUR: *(After a moment, raising himself on his elbows)* What'll I do, Ernie? Just go up right now?

ERNIE: Sure.

ARTHUR: And just—just *tell* 'em!

ERNIE: Why not? You didn't kill anybody!

ARTHUR: I'm not even gonna stop to think about it!

ERNIE: Art! You're doin' the right thing. You won't be sorry.

(ARTHUR quietly ascends the stairs and exits into the kitchen. ERNIE climbs the steps into the yard and exits. ARTHUR appears in the hallway.)

THE CHOPIN PLAYOFFS
by Israel Horovitz
Stanley (16) - Irving (16)

The Play: This is play number three in a trilogy by Mr. Horovitz based on stories by Morley Torgov. At the heart of the play is a piano contest between Irving Yanover and Stanley Rosen, two sixteen-year-old boys living in Sault Ste. Marie, Ontario, Canada in 1947. More precisely, the "playoffs" occur between the Rosen and Yanover families for their position in the Jewish community, between the two boys in their private struggles to each win the heart of Fern Fipps, a very Protestant girl (much to the horror of the two very Jewish families), and between Fern and the boys as she attempts to make the right decision and please everyone. The play snaps and crackles with these individual playoffs as the boys battle, the parents battle, the boys battle with the parents, and Fern becomes the ultimate judge on the entire proceedings. Added to the mix of children and parents, Horovitz weaves two billiant characters: Ardenshensky, an old Jew, and Uncle Goldberg, Irving's old Jewish uncle (both roles played by the same actor). Here the wisdom of age and a sense of the struggle between the old world and the new offers a balance and much fun. As Fern promises her heart to the winner of the playoffs, the play serves almost as a boxing ring (Horovitz even calls for a prizefight bell to ring the transitions between scenes). The play concludes with lessons for everyone. Young and old alike question the decisions made in youth that will effect one's life forever.

The Scene: Prior to this scene, Stanley and Irving have been literally fighting for the heart of Fern Fipps. Not only do they compete in piano competitions, but throughout their lives, they have been in a constant struggle to be number one. At times these fights have been physical, something Fern has forbidden. What they have in common, besides their love for Fern and their interest in music, are parents who insist on the traditions of the old world, an ill-fit for the boys. This scene shows the two boys actually sharing a common set of problems. At this point in the play, there is no one else to turn to but each other.

Special Note: Mr. Horovitz cautions actors to avoid any stereotypical behavior with the characters in this play. In addition, Yiddish or Eastern European accents—"or stereotypically 'Jewish' intonation" should be avoided.

176

THE CHOPIN PLAYOFFS

(Stanley moves downstage, talks as if on telephone)
STANLEY: Yanover? I'm coming over. *(Lights fade up on an amazed Irving Yanover, in Yanover living room)*
IRVING: Who's this?
STANLEY: Stanley Rosen. *(The fight bell sounds as Stanley crosses into Yanover house)* She's nuts, you know. We don't look anything alike.
IRVING: Of course she's nuts. Nuts is the Human Condition. Have you read Camus?
STANLEY: *(Lying through his teeth)* Most of Camus. But it's been a long time.
IRVING: Uh hahhh! A blind spot in your intellectual growth, Rosen! Now that I know your weakness, I shall leap in and triumph...
STANLEY: I never saw two men look less alike!
IRVING: I agree.
(Stanley crosses to table)
STANLEY: Do you think Fern's father is really a Nazi?
IRVING; Naw, I don't think he's so much a Nazi as he is a Nazi supporter.
STANLEY: Mmm. *(Nods in agreement)*
IRVING: It's exactly like you not being so much an athlete as an athletic supporter...
STANLEY: *(They both squeeze invisible horns and make "nahn-nah" sound)* Ho, ho! That was rich. *(Pause)* Could we leap over the small talk, up to some medium talk, Yanover?
IRVING; Be my guest: leap.
STANLEY: How'd you get your parents around the idea of Fern Fipps being somebody you date?
IRVING: Parents, my dear Rosen, have a strong tendency to see life *as they want it to be*, rather than life as it most obviously *is*...until, of course, a Stanley Rosen comes along and takes the truth and tries to *rub it in my parents' eyes*!
STANLEY: A basic survival technique, my dear Yanover. Blind the enemy parent with the truth and your own parents will never see the *truth*...

177

THE CHOPIN PLAYOFFS

IRVING: If I were you, I wouldn't go into philosophy for a living...

STANLEY: You know what Plato said?

IRVING: Remind me.

STANLEY: Plato said, "Never wear argyle socks with a glen-plaid suit."

IRVING: Plato was in the menswear business?

STANLEY: "Morris Plato's Togary"

IRVING: Is is true what my father said? That you wrote a song called "Prelude to the Sale of a Pair of Pants"? That's what your father told *my* father, anyway...

STANLEY: I did. I did that.

IRVING: I composed a tune called "Fanfare for Five Flannel Sheets and a Pillowcase."

STANLEY: You ever play four-handed Gershwin?

IRVING: Is that like doubles pinochle?

STANLEY: Aha! A major blind spot! Do you know Oscar Levant?

IRVING: Didn't he live over on Pim Street?

STANLEY: Get serious, Yanover! Oscar Levant is just about the greatest mind in the twentieth century, that's all... He wrote a book called *A Smattering of Ignorance*, about how he and Gershwin fought all the time.

IRVING: They fought too, huh!

STANLEY: Oil and water... I'll loan you the book. It's just probably the greatest book ever written in English, that's all.

IRVING: No kidding?

(Stanley produces a dog-eared copy of a book by Levant)

STANLEY: *A Smattering of Ignorance*. Be my guest, Yanover. Just read the opening paragraph. *(Stanley tosses book across store to Irving, who catches it)* My life was changed by Oscar Levant. There's more to life than Frédéric Chopin, m'boy. *(Irving is reading; pretends to be engrossed totally)*

IRVING: Shhh. I'm reading...

STANLEY: Some middlebrow would-be pseudointellectuals claim *Camus* has a brain, but history will prove that the *great* thinker of the twentieth century was, unquestionably, Oscar Levant...

THE CHOPIN PLAYOFFS

IRVING: *(Looks up. Playacts exasperation)* Will you *please*? I am reading. If you think this is a good book, Rosen, you're out of your mind! This is a great book, Rosen! A Great Book!

STANLEY: I gave this book to my father to read.

IRVING: What did he say?

STANLEY: Obvious line: "I used to think you were a lunatic. Now I'm *convinced*!"

IRVING: Lunacy is a son's birthright...

STANLEY: It's in the Talmud. Page eight...

IRVING: Page *nine*.

STANLEY: You know your Talmud...

IRVING: Back to front...

STANLEY: *(Masturbation joke)* Like the front of your hand...

IRVING: That was funny. Maybe I was Levant in an earlier life?

STANLEY: This is true, you were Levant and I was Gershwin. You see, my dear Yanover, the subtle difference between Levant and Gershwin is the subtle difference between talent and genius...

IRVING: Really?

STANLEY: Really.

IRVING: You wanna try to back up your fancy talk with fancy action?

STANLEY; Okay, palley-pal. You see these mitts? *(Makes two fists)*

IRVING: Yuh, so?

STANLEY: Watch 'em and weep. *(Stanley walks to Irving's piano and plays Gershwin's Rhapsody in Blue)*

IRVING: That is just great, Rosen. Just *goddam great*!

THE CONTRAST
by Royall Tyler
Jessamy (19) - Jonathan (18)

The Play: Written in 1787 and most likely patterned after Richard Brinsley Sheridan's *The School for Scandal*, *The Contrast* is considered to be the first American comedy. Dimple, just back from a trip to Europe, scorns all things American. His silly affectation is in sharp contrast with the more rough-and-ready character of Colonel Manly, who served under Washington, and is the brother of Charlotte, whom Dimple hopes to take as his mistress. After Dimple breaks off his engagement with Maria, a girl of simple means, he attempts to marry the wealthy Letitia and woo Charlotte. Colonel Manly comes to his sister's aid, however, foils Dimple, and wins the hand of Maria for himself. In the process, the play attempts to answer the question: should Americans cultivate their own customs and manners, or should they follow the fashions of the Continent? Much of the play's humor derives from the contrast between Jessamy, Dimple's affected servant, and Jonathan, Manly's bumbling but true, blue Yankee servant—the first of his type in American theater, and one which was popular on the stage throughout the 19th centruy.

The Scene: Dimple's servant, Jessamy, is walking on the Mall hoping to find some pretty girls when he encounters Jonathan, Colonel Manly's "waiter." Jessamy seizes the opportunity to have some fun with his less sophisticated counterpart.

THE CONTRAST

(The Mall.   Enter Jessamy.)

JESSAMY: Positively this Mall is a very pretty place. I hope the cits won't ruin it by repairs. To be sure, it won't do to speak of in the same with Ranelagh or Vauxhall; however, it's a fine place for a young fellow to display his person to advantage. Indeed, nothing is lost here; the girls have taste, and I am very happy to find they have adopted the elegant London fashion of looking back, after a genteel fellow like me has passed them. —Ah! who comes here? This, by his awkwardness, must be the Yankee colonel's servant. I'll accost him.

JESSAMY: *Votre trés-humble seviteur, Monsieur.* I understand Colonel Manly, the Yankee officer, has the honour of your services.

JONATHAN: Sir!—

JESSAMY: I say, Sir, I understand that Colonel Manly has the honour of having you for a servant.

JOHATHAN: Servant! [Sir, do you take me for a neger,]—I am Colonel Manly's waiter.

JESSAMY: A true Yankee distinction, egad, without a difference. Why, Sir, do you not perform all the offices of a servant? do you not even blacken his boots?

JONATHAN: Yes; I do grease them a bit sometimes; but I am a true blue son of liberty, for all that. Father said I should come as Colonel Manly's waiter, to see the world, and all that; but no man shall master me. My father has as good a farm as the colonel.

JESSAMY: Well, Sir, we will not quarrel about terms upon the eve of an acquaintance from which I promise myself so much satisfaction;— therefore, *sans cérémonie—*

JONATHAN: What?—

JESSAMY: I say I am extremely happy to see Colonel Manly's waiter.

JOHATHAN: Well, and I vow, too. I am pretty considerably glad to see you; but what the dogs need of all this outlandish lingo? Who may you be, Sir, if I may be so bold?

JESSAMY: I have the honour to be Mr. Dimple's servant, or, if you please, waiter. We lodge under the same roof, and should be glad of the honour of your acquaintance.

JOHATHAN: You a waiter! by the living jingo, you look so topping,

181

THE CONTRAST

I took you for one of the agents to Congress.

JESSAMY: The brute has discernment, notwithstanding his appearance. —Give me leave to say I wonder then at your familiarity.

JOHATHAN: Why, as to the matter of that, Mr.———; pray, what's your name?

JESSAMY: Jessamy, at your service.

JONATHAN: Why, I swear we don't make any great matter of distinction in our state between quality and other folks.

JESSAMY: This is, indeed, a levelling principle. —I hope, Mr. Jonathan, you have not taken part with the insurgents.

JONATHAN: Why, since General Shays has sneaked off and given us the bag to hold, I don't care to give my opinion; but you'll promise not to tell—put your ear this way—you won't tell? —I vow I did think the sturgeons were right.

JESSAMY: I thought, Mr. Jonathan, you Massachusetts men always argued with a gun in your hand. Why didn't you join them?

JONATHAN: Why, the colonel is one of those folks called the Shin—Shin—dang it all, I can't speak them lignum vitae words—you know who I mean—there is a company of them—they wear a china goose at their button-hole—a kind of gilt thing. —Now the colonel told father and brother,—you must know there are, let me see—there is Elnathan, Silas, and Barnabas, Tabitha—no, no, she's a she—tarnation, now I have it— there's Elnathan, Silas, Barnabas, Jonathan, that's I—seven of us, six went into the wars, and I staid at home to take care of mother. Colonel said that it was a burning shame for the true blue Bunker Hill sons of liberty, who had fought Governor Hutchinson, Lord North, and the Devil, to have any hand in kicking up a cursed dust against a government which we had, every mother's son of us, a hand in making.

JESSAMY: Bravo! —Well, have you been abroad in the city since your arrival? What have you seen that is curious and entertaining?

JONATHAN: Oh! I have seen a power of fine sights. I went to see two marble-stone men and a leaden horse that stands out in doors in all weathers; and when I came where they was, one had got no head, and t'other wern't there. They said as how the leaden man was a damn'd tory, and that he took wit in his anger and rode off in the time of the troubles.

JESSAMY: But this was not the end of your excursion?

JONATHAN: Oh, no; I went to a place they call Holy Ground. Now I counted this was a place where folks go to meeting; so I put my hymnbook in my pocket, and walked softly and grave as a minister; and when I came there, the dogs a bit of a meeting-house could I see. At last I spied a young gentlewoman standing by one of the seats which they have here at the doors. I took her to be the deacon's daughter, and she looked so kind, and obliging, that I thought I would go ask her the way to the lecture, and—would you think it?—she called me dear, and sweeting, and honey, just as if we were married; by the living jingo, I had a month's mind to buss her.

JESSAMY: Well, but how did it end?

JONATHAN: Why, as I was standing talking with her, a parcel of sailor men and boys got round me, the snarl-headed curs fell a-kicking and cursing of me at such a tarnal rate, that I vow I was glad to take to my heels and split home, right off, tail on end, like a stream of chalk.

JESSAMY: Why, my dear friend, you are not acquainted with the city; that girl you saw was a—*(Whispers)*

JONATHAN: Mercy on my soul! was that young woman a harlot!— Well! if this is New-York Holy Ground, what must the Holy-day Ground be!

JESSAMY: Well, you should not judge of the city too rashly. We have a number of elegant, fine girls here that make a man's leisure hours pass very agreeably. I would esteem it an honour to announce you to some of them. —Gad! that announce is a select word; I wonder where I picked it up.

JONATHAN: I don't want to know them.

JESSAMY: Come, come, my dear friend, I see that I must assume the honour of being the director of your amusements. Nature has given us passions, and youth and opportunity stimulate to gratify them. It is no shame, my dear Blueskin, for a man to amuse himself with a little gallantry.

JONATHAN: Girl huntry! I don't altogether understand. I never played at that game. I know how to play hunt the squirrel, but I can't play anything with the girls; I am as good as married.

JESSAMY: Vulgar, horrid brute! Married, and above a hundred miles from his wife, and thinks that an objection to his making love to every woman he meets! He never can have read, no, he never can have been in a room with a volume of the divine Chesterfield. —So you are married?

JONATHAN: No, I don't say so; I said I was as good as married, a kind of promise.

JESSAMY: As good as married!—

JONATHAN: Why, yes; there's Tabitha Wymen, the deacon's daughter, at home; she and I have been courting a great while, and folks say as how we are to be married; and so I broke a piece of money with her when we parted, and she promised not to spark it with Solomon Dyer while I am gone. You wou'dn't have me false to my true-love, would you?

JESSAMY: May be you have another reason for constancy; possibly the young lady has a fortune? Ha! Mr. Jonathan, the solid charms: the chains of love are never so binding as when the links are made of gold.

JONATHAN: Why, as to fortune, I must needs say her father is pretty dumb rich; he went representative for our town last year. He will give her—let me see—four times seven is—seven times four—nought and carry one,—he will give her twenty acres of land—somewhat rocky though—a Bible, and a cow.

JESSAMY: Twenty acres of rock, a Bible, and a cow! Why, my dear Mr. Jonathan, we have servant-maids, or, as you would more elegantly express it, waitresses, in this city, who collect more in one year from their mistresses' cast clothes.

JONATHAN: You don't say so!—

JESSAMY: Yes, and I'll introduce you to one of them. There is a little lump of flesh and delicacy that lives at next door, waitress to Miss Maria; we often see her on the stoop.

JONATHAN: But are you sure she would be courted by me?

JESSAMY: Never doubt it; remember a faint heart never—blisters on my tongue—I was going to be guilty of a vile proverb; flat against the authority of Chesterfield. I say there can be no doubt that the brilliancy of your merit will secure you a favourable reception.

JONATHAN: Well, but what must I say to her?

JESSAMY: Say to her! why, my dear friend, though I admire your profound knowledge on every other subject, yet, you will pardon my saying that your want of opportunity has made the female heart escape the poignancy of your penetration. Say to her! Why, when a man goes a-courting, and hopes for success, he must begin with doing, and not saying.

JONATHAN: Well, what must I do?

JESSAMY: Why, when you are introduced you must make five or six elegant bows.

JOHATHAN: Six elegant bows! I understand that; six, you say? Well—

JESSAMY: Then you must press and kiss her hand; then press and kiss, and so on to her lips and cheeks; then talk as much as you can about hearts, darts, flames, nectar, and ambrosia—the more incoherent the better.

JONATHAN: Well, but suppose she should be angry with I?

JESSAMY: Why, if she should pretend—please to observe, Mr. Jonathan—if she should pretend to be offended, you must— But I'll tell you how my master acted in such a case: He was seated by a young lady of eighteen upon a sofa, plucking with a wanton hand the blooming sweets of youth and beauty. When the lady thought it necessary to check his ardour, she called up a frown upon her lovely face, so irresistibly alluring, that it would have warmed the frozen bosom of age; remember, said she, putting her delicate arm upon his, remember your character and my honour. Mr master instantly dropped upon his knees, with eyes swimming with love, cheeks glowing with desire, and in the gentlest modulation of voice he said: My dear Caroline, in a few months our hands will be indissolubly united at the altar; our hearts I feel are already so; the favours you now grant as evidence of your affection are favours indeed; yet, when the ceremony is once past, what will now be received with rapture will then be attributed to duty.

JONATHAN: Well, and what was the consequence?

JESSAMY: The consequence! —Ah! forgive me, my dear friend, but you New England gentlemen have such a laudable curiosity of seeing the bottom of everything;—why, to be honest, I confess I saw the blooming cherub of a consequence smiling in its angelic mother's arms, about ten months afterwards.

JONATHAN: Well, if I follow all your plans, make them six bows, and all that, shall I have such little cherubim consequences?

JESSAMY: Undoubtedly. —What are you musing upon?

JONATHAN: You say you'll certainly make me acquainted? —Why, I was thinking then how I should contrive to pass this broken piece of silver—won't it buy a sugar-dram?

JESSAMY: What is that, the love-token from the deacon's daughter?— You come on bravely. But I must hasten to my master. Adieu, my dear friend.

JONATHAN: Stay, Mr. Jessamy—must I buss her when I am introduced to her?

JESSAMY: I told you, you must kiss her.

JONATHAN: Well, but must I buss her?

JESSAMY: Why kiss and buss, and buss and kiss, is all one.

JONATHAN: Oh! my dear friend, though you have a profound knowledge of all, a pugnency of tribulation, you don't know everything. (Exit)

JESSAMY: (Alone) Well, certainly I improve; my master could not have insinuated himself with more address into the heart of a man he despised. Now will this blundering dog sicken Jenny with his nauseous pawings, until she flies into my arms for very ease. How sweet will the contrast be between the blundering Jonathan and the courtly and accomplished Jessamy!

THE DIVINERS
by Jim Leonard, Jr.
Buddy (mid-teens) - Showers (30)

The Play: Set in a small town in Indiana in the 1930's, the play deals
with events leading to the death of Buddy, a young, troubled, boy.
When he was very little he and his mother were in a traumatic accident
that resulted in his mother drowning. Since the accident, he has
developed a phobia of water, so much so that he doesn't even wash.
However, Buddy's accute fear had lead to his ability to "divine" water.
Raised by his father and sister, he needs more help than they can
provide to overcome his fears. These are poor people living in difficult
times with little if any assistance available for troubled children. Seen
as the "idiot boy" by the twonspeople, life has stopped going forward
for Buddy until Showers, a young preacher, comes into his life.
Doubting his faith and his ability to preach, Showers has left his home
and family in search of a new purpose in life. He secures a job as a
mechanic working for Buddy's father and becomes involved with
Buddy's sister. The town, in need of a good preacher, tries to persuade
Showers to take on the responsibility. As the play progesses, Showers
resists the townspeople, while at the same time becoming more and
more determined to help Buddy overcome his fears. The play reaches
its startling climax at the river when finally Showers persuades Buddy
to let him help him wash. The town sees this as a baptism and startles
the boy who eventually slips away and drowns. This very human story
of youth, troubled by circumstances beyond their control, is told
theatrically and poetically. The characters are rich and the relationships
intriguing and sensitive.

The Scene: It is early in the morning. By this time in the play's
action, Buddy has begun to place some trust in Showers. They are
outdoors.

THE DIVINERS

(Morning. Faint sounds of birds. As the light rises we see BUDDY creeping onto the stage, bent low with one hand held out as he tries to befriend a small bird:)

BUDDY: Ain't you so pretty, huh? Ain't you so pretty. You're the color a the sky. Yes, you are. You want a be up there, now, don't you. In the sun and the wind. Well, hold still, now. Hold still. He ain't gonna hurt you. *(SHOWERS enters as the boy catches the bird.)* You're too little to fly. Shhh, you're alright.

SHOWERS: Is he hurt?

BUDDY: Look at him, C.C. He's little.

SHOWERS: It's an awful pretty bird.

BUDDY: See his feathers?

SHOWERS: Those're blue.

BUDDY: Blue?

SHOWERS: Blue like your eyes.

BUDDY: His eyes is blue?

SHOWERS: Like the bird, like the sky—that's all blue.

BUDDY: Boy. You want a lift him, C.C.? Put him back to his Mama? *(BUDDY climbs on SHOWERS' shoulders and they move downstage to the edge of the stage.)*

SHOWERS: Careful, now, pal. You alright?

BUDDY: Yeah. How bout you?

SHOWERS: Oh, you're awful heavy! Now watch yourself up there. You got him?

BUDDY: *(As he places the bird in the tree.)* What color's that?

SHOWERS: That's green.

BUDDY: Green? Trees is green. Weeds is green. Grass is green. And birds're blue.

SHOWERS: *(Letting the boy down.)* You're awful smart first thing in the mornin.

(BUDDY lies on the stage floor looking up at the trees.)

BUDDY: Like to live up there with him. His arms turn to wings and his wings turn to feathers.

SHOWERS: How'd you get down?

BUDDY: He'd just fly down, C.C.

SHOWERS: Well, if you're gonna be barnstormin you'd best get your wings out.

BUDDY: Like a bird?

(SHOWERS holds onto the boy's arms, slowly lifting his upper body until the boy stands on his toes with his arms extended.)

SHOWERS: Like a bird.

BUDDY: Is he flyin?

SHOWERS: Shut your eyes, now.

BUDDY: Is he flyin?

SHOWERS: If you're willin to fly, pal, I'm willin to witness.

BUDDY: Lift him higher.

SHOWERS: Higher?

BUDDY: Lift him way up the sky! Clear up the sky!

SHOWERS: Higher?

BUDDY: Higher! *(BUDDY runs to a high platform.)*

SHOWERS: *(As if calling a great distance.)* How's the air up there?

BUDDY: Blue!

SHOWERS: Where's Buddy Layman?

BUDDY: He's flyin!

SHOWERS: Flyin!

BUDDY: Flyin clear up the sky! Way up the sky!

SHOWERS: Have you seen Mr. Lindbergh? Any word from Mr. Lindbergh?

BUDDY: Mr. Who?

SHOWERS: Mr. Lindbergh!

BUDDY: Ain't nobody flyin but birds.

SHOWERS: Any sign a Buddy Layman?

BUDDY: Who's Buddy Layman!

SHOWERS: He's a good boy.

BUDDY: *(Pleased.)* He is?

SHOWERS: He's a smart boy. I know him.

BUDDY: Have you seen Mr. C.C.?

SHOWERS: Mr. Who?

BUDDY: Mr. C.C.?

SHOWERS: Who's Mr. C.C.?

BUDDY: He's a bird!

(SHOWERS has spread his arms and moved up behind the boy. The distance games with their voices stop.)

SHOWERS: A bird brain, you mean.

BUDDY: Hey, C.C.? You flyin?

SHOWERS: Keep your eyes closed.

BUDDY: *(Amazed.)* You're flyin.

SHOWERS: Want to go higher?

BUDDY: He wants to go where you go, C.C.

SHOWERS: I'm stayin right here with you.

BUDDY: You like it here?

SHOWERS: I like it just fine.

BUDDY: *(Softly.)* You like the wind?

SHOWERS: Feels nice...

BUDDY: Feels soft...

SHOWERS: That's a nice sort a feelin.

BUDDY: His Mama's soft like the wind. Her voice's soft when he's sleepin.

SHOWERS: That's a dream, my friend.

BUDDY: *(Concerned.)* Is angels a dream?

SHOWERS: Buddy.

BUDDY: How come he can't find her?

SHOWERS: Your Mama's been gone a long time now.

BUDDY: He wants her so bad.

SHOWERS: I know.

BUDDY: If his arms turn to wings and his wings turn to feathers he could find her in the sky, maybe, C.C. *(The boy moves away from SHOWERS.)* If he's flyin he could be with his Mama.

SHOWERS: Buddy, listen to me...

BUDDY: *(Overlapping.)* They could fly in the sky, in the wind, in the sun! He could be with his Mama! They could fly and they fly and they fly!

SHOWERS: *(Overlapping from the next to last "fly".)* Your Mama's not here anymore!

BUDDY: He has to find her!

SHOWERS: *(Forceful.)* No! You have to remember! She's left you a father and a sister and there's friends here for Buddy! And they want him and need him and love him! And he isn't a bird—he's a boy! You're a boy. You're a son. You're a brother. And you're a friend.

BUDDY *(Moved.)* And you like him?

SHOWERS: I like him a lot.

BUDDY: That's somethin, huh?

SHOWERS: You know it is.

BUDDY: Hey C.C.? You know what?

SHOWERS: What?

BUDDY: *(Shakes his hand.)* You're a good guy.

SHOWERS: I am, huh? Well you too!

BUDDY: Buddy is?

SHOWERS: Sure you are.

BUDDY: You know what else he is, C.C.? He's itchin.

SHOWERS: Still itchin?

BUDDY: Right there, C.C. Itchin right there.

SHOWERS: Well, the skin looks a little red yet.

BUDDY: He don't want no more itch-juice.

SHOWERS: You'll never get better if you keep scratchin, Bud.

BUDDY: Well it itches!

SHOWERS: I know—but anytime your legs start to get at you, you say "I'm gonna save this scratch for another time." *(SHOWERS starts to cross away.)*

BUDDY: Hey, C.C.? When's it gonna be another time?

SHOWERS; After you're better.

BUDDY: Is he better now?

SHOWERS: Nope.

BUDDY: Not yet?

SHOWERS: Not quite.

ENTER LAUGHING
by Joseph Stein
adapted from Carl Reiner's novel
David Kolovitz (18) - Marvin (18)

The Play: Joseph Stein's stage adaptation of Carl Reiner's marvelously funny autobiography is as hilarious as the original. Set in New York City in the mid-1930's, it is the story of David, a stage-struck young Jewish boy from the Bronx who works as a delivery boy in a sewing machine factory. The problem is David's parents want him to become a druggist, and he'll have none of it; he's determined to become an actor. As soon as he's earned enough money, he joins a semi-professional theater company, which, as it turns out, will cast anyone for the right amount. David is as bad an actor as the others are hammy, and his debut on stage brings down the house. In the process David falls in love with the manager's overly dramatic daughter, someone else's girlfriend, and finally an office girl who seems to have been meant for him all along. Before the curtain comes down, David has learned much about life and the business of show business.

The Scene: David is at the sewing machine factory. His boss, Mr. Foreman, has just informed him that he has had a phone call from a girl. Foreman, who hopes David might take over the business one day, has advised David to stay away from girls for now, especially ones who aren't Jewish. David's hormones tell him otherwise, and in the scene that follows, he and his friend, Marvin (who admires David "just this side of hero worship"), have girls on their mind, as usual. But more than that, David discloses that he wants to become an actor.

Special Note: As David and Marvin are two Jewish boys from the Bronx, every effort should be make to capture the genuine flavor of their ethnicity, while resisting stereotypes.

ENTER LAUGHING

(MARVIN enters. MARVIN is David's age; he is not too good-looking, a little timid, unsure of himself. He admires David, just this side of hero worship. He carries his lunch, wrapped in a newspaper.)

DAVID: Hi, Marv.

MARVIN: Hi. *(Crossing to L. of table, gets chair from U.L., moves it to L. of table. Sits and eats.)*

DAVID: I'm calling Wanda. *(Into phone.)* Hello, Wanda? Did you call me?... He told me... No, he went out... Yeah, Marvin just came down. He's having his lunch... Saturday night? Gee, I'd love to, Wanda, only my mother and father are visiting some relatives in Flatbush, and I've got to mind my stupid kid sister. Who's giving the dance?... Well, listen, Wanda, maybe after the dance, you and me could get together and have a little tete-a-tete. *(Imitating Ronald Colman.)* "It will be a far, far better thing that you and I will do on Saturday night than has ever been done before."... Yes, Ronald Colman, that's right!... Goodbye. *(Hangs up and moves chair from U.R. to S. R. of table.)*

MARVIN: Boy, the way you do those imitations. You're great, you know that, Dave? *(DAVID then goes into a Louis Armstrong routine in midst of which MARVIN says: "Louis Armstrong." At end of it he takes rag from bench and dabs face.)* Great!

DAVID: I know. *(He sits R. of table.)*

MARVIN: And the way you talk to girls. Boy, I wish I had a steady girl, like you.

DAVID: You do?

MARVIN: I sure do. A steady girl, boy.

DAVID: I'll tell you, Marv, even though I got a steady girl, I think about other girls.

MARVIN: You do?

DAVID: Yeah, a lot. Do you think about girls a lot?

MARVIN: Me? I don't know what you mean by a lot. Sometimes I think about other things.

DAVID: Like what?

MARVIN: *(Considers.)* Oh, you know, other things—food.

DAVID: *(Rises. Crosses L. below table, above it, then to S.R. of it.)*

193

I think about girls a lot. I admit it. Like if I'm walking down the street, I see a girl swinging along—you know the way they do when they're walking, the way they walk.

MARVIN: Yeah—

DAVID: *(Crossing U.S. and D.S.)* Sometimes I go two, three blocks out of my way, just to watch the way they walk. What the heck, it's better than looking at nothing. Right?

MARVIN: Me, too.

DAVID: *(U.S.C. of table.)* I think about it a lot. Like there's this bookkeeper at the LaTesh Hat Company. Her name is Miss B., she's the mosts zaftig thing you ever saw, Marve, I mean it—

MARVIN: Her name is Miss B.?

DAVID: *(At R. of S.R. chair.)* That's what they call her. Anyway, she'd drive you crazy if her name was Irving. I go up there sometimes I forget to get a receipt.

MARVIN: I thought you're crazy about Wanda.

DAVID: I am. I'm crazy about Wanda. And I'm crazy about Miss B. And I'm crazy about strange girls on the street. Sometimes I think I'm a sex maniac.

MARVIN: Yeah, me, too.

DAVID: *(Crossing R. to U.R. Then D.S.)* Only one thing, I talk a lot, but I don't do anything. Not that I don't want to, I just don't. *(Sits chair R. of table.)* I'm a big talker.

MARVIN: Me, too.

DAVID: *(Rises above table.)* Another thing. What am I doing in this crummy job? I mean, okay, just for a while, but Mr. Foreman thinks I want to learn the business—what do I want to be a machinist on ladies hats for? *(Picks up two files from table.)*

MARVIN: Then don't.

DAVID: Okay, then why don't I tell him? He keeps saying, you'll work hard, be a good machinist, and I say, sure, Mr. Foreman....

MARVIN: Do you want an apple?

DAVID: No. *(Drumming on shelves with files.)* And my parents, they want me to be a druggist. *(Drums.)* They want me to register in night school for September, to be a druggist. *(Drums.)* I don't want to be

194

a druggist.

MARVIN: Then why don't you tell them?

DAVID: *(Drumming.)* I did tell them. I kind of told them. So they say, what do you want to be? You can't be a nothing. Everyone calls me a nothing. *(Throws files in tray on table. Sits S.R. of table.)*

MARVIN: Why don't you want to be a druggist?

DAVID: Because I don't want to. Does everybody have to want to be a druggist?

MARVIN: You know, I wouldn't mind being a druggist.

DAVID: You? You'd poison the whole neighborhood. *(Rises to U.S. C. of table.)* The thing is, I want to be something. Something, so people will say, there goes Dave Kolovitz, the something.

MARVIN; What's the matter with "there goes the druggist?"

DAVID: *(Crosses R.)* Naah.

MARVIN; *(Offering apple.)* You sure you don't want an apple?

DAVID: *(Crosses to above table.)* What's with you and the apple? What's it got, worms or something?

MARVIN: No, my mother just put in two today, that's all. *(Bites second apple.)*

DAVID: *(Crosses L. above table to L. of table.)* If I had any guts, I'd pack up and go to Panama or someplace.

MARVIN: Why don't you?

DAVID: *(At S.L.; shouts.)* Because I have to mind my stupid kid sister Saturday night, that's why.

MARVIN: *(Rises, steps L. to DAVID with apple.)* Okay, you don't have to bite my head off.

DAVID: *(Pause.)* Give me the apple.

MARVIN: I bit it already.

DAVID: What are you giving me an apple for and then eating it yourself?

MARVIN: It ain't my fault you don't know what you want to be.

DAVID: Did I say I don't know what I want to be? I know what I want to be.

MARVIN: Yeah—a something!

DAVID: *(Crosses R. below table to R. of table.)* No. I'll tell you what I want to be. I want to be an actor.

MARVIN: An actor?

DAVID: *(Crosses D.S.R. of table.)* Sure. Why not? An actor! *(Faces audience, poses.)*

MARVIN; You know something? You'd be great!

DAVID: I know. But you can't just be an actor. You can't just go around and tell people—hello, I'm an actor!

MARVIN: *(Crossing R. to DAVID.)* Hey, I saw this ad in today's paper. I saw it yesterday, too. I saw it both days.

DAVID: An ad? For what?

MARVIN: For actors.

DAVID: For actors?

MARVIN: For actors.

DAVID; You're crazy! *(Goes U.S., takes newspaper from shelf on C. wall. MARVIN crosses L. of table to above it.)*

MARVIN: *(Taking paper from DAVID, finds ad.)* It's here, right here in the paper. I saw it yesterday, I saw it today.... Here. When I saw it I even thought about you.

DAVID: *(Reads; U.S. of S.R. chair.)* "Marlowe Theatre and School for Dramatic Arts... Scholarships for Promising Young Actors..."

MARVIN: *(At S.L. of DAVID.)* Just do your Ronald Coleman or your Humphrey Bogart.

DAVID: "Learn to act before audiences."

MARVIN: No kidding, you're a cinch.

DAVID: *(Crossing S.R. MARVIN follows.)* They'll see applicants at six o'clock.

MARVIN: What do you say, will you go?

DAVID: Sure. Why not?

MARVIN: Bet you a dime you don't.

DAVID: It's a bet.

(They shake hands.)

MARVIN: *(Gets apple from table.)* Here. I only took one bite.

DAVID: Thanks—I can't make it, though. I don't get out of here till six o'clock—

MARVIN: Listen, you don't want to be a machinist or a druggist all

196

your life?

DAVID: Besides, I got to be home tonight. What will I tell my mother?

MARVIN: Okay, okay, you lose; give me the dime.

DAVID: Besides it's in the paper. There'll be a thousand guys.

MARVIN: Okay, give me the dime.

ORPHANS
by Lyle Kessler
Treat (early twenties) - Phillip (late teens)

The Play: Treat and Phillip were orphaned at an early age. Somehow they have managed to escape the various governmental agencies who look after orphaned children, in great part due to Treat's cunning ability to look after his younger brother. Treat has been the provider. So concerned that they might loose their freedom to be together, Treat has raised his little brother to fear the outside world. He has laid out strict rules about Phillip's health, making Phillip completely dependant on him for his very life. Treat "makes the living" by stealing. It is clear that their home situation, although stable, is bizarre. Phillip watches television all day—and reads, although Treat has forbidden this. We aren't sure if Phillip is genuinely suffering from retardation or if the circumstances of his protective and disfunctional upbringing has lead to this extraordinary behavior. Treat is like a cornered animal, constantly doubting life and expecting the rug to be pulled from under their feet at any moment. Into this relationship comes Harold, a drunk businessman, who Treat brings home to hold for ransom. Harold, however, succeeds at befriending both Treat and Phillip and sets up his own questionable business in their house, taking on Treat as a sort of helper. He too was orphaned and he seems touched and moved by their situation. As he helps the two clean up their lives, including cleaning up and refurnishing their home and buying them new clothes, Phillip warms up to Harold and begins to grow and question the status of his stifled life. In a highly dramatic conclusion, Phillip becomes the catalyst for Treat to finally get in touch with the feelings that he has covered since the loss of their mother many years ago.

The Scene: This is the very first scene in the play. Treat has been out all day, "making a living." Phillip is in another part of the house. The time is the present, the play is North Philadelphia ("Philly").

198

ORPHANS

(A spring day. An old row house. Wallpaper, faded, peeling. A cluttered living room, stacks of newspapers, a worn, frayed couch, old, broken furniture, and other litter. A small television set on the floor in the middle of the room. A table with a large empty bottle of Hellman's mayonnaise on it. On a shelf, stacks of Star Kist tuna cans. The front door opens. TREAT enters out of breath. He wears a dungaree jacket, faked khaki pants, and a bandanna around his neck. He catches his breath, looks out the window down the street, relaxes, snaps his fingers, and enters the living room. He picks up the empty mayonnaise bottle and looks at it.)

TREAT: *(calling)* Phillip? Phillip? *(Yells.)* Phillip, you hear me! *(He begins to empty his pockets of bracelets, wallets, and rings.)* You home, Phillip! I imagine you're home! Where the hell else you gonna be, huh! I imagine you're hiding from your big brother Treat! *(He inspects the jewelry.)* Come on out, Phillip! I ain't in the mood for no hide-and-go-seek game. You hear me! *Come on the fuck out!*

(PHILLIP appears from upstairs. He wears an old tattered shirt, dirty sweatpants, green sneaks with open hanging shoelaces.)

PHILLIP: Don't tag me.

TREAT *(preoccupied with jewelry)*: I ain't gonna tag you.

PHILLIP: 'Cause I'm sick and tired of being *it*, Treat.

TREAT: I ain't gonna tag you. I told you. I ain't playing no games. *(He takes out a large, colored brooch and holds it up to the light. The jewels sparkle. PHILLIP stares at it.)*

PHILLIP: You said that yesterday.

TREAT: Yesterday's yesterday. Today's today. *(Places brooch on table.)*

PHILLIP: You promise?

TREAT: I promise. How long you been hiding?

PHILLIP: I don't know.

TREAT: Half the day, I bet.

PHILLIP *(moves closer to the brooch)*: I didn't keep count.

TREAT: You eat lunch?

PHILLIP: Uh huh.

TREAT: What you have?

PHILLIP: I had Star Kist tuna.

TREAT: Mayonnaise?

PHILLIP *(closer to brooch, TREAT watches him)*: Uh huh. Hellman's.

TREAT: How much mayonnaise you have?

PHILLIP: Couple of tablespoons.

TREAT: If you only had a couple of tablespoons, how come we're out of it?

PHILLIP: Hellman's goes fast, Treat.

TREAT: It goes fast, all right. A half a bottle a day. *(TREAT tags PHILLIP suddenly.)* You're it, Phillip.

PHILLIP: *No!*

TREAT: You're fucking it! *(He runs to the other side of the room, laughing.)*

PHILLIP: You promised.

TREAT; I had my fingers crossed.

PHILLIP: I come out 'cause you said you wouldn't.

(PHILLIP chases TREAT around the room. He catches him and tags him.)

TREAT: Time out!

PHILLIP: No!

TREAT: Fucking time out, Phillip. The game's over. *(PHILLIP throws himself down on the couch, sulking.)* Where were you?

PHILLIP: I ain't telling.

TREAT: Come on.

PHILLIP: No, it's my secret.

TREAT: I know where you been anyway.

PHILLIP: Where?

TREAT; In the closet.

PHILLIP: How you know that?

TREAT: It's your favorite hiding place. *(He pulls more booty out of his back pocket, a couple of wallets, a gold chain.)*

PHILLIP: I was hiding in there waiting for you to come home.

TREAT: Just standing and waiting, huh?

PHILLIP: Uh, huh.

ORPHANS

TREAT: Just standing and hiding in the darkness, waiting for your big brother Treat to come home.
PHILLIP: I like it in there. It's warm.
TREAT: I wouldn't know.
PHILLIP: It's got all of Mom's coats in there.
TREAT: We ought to get rid of them.
PHILLIP: No!
TREAT: What good they doing hanging there all these years?
PHILLIP: I want them.
TREAT: They ain't doing nobody any good.
PHILLIP: They're not bothering anybody, Treat. They're just hanging there.
TREAT: People find out about you, they're gonna put you away.
PHILLIP: They won't put me away!
TREAT: A grown man standing all day in a dark closet.
PHILLIP: I done other things.
TREAT: What other things you do?
PHILLIP: I looked out the window.
TREAT; Good.
PHILLIP: I seen some things.
TREAT: What you see?
PHILLIP: I seen a man and a dog, a man walking a big black dog. *(PHILLIP gets on his hands and knees and imitates the dog, crawls a few steps, raises one leg. TREAT, inspecting the booty, half watches, mildly amused.)*
TREAT: What else?
PHILLIP: I seen a woman, a tiny, tiny woman. *(Compresses his body, and walks with tiny steps.)*
TREAT: Anything else?
PHILLIP: Plenty else.
TREAT: Go on.
PHILLIP: A man with two big boys, man in the middle, a boy on each side.
TREAT: What were they doing?
PHILLIP *(walking like man)*: Goin' swimming maybe, goin' to the

movies, probably. Gonna see John Wayne in *The Halls of Montezuma*.
TREAT; You got an imagination.
PHILLIP: I seen other things. I seen a man with a woman, man walking arm and arm with a woman. Woman had long red hair. *(Strokes his hair like the woman, walks, swishing from side to side.)*
TREAT: Long red hair, huh. Was the man balding?
PHILLIP: Man was balding, right.
TREAT: Woman had bangles dangling from her wrist, woman loaded with bangles, am I right?
PHILLIP: You're right, Treat.
TREAT; I seen that couple! *(He holds up a piece of jewelry.)* What else you do?!
PHILLIP: I watched TV.
TREAT: What did you watch?
PHILLIP: I watched reruns. I watched "The Price is Right."
TREAT *(turns to him):* That's a woman's show!
PHILLIP: They have fabulous prizes, Treat.
TREAT: You'd like to win one, I bet.
PHILLIP: They won a hi-fi stereo combination, a year's supply of l.p.'s and cassettes; they won a mahogany dining room set, they won an Electro Lux golf cart and a Bendix freezer filled with five hundred filets mignons.
TREAT: You remember all that.
PHILLIP: They won a year's subscription to *National Geographic*. They won a ...
TREAT: That's enough!
PHILLIP: I'd like to get that *National Geographic*.
TREAT *(stops and stares at him):* What would you do with it?
PHILLIP: I'd look at it.
TREAT: You'd read it?
PHILLIP: You know I couldn't read it, Treat. I'd look at the pictures, though. They got real nice pictures, pictures of all kinds of animals and primitive tribes.
(PHILLIP, crawling hand over hand, makes jungle sounds: birds, monkeys... TREAT begins to put the booty away.)

ORPHANS

TREAT: I bumped into that woman and man today. Man was balding, woman had long red hair.

PHILLIP: That's right.

TREAT: I had a real good day today, Phillip. I'm gonna go out, tonight, gonna celebrate!

PHILLIP: We all outta mayonnaise, Treat. You go out, will you bring home an extra large bottle of Hellman's Mayonnaise?

TREAT: Yes sirree, had a hell of a day, Phillip. You interested? *(He gathers the jewelry, and places it in a dresser drawer.)*

PHILLIP: I'm interested, Treat. Only thing is I got a real taste in my mouth for that Hellman's.

TREAT *(picks up more jewelry):* Guy wasn't carrying much, just a few bucks, but he had a real nice wristwatch. Whadaya think?

PHILLIP: It's nice.

TREAT: Man had good taste, woman didn't have bad taste either. Look at this! *(a woman's wristwatch)* Tiny little wrists, tiny little dainty little wrists.

PHILLIP: She wore this?

TREAT: No more! Bumped into another fellow earlier today, Fairmount Park. Fellow put up a struggle.

PHILLIP: No kidding.

TREAT: I said, "What you gettin' violent about, Mister, no point in gettin' violent!"

PHILLIP: What did he say?

TREAT; He kicked at me.

PHILLIP: He kicked you?

TREAT: Right in the shin. *(He rolls up his trouser.)* See. Gonna be fucking black and blue.

PHILLIP: I'll get the hydrogen perioxide. *(He dashes off.)*

TREAT *(calling after):* You remember all them brand names!

PHILLIP *(off):* Uh huh.

TREAT: How come you can do that?

PHILLIP *(returns with bottle):* I don't know.

TREAT: I mean you don't have much of an intellect for anything else, but you know them brand names and the names of all them various

prizes. *(He pours hydrogen peroxide over his leg.)*
PHILLIP: It just comes to me.
TREAT: I said, "Listen, Mister, I don't appreciate getting kicked in the shins like that."
PHILLIP: What did he do?
TREAT: He cursed at me.
PHILLIP: He cursed you?
TREAT: All kinds of names, names I wouldn't even repeat. Terrible fucking filth came out of that man's mouth.
PHILLIP: What did he look like?
TREAT: Dressed real nice, had on a suit and tie. Must have driven over to Fairmount Park. It was a real nice spring day, today, Phillip. Too bad you couldn't go out and enjoy it. Man figured he'd take a little walk in Fairmount Park.
PHILLIP: What happened?
TREAT: Had a lot of money on him, that's why he put up a struggle, I guess, must've had three, four hundred dollars.
PHILLIP: Where is he?
TREAT: Left him there, had to cut him though. Not bad, just superficial. Warned him! In fact, said, *"Mister, you're gettin' me pissed off kickin' me like that."*
PHILLIP: Did you show him the bruise?
TREAT; I didn't have to show him the bruise. Got me pissed off. I had to take out my knife, had to cut him. *(He takes a switchblade out and demonstrates.)*
PHILLIP: Did he bleed?
TREAT; Just a little bit, Phillip. It's amazing, how people stop struggling once there's a little blood. *(Sticks switchblade into the table.)* Paper come?
PHILLIP: Uh huh.
TREAT: Let's have it.
PHILLIP: Come early this morning. *(Hands it to TREAT.)*
TREAT *(reading it)*: What's this, Phillip?
PHILLIP: What's what?
TREAT: How come this word is underlined?

PHILLIP: I don't know.

TREAT *(scanning paper)*: How come there are underlined words in this here *Philadelphia Inquirer*!

PHILLIP: I have no idea, Treat.

(TREAT crosses to PHILLIP, holding the paper.)

TREAT: Here's a word, *dispensation*. You underline this word?

PHILLIP: I didn't touch that word.

TREAT: You read this word?

PHILLIP: No.

TREAT: You got a dictionary, Phillip?

PHILLIP: I got no dictionary.

TREAT *(stalking him)*: You sure you don't have no pocket dictionary somewhere in this house? You sure you ain't spending the day reading the newspaper and books, underlining words, looking up the meaning of particular words, getting yourself an education?

PHILLIP *(running from him)*: I got no education!

TREAT: You know the alphabet?

PHILLIP: No!

TREAT; I bet you know the fuckin' alphabet. *(Hits him with the rolled up newspaper.)* I bet you're holding out on me.

PHILLIP: I ain't holding out on you, Treat.

TREAT: What's this word mean, what's this fuckin' *dispensation* mean?

PHILLIP: I don't know, Treat.

TREAT *(hitting him)*: Who underlined this fuckin' dispensation!

PHILLIP: It wasn't me! *(He pulls away.)*

TREAT: Someone come in the house while I was away?

PHILLIP: I don't know.

TREAT: You would have heard him.

PHILLIP: I was in the closet.

TREAT: Someone steal in the house while you were standing in the closet and underline this word?

PHILLIP: Maybe.

TREAT: Where is he?

PHILLIP: I don't know.

ORPHANS

TREAT: Is he still here?

PHILLIP: He might be.

TREAT: Find him.

PHILLIP: All right.

TREAT: Kill him! *(Hands PHILLIP the knife.)* I want him dead, you understand! Man stealing in my house like that.

(PHILLIP runs around the room looking under tables and chairs and other unlikely places.)

PHILLIP *(stops)*: Maybe he's upstairs.

TREAT: Yea, maybe.

PHILLIP: Maybe he's hiding under the bed.

TREAT; I wouldn't put it past him, hiding under the bed, waiting for us to go to sleep.

PHILLIP: I'll get him!

(PHILLIP rushes upstairs, holding out the knife like a sword. TREAT sits on the couch, lights a cigarette. The sound of a crash is heard from upstairs. TREAT doesn't react. More noise, something breaking.)

PHILLIP *(off)*: Son of a bitch!

(PHILLIP appears, disheveled, holding his arm. He walks unsteadily a couple of steps, then slips, slides, tumbles down the stairs. A great death scene. TREAT, smoking, ignores him. PHILLIP on the floor.)
That son of a bitch!

TREAT: You get him?

PHILLIP: No Treat, he got me.

TREAT: Whadaya mean?

PHILLIP: I'm bleeding. I was looking under the bed and he came out of the closet.

TREAT: Let's see. *(PHILLIP shows his arm to TREAT.)* That ain't bad. That's just a scratch.

PHILLIP: I jumped back and banged into the night table. The lamp fell over.

TREAT: I heard it.

PHILLIP: If I hadn't jumped back he would have stabbed me right through the back, Treat.

TREAT: Lucky for you. Where is he?

PHILLIP: He leaped out the window.

TREAT: He got away?

PHILLIP: Yes.

TREAT: What did he look like?

PHILLIP: Errol Flynn.

TREAT: Errol Flynn?

PHILLIP: The movie actor.

TREAT: I know Errol Flynn!

PHILLIP: He could've broke a leg leaping outta the window like that, Treat. He must be some kind of athlete.

TREAT: Maybe I better put on some hydrogen peroxide.

PHILLIP: No, Treat, it burns.

TREAT: You don't want it to get infected. *(He picks up the hydrogen peroxide.)*

PHILLIP: It's not gonna get infected.

TREAT: You don't wanna lose your arm.

PHILLIP: I ain't gonna lose my arm.

TREAT: Come here, Phillip. Let me help you. Let your big brother Treat take care of you.

(TREAT stands holding the bottle of hydrogen peroxide. PHILLIP walks slowly toward him.)

SCOOTER THOMAS MAKES IT TO THE TOP OF THE WORLD
by Peter Parnell
Scooter (various ages) - Dennis (various ages)

The Play: Peter Parnell often deals with the loss of the magic of youth as one grows into adulthood (see the scene and introduction from *The Rise and Rise of Daniel Rocket* in the first section of this book). In *Scooter Thomas Makes it to the Top of the World*, Mr. Parnell examines what leads to the suicide of a young man who seemed to have started life with so much to offer—so much to live for. This play, presented as a memory from Dennis's point of view, reconstructs a series of life-moments shared by Dennis and Scooter as they grew up as best of friends. When the play begins, Dennis has just received the news of his friend's suicide. The theatrical device of flashback, showing various scenes from the two friends' lives, allows us to look at a delightful, often touching, journey from youth through adolescents. Along with Dennis, we see, little by little, Scooter's fragile collapse. We know at the beginning where his life is going, but somehow, as the play progresses, we hope for a change in the outcome. In this, Mr. Parnell has given a truly affecting drama, filled with humor, but clearly a statement about the loss of our dreams.

The Scene: One of many scenes in the play where Scooter and Dennis are together, recreating a number of events shared in life.

SCOOTER THOMAS MAKES IT TO THE TOP OF THE WORLD

SCOOTER: Pizarro discovered the Inca Indians... Ponce de Leon discovered Florida looking for the Fountain of Youth...! Florida...is where my uncle Simon lives... John Smith discovered Pocahantas and married her... Miles Standish asked Priscilla Armstong to... Give me liberty or give me death...?

DENNIS: Psst! Hey, Scooter! Psst!

SCOOTER: Eddie! Whadda you doin' here?

DENNIS: I'm lookin' fer PeeWee. We're goin' out drivin' an' I figgered we'd take him along.

SCOOTER: You cuttin' class in *high school*?

DENNIS: I gotta be back by lunch.

SCOOTER: Is Wally goin' with ya?

DENNIS: He's waitin' outside.

SCOOTER: Oh boy, I'm comin' too.

DENNIS: You can't, ya little creep. Your brother told me definitely no.

SCOOTER: Look Eddie, I gotta go Wally never takes me out drivin' an I'm sicka studyin' stupid history for this stupid test an...

DENNIS; N-O.

SCOOTER: I'll tell my Dad that you an' he...

DENNIS: You say anything to anyone an' I'll personally drive a Mack truck over your face, understand?

SCOOTER: Eddie, lemme come with ya!

DENNIS: Just SHUT UP, ya little moron, OKAY? Nobody'd want to go drivin' with you! You're just your brother Wally's creepy kid brother, ya little creep! *(Dennis turns and Scooter plows into him from the side. Dennis goes to the floor, and Scooter pummels him about the head and waist. Breaks.)* Okay man, that's enough, enough!

SCOOTER: Sorry. I got carried away.

DENNIS: I'll say. Nearly fractured my skull.

SCOOTER: He really got me angry when he said that. About me being my brother Wally's kid brother. I mean, who did he think he was? I should have busted his—agh, knocked his block off!

DENNIS: *(Adult, authoritarian voice.)* ...And the nurse seems to think you might have even broken one of his ribs. Do you have any idea what that means?

SCOOTER: He might be permanently paralyzed from the neck down?

DENNIS: This isn't something to laugh at, young man.

SCOOTER: Sorry Mr. Greenbaum, sir.

DENNIS: Naturally I can't have too much pity for Mr. Marcus either. He's going to have to answer some serious charges once he gets up from that hospital bed. But as for you, Scooter. What seems to be the problem?

SCOOTER: Problem? There is no problem, sir.

DENNIS: Let me tell you something, Scooter. You are a very bright young boy. You could go far. But when will you learn to follow instructions? Sixth grade isn't the end of the line. After you graduate—*if* you graduate—you will have three years of junior high school to face. And believe me, they won't take any fooling around in junior high, Scooter. Then there'll be three more of high school, and *that* will be more difficult and disciplined than anything you will have encountered before. High school is going to make you into a responsible person, so that you will go on through four rigorous years of college and emerge—we hope—as something resembling an adult. And being an adult, Scooter, will be the toughest, most demanding thing of all. A job, a house, a wife, a little Scooter of your own. So I ask you: how are you ever going to expect to get anywhere, son, if you can't even make it through the sixth grade? You've got a long hard road ahead of you. Why do you want to blow it all now?

SCOOTER: I didn't start that fight, Mr. Greenbaum.

DENNIS: But you certainly finished it, didn't you?

SCOOTER: Eddie Marcus started it. And he should know better. He's a lot older and a lot smarter than me. I'm just my brother Wally's kid brother.

DENNIS: Then why don't you start acting like him, young man? Wallace was always one of my favorite students.

SCOOTER: *(Breaks.)* Jesus, why couldn't they have nabbed him, too! He was standing right outside the building!

DENNIS: *(To audience.)* Years later—after he'd told me all about the particulars of that interview—Scooter confessed to having wanted to ask

Mr. Greenbaum something, but failed to find the courage or even—so rare for him—the sheer audacity. It was:

SCOOTER: When did *you* start to blow it, Mr. Greenbaum?

DENNIS: I beg your pardon?

SCOOTER: You couldn't have been very happy in the sixth grade.

DENNIS: Well, I—don't know. I don't really—remember...

SCOOTER: Are we all through now?

DENNIS: All...? Er, yes, I suppose we— Naturally, I'll have to call your parents and tell them...

SCOOTER: Naturally. Good afternoon, sir.

DENNIS: Good afternoon. And. Take care, son. *(Scooter has turned away. Dennis stands and blows a whistle.)* All right you guys, I want you doin' jumping jacks high into the air! On the double! One-two-three-four, One-two-ready-begin... *(Scooter starts jumping.)* Side-up-side-down, side-up-side-down, side-up-side down, one-two-three-four, one-two-three-four, one-two-ready-stop... All right, now listen up, you guys. This is a junior high gym class, not a sewing class for pansies and queers. In this class we are here to develop sound bodies, because a sound mind must have a sound body to go with it, or else it shrivels up and turns to jelly and you find yourself dead before you're thirty. And that is the simple truth, you understand? Now I take it that nobody here wants to die before they're thirty. Is that right? Is there anyone here who wants to be dead before they are thirty? I didn't think so. So what this means is I want you all to bust your asses in this class. You'll be thankful for it later. Twenty years from now you'll see me on the street and you'll say, "Mr. Tartarian, I never realized how important it was for me to keep in shape. I'm glad you scared the piss outa me when you did." And believe me, I'll understand. But right now I don't want to hear a sound out of any of you, got me? Not a sound. Okay. Now when I blow this whistle—and not before—I want you to get down on the floor and do twenty push-ups on the double. *Quietly.* Okay.

SCOOTER: *(Falsetto, between his teeth.)* Okay.

DENNIS: Who said that? Who just opened his—Pee Wee, was that you? Who just said okay?

SCOOTER: I did. I cannot tell a lie. It was I, Mr. Tartarian, sir.

DENNIS: And who are you, shrimphead?

SCOOTER; Scooter Thomas, sir.

DENNIS: Thomas. Thomas. You have an older brother?

SCOOTER: Always have, sir.

DENNIS: He was a good man. Ran a good mile, Scooter. He'll be a tough man to follow—even tougher to beat.

SCOOTER: Then I won't plan on trying, sir.

DENNIS: What's that, Scooter?

SCOOTER: Nothing, Mt. T. Sir.

DENNIS: I bet you must think you're pretty funny, don't you?

SCOOTER: Not especially, sir.

DENNIS: Oh yes. I think you think you're very funny. Well let me tell you something Scooter Thomas: you may think you're funny, and everybody else may think you're funny, but I don't think you're funny, and you know what that means? It means you don't ever do that again, okay?

SCOOTER: Okay.

DENNIS: Or else you may just find yourself dead before you're thirty. And *that* would be just about the un-funniest thing of all. *(Blows his whistle.)* Ready, AND—One-two-three-four, One-two-ready-begin... *(Scooter gets down and starts doing push-ups. After several, he rolls over onto his stomach. He looks out into the audience a moment. Then he takes a pea-shooter, aims it out and starts firing, still on the floor. Dennis stands watching him for a moment, then walks over to him.)* Hey there. Whaddya doin'?

SCOOTER: Watching for puffins.

DENNIS: Oh. Yeah?

SCOOTER: Yeah. Puffins. You know. Little seabirds.

DENNIS: Puffins. Yeah. *(Scooter fires pea-shooter. Beat.)* Didn' year hear me? I kept calling and calling down there. *(Scooter fires.)* Nobody knew where you—figured I'd try Hatch's Cliff.

SCOOTER: I thought it'd be nice to come up.

DENNIS: Then why you weren't at practice?

SCOOTER: I didn't even know there was a game.

ENNIS: Whaddya talkin'. I told ya yesterday.

COOTER: So maybe I forgot.

ENNIS: So maybe you did. And then again, maybe you didn't.

COOTER: What's that supposed to—

ENNIS: You know what I mean—the gang's played four games in ve days, and you haven't been to one of 'em.

COOTER: I've been busy.

ENNIS: Sure you have. Watching for puffins.

COOTER: You wanna make something of it?

ENNIS: (Laughs.) Sure. Why not? (Beat. Scooter fires.) Did azorhead send you to Brownstein again?

COOTER: What d'you think? Yeah, that Brownstein—he's worse aan Greenbaum ever was.

ENNIS: I see he didn't take away your pea-shooter.

COOTER: He tried to. I told him I needed it for the All-State hampionships next Saturday.

ENNIS: (Laughs.) And he believed you?

COOTER: That's why I hit Razorhead in the neck—needed the ractice. (They laugh.) Razorhead didn't say anything after I left?

ENNIS: (Guilty.) I don't think he felt the second one.

COOTER: Yours was a direct hit.

ENNIS: Yeah, I know, but...

COOTER: It was an even better hit than mine.

ENNIS: But yours came first.

COOTER: (Laughs.) Yeah, we got him from both sides, didn't we!

ENNIS: Look, I'm sorry I didn't raise my hand or anything when he sked who else—I mean, I wanted to go up to him after, I really did.

COOTER: (Shrugs.) He likes you. He wouldn't have gotten mad.

ENNIS; No, he'd have remembered from the last time. When we ut chalk in his erasers.

COOTER: (Laughs.) Yeah, what did he—

ENNIS: (Does Razorhead.) I'm very disappointed in you, Dennis. Associating yourself with the likes of Scooter Thomas. I should think you'd be embarrassed... (Scooter looks at Dennis. Dennis stops. Scooter smiles and turns out. Fires.)

SCOOTER: Got the bastard! Got him again! (Pause.) Y'know, the interesting thing about puffins, Dennis, is that for birds they're terrible flyers. Can't fly worth shit. They always end up crashing into things whenever they try to land. Sort of a funny little problem to have for a seabird, don't you think?

DENNIS: I guess.

SCOOTER: What'd you do with your shooter?

DENNIS; Threw it out with my lunch-bag.

SCOOTER: Oh geez. I'll have to make you another one. Take mine for now.

DENNIS: What?

SCOOTER; Take mine. I'll make myself a new one as soon as I get home. *(Pause.)* What's the matter? Not good enough for ya?

DENNIS: What? No, Scoots, sure I...

SCOOTER: Don't you want it?

DENNIS: Yeah. Thanks. *(Pause.)*

SCOOTER: I'll see ya later. *(He gets up to go.)*

DENNIS: Yeah, see ya. Hey, Scoots?

SCOOTER: *(Stops. Turns.)* Yeah?

DENNIS: See ya later. *(Scooter nods. Goes. Dennis looks out beyond the audience for a moment. Shouts.)* Hey, Scoots! Scoots! I think I just saw a puffin!

SCOOTER: *(Rushing in.)* Where? Where? *(Looks out.)* Nah. That's a Tibetan Spiny-babbler. It's not the same thing at all...

DENNIS: *(Reads.)* When walking in the wilderness, always relate your route to something else. If you walk in a circle, you'll only end up back where you started. Follow these simple rules and you should never get lost... *(Scooter points. Dennis follows.)*

SPRING AWAKENING
by Frank Wedekind
translated by Tom Osborn
Melchior (15) - Moritz (15)

The Play: Frank Wedekind's *Spring Awakening* is a pre-expressionistic tragedy about young people searching for knowledge about sex. Set in the bourgeois society of late 19th-century Germany, the hypocritical morality and stultifying attitudes of the children's parents and teachers choke them off in the very springs of their lives. The story focuses on two friends, Melchior and Moritz, who are just beginning to experiment with sexual activity. Like their fellow classmates, they only receive vague, foolish answers to their questions. Wendla and her girlfriends find it even more difficult to gain information. She and Melchior begin to fall in love, and, after succumbing to a moment of passion, Wendla becomes pregnant—yet she does not understand why. Her horrified mother arranges an abortion for the girl, and she dies. Moritz, confused by his sexual feelings, begins to fail in his studies and doesn't graduate. Troubled and disturbed, he commits suicide. There is no sympathy from his father and teachers, however, only contempt. Later, Melchior, who has been sent to a reformatory, is driven to escape and find Wendla's grave. The specter of Moritz appears and encourages the boy to join him in death, but a stranger—the force of life—intervenes.

The Scene: Sunday evening. Melchior and Moritz, bored with doing their homework, go for a walk.

Special Note: Students may want to look at Eric Bentley's translation of the play, as well as Edward Bond's.

MELCHIOR: I'd really like to know what we're supposed to be doing in this world.

MORITZ: What are we supposed to be doing at school? I'd rather have been a cart-horse. I'd like to know what exams are for. So they can fail us. Seven of us have got to fail anyway, the next classroom only holds sixty... Ever since Christmas everything's felt strange—I'm so separate... God, if it wasn't for Father I'd just go away, pack up my rucksack and go off walking.

MELCHIOR: Let's talk about something else.

(They walk)

MORITZ: A bird flew in through my window this morning. That means bad luck of some sort.

MELCHIOR: D'you believe in all that?

MORITZ: I don't really know. It flew out again without going round the room. I think that makes it all right.

MELCHIOR: It's as bad as religion. Like Scylla and Charybdis. You think you're safe, sailing untouched past the Scylla of all that religion nonsense, and there's the Charybdis of omens and superstitions waiting to suck you down. Let's sit under this tree. There's a warm wind blowing down from the hills. All the snow must be melting. That's where I'd like to be now, up there—all night in the treetops—rocking and swaying in the wind.

MORITZ: Undo your collar, Melchior.

MELCHIOR: Yes...let the wind in.

MORITZ: It's getting so dark—I can hardly see you. Melchior...d'you think the feeling of shame—in man—d'you think it's because of his upbringing?

MELCHIOR: I was thinking about that only the other day. It's deeply rooted in human nature. I mean—if you think of yourself with nothing on—undressing in front of your best friend. You wouldn't do it. Not unless he was undressing at the same time. Of course convention must have a lot to do with it.

MORITZ: If I ever have to bring up children I've worked out what I'm going to do. They'll all live together in the same room, boys and girls, all sleep in one big bed. They could help each other to dress and

216

undress. And when the warm wind comes all they'll need to wear is a short tunic—plain white—with a leather belt. If they grew up like that I'm sure they'd be less ashamed than us.

MELCHIOR: Fine. And tell me what you'll do when the girls have babies?

MORITZ: What d'you mean, have babies?

MELCHIOR: Don't you think there'd be a certain instinct at work? Suppose you took two kittens—a boy and a girl—and shut them away—left them. Sooner or later you'd have a litter on your hands, wouldn't you, even with no grown-up cats to show them how.

MORITZ: I suppose with animals it just happens.

MELCHIOR: I think humans are just the same. Look here, Moritz, those boys and girls of yours in the same bed—and then, out of the blue, out of the dark, the first—you know—effects of puberty... I'd give you any odds...

MORITZ: *(Doubtful)* I'm sure your right—but all the same...

MELCHIOR: And it won't be just the boys, you know. Not that all girls are the same...probably you can't always tell... Oh it's a safe bet. And you'd have curiosity on your side.

MORITZ: Yes... By the way I rather want to ask you something...

MELCHIOR: All right.

MORITZ: You will answer, won't you?

MELCHIOR: Of course I will.

MORITZ: The truth?

MELCHIOR: Of course. Well, Moritz?

MORITZ: ...Have you done that Latin composition yet?

MELCHIOR: You don't need to change the subject you know. There's no-one here.

MORITZ: Of course my children would be working, all day long. Farming or in the garden, or strenuous games—gym, riding, rock-climbing. And they'd have to sleep on the floor, or in the open, not in soft beds like us—that's what makes us weak... I'm certain we wouldn't dream, sleeping rough.

MELCHIOR: Yes. I'm sleeping in my hammock. I've put my bed away and I won't use it again till the wine harvest's over. Last winter—I dreamt once—I was whipping our dog. I whipped him so much he couldn't move—he was lying there... That's the worst dream I've ever had. Why are you looking at me like that?

MORITZ: So it has happened to you?

MELCHIOR: What?

MORITZ: What you said.

MELCHIOR: The effects of puberty.

MORITZ: Yes.

MELCHIOR: Certainly.

MORITZ: Me too...

MELCHIOR: Ages ago.

MORITZ: It hit me like a thunderbolt.

MELCHIOR: Have you dreamt?

MORITZ: Just once. Quite short. Legs in knitted stockings—bright blue—rising up over my desk... Actually I think just climbing over. I only saw them for a moment.

MELCHIOR: Georg Tirschnitz dreamt about his mother.

MORITZ: Did he tell you that himself?

MELCHIOR: Yes, why not?

MORITZ: If you knew what I've been through since that night.

MELCHIOR: Guilt?

MORITZ: Guilt? No, no... I've realized what Hell means...and if I died...

MELCHIOR: Good God.

MORITZ: It felt like some poison—a poison from inside. I started a journal. I've written down my whole life. It was the only thing that made me feel better. Honestly, Melchior—the Garden of Gethsemane must have been rather like this...

MELCHIOR: It didn't take me like that. It was a bit shaming, but that's all.

MORITZ: And you're almost a year younger than me.

MELCHIOR: That doesn't mean a thing. It can start at any age. That blond lout Lammermeier, he's three years older than us and Hans Rilow says he still dreams about fruit cake and chocolates.

MORITZ: How did he find that out?

MELCHIOR: He asked him.

MORITZ: I couldn't ask anybody that.

MELCHIOR: You just asked me.

MORITZ: My God, yes, so I did. Perhaps Hans has written his journal too. Honestly, life... What a game... We're pushed into it, and then we're expected to give thanks to God. I didn't ask for all this. Why can't I just sleep, till the silence comes back. My parents could have had any one out of a hundred children—and they got me. And I don't even know how. I'm just here—being made to suffer because I didn't stay away. Melchior...don't you ever wonder—I mean in what way—we manage to get here—into this whirlpool?

MELCHIOR: So you really don't know then?

MORITZ: How d'you expect me to know? All right, chickens lay eggs, and I was once told Mother carried me near her heart. And I can remember being five and looking the other way when someone turned up that queen of hearts with the low neckline. I don't have to do that any more—but nowadays I can hardly speak to a girl without feeling as if I'm loathsome—and I don't know why...

MELCHIOR: I'll tell you. I've learnt all about it, from books, from pictures, partly from observing nature. It'll surprise you. I turned atheist. I told Georg Tirschnitz. He wanted to tell Hans Rilow, but Rilow was shown everything long ago by his governess.

MORITZ: I looked through the whole of Meyer's shorter encyclo-paedia. Nothing but a lot of words, they don't tell you a thing. Just—shame. What's the use of an encyclopaedia that doesn't answer the real questions?

MELCHIOR: Well. You've seen two dogs playing in the street...

MORITZ: No... Don't go on, not now. I've still got Central America and Ludwig the Fifth, and then those sixty verses of Homer and seven equations, and the Latin composition—I'd only do badly again tomorrow. If I'm going to keep working I've got to be a cart-horse—an ox—with blinkers on.

MELCHIOR: Come home with me. It'll only take me an hour for the whole lot. I'll put a few mistakes in yours and we've finished. Then Mother can make us some lemon tea and we'll settle down for a nice cosy chat about reproduction.

MORITZ: I can't chat about reproduction, Melchior. No...no, couldn't you write it all out, everything you know—clear, unambiguous—stick it in one of my books during break and I'll take it home without knowing. One day it'll just turn up. So I'll have to look through it however much work there is piling up. And if it's absolutely essential—you could put a few diagrams in the margin.

MELCHIOR: You're a little girl, Moritz. Still, it'll be an interesting piece of work. You haven't ever seen a girl, I suppose?

MORITZ: Yes, I have.

MELCHIOR: All over?

MORITZ: Completely. On Shrove Tuesday I slipped into the anatomy museum. If anyone had caught me I'd have been expelled. It was like waking up on a new day...everything there, it was the truth—such beauty...

MELCHIOR: Oh. Well, then illustrations won't be necessary.

MORITZ: No...of course not... Of course you've seen it...

MELCHIOR: That time in Frankfurt, when I was there with Mother last summer, one day... You're going, Moritz?

MORITZ: I must work... Good night.

MELCHIOR: See you tomorrow.

ASCENSION DAY
by Timothy Mason
Faith (18) - June (18) - Mary-Lois (17) - Joyce (16)

The Play: Life often takes a turn when we are young that affects us
forever. This theme is explored with an edge in Timothy Mason's short
play set in a Lutheran Bible camp in Wisconsin, late in May, 1947.
The story centers around nine teenagers spending a week at camp,
strengthening their faith through testimonials, enriching the quality of
their lives by study (everything from "nature tips" to lifesaving), and
having time to spend with each other, sharing life experiences. If all
of this seems like expected church camp business, what is underneath
this engrossing drama certainly isn't. In this seemingly tranquil
environment, on the shores of a beautiful lake, loon song abounding, a
series of moments compose a score that will not only change many
lives, but will allow us the opportunity to reflect on the path our lives
have taken. Written with economy, the issues are significant, the
characters crystalline. The week is seen through the eyes of the young
people. In fact, the adults at camp never appear—but are always a
threatening presence. Specifically we follow the story of two sisters.
Faith and Charity. Faith, the older of the two, is returning to camp—
this year as a junior counselor. Last year at camp, her life began to
change. Having been brought up in a strict home, overseen by a
demanding, single-minded father, Faith found her experiences at camp
exciting but disturbing. She met a boy, a boy who has returned this
year. Faith struggles to handle the feelings in her heart, while at the
same time, striving for perfection in the eyes of her parents, her sister,
and herself. Her rigid instincts for right and wrong (influenced by her
father) have driven away the boys and, during the course of the play,
will sever the close bond that for years had held her and Charity
together. Charity wants the freedom to explore a new-found excitement
away from the watchful eye of her parents and resists Faith's firm
governance. Perhaps seeing her own choices in Charity's actions, Faith
drifts further away until the desperation demands action. A rekindled
spark with Wesley, last year's boyfriend, ends in disaster. Those
around her seem shallow, mindlessly content for the same kind of life
that their parents live. Faith somehow demands more from life. As the

221

loons cry on the lake, Faith shatters inside, unable to maintain her fragile facade. Her final fateful move brings the play to its startling climax, and forever changes the course of her life.

The Scene: A few days have gone by, rather uneventfully, and the girls take a moment to finish their hot chocolate on the back steps of the dining hall. It is a moonlit night. Among the thoughts on the minds of the girls is Faith's concern that these few days have passed without Wesley, her boyfriend from last summer, so much as saying hello.

ASCENSION DAY

(Wednesday night. Faith, June, Mary-Lois and Joyce sit and stand on a flight of steps behind the dining hall, drinking hot chocolate. Over the lake, there's a moon.)

JOYCE: On a night like tonight I can't imagine a thing wrong with the world.

FAITH: You should get a better imagination.

JUNE: Faith, she's fine, stop worrying.

FAITH: It's ten-thirty.

MARY-LOIS: Gosh, I had no idea.

JOYCE: When do you suppose the moon'll be full? It's pretty close.

FAITH: Full moon, June the first—first quarter, June the ninth—new moon, sixteenth of the month.

JOYCE: How do you keep track of things like that?

FAITH: I pay attention. If I hadn't promised her I wouldn't act like her sister while we're here, I'd kill her.

JUNE: When are you going to talk to Wesley?

FAITH: June, just don't.

MARY-LOIS: *(To Joyce.)* Are you going with us into town in the morning?

JOYCE: No, I've got Junior Lifesaving. It's strange, when you're out here it's as though things like towns don't exist, the rest of the world doesn't exist.

MARY-LOIS: Oh, I know.

FAITH: It's been nearly a week, if he wants to talk to me he can come up and talk to me.

JUNE: Not when you've got a look like that on your face.

FAITH: A look like what?

JUNE: I don't know. Mount Rushmore.

FAITH: I am sick to death of people telling me I turn to stone, I don't turn to stone, I am not made of stone, I am made of all the ordinary things people are made of. *(Beat.)*

JUNE: Pardon me. *(Long uncomfortable pause, which Joyce tries to cover with a song, unsuccessfully.)*

JOYCE: *(Singing.)* "K-k-k-Katie, K-k-k-Katie, You're the only g-g-g-girl that I adore..." *(She trails off. Long pause.)*

223

ASCENSION DAY

FAITH: *(To June.)* What are you doing in the fall?

JUNE: Oh, it's going to be crazy. George gets demobilized at the end of August, we figure he'll be back home by the first week of September, just in time to help finish getting the crops in. Mom's already working on the dress, and I'll start sending out the invitations and working on the bridesmaids' dresses and turning Dad's den into a home for George and me and that's going to be no picnic, believe me, I think Dad wishes he'd never said okay, he's really going to miss that den. You're going to like your dress, I think, at least I hope, just a very pale purple taffeta with a delicate white lace. The groom's dinner'll be at Weston's Steak House and the rehearsal dinner'll be at the hotel, and we're renting the American Legion club for the reception, and by the thirty-first of October I'll be Mrs. George Nyquist.

FAITH: Oh, yeah, I forgot. *(Beat.)*

JUNE: Faith, you just say things like that to annoy people, you didn't forget my wedding for goodness sake.

JOYCE: *(To June.)* Gosh, I envy you.

JUNE: *(To Faith.)* What are you doing this fall?

FAITH: I don't know. Dad'll hire me at the feed-store, I guess.

JOYCE: Marrying a *soldier*.

JUNE: What about college? Out of our whole class, you were going to be the one who went to college.

FAITH: Out of our whole class, you mean all nine of us? Yeah, I guess I thought so, too. Chippewa County Community College. Maybe I still will. Dad doesn't see the point of it. At first I was upset, but now I'm not sure I can see any point either.

MARY-LOIS: I can't help it, I want to start having babies. As long as I can remember I've just wanted a baby, a whole lot of babies, I love babies.

FAITH: Did you ever wonder, if we didn't happen to be born here, if we were born somewhere else, everything would be different?

MARY-LOIS: What do you mean?

FAITH: I don't know. *(Pause.)*

JOYCE: What is it about a moon that makes you want to be with someone so bad?

ASCENSION DAY

MARY-LOIS: I asked my Aunt Elinor, she's a spinster, I asked her if she ever missed having children, gosh, I could have bit my lip. She said, No, I've got my nieces and my nephews, and then she went upstairs to bed with a migraine headache for the rest of the day.

JOYCE: When I said the moon made me want to be with someone, I wasn't talking about children.

JUNE: Joyce, we know what you were talking about.

JOYCE: Or your Aunt Elinor. *(The girls laugh a little. Long pause.)*

JOYCE: *(Singing.)* "K-k-k-Katie... "

JOYCE & MARY-LOIS: "K-k-k-Katie....

> You're the only g-g-g-girl
> That I adore.
> When the m-m-moon shines
> Over the cowshed,
> I'll be waiting by the k-k-k-kitchen door. "

THE CHOPIN PLAYOFFS
by Israel Horovitz
Fern (16) - Stanley (16) - Irving (16)

The Play: This is play number three in a trilogy by Mr. Horovitz based on stories by Morley Torgov. At the heart of the play is a piano contest between Irving Yanover and Stanley Rosen, two sixteen-year-old boys living in Sault Ste. Marie, Ontario, Canada in 1947. More precisely, the "playoffs" occur between the Rosen and Yanover families for their position in the Jewish community, between the two boys in their private struggles to each win the heart of Fern Fipps, a very Protestant girl (much to the horror of the two very Jewish families), and between Fern and the boys as she attempts to make the right decision and please everyone. The play snaps and crackles with these individual playoffs as the boys battle, the parents battle, the boys battle with the parents, and Fern becomes the ultimate judge on the entire proceedings. Added to the mix of children and parents, Horovitz weaves two brilliant characters: Ardenshensky, an old Jew, and Uncle Goldberg, Irving's old Jewish uncle (both roles played by the same actor). Here the wisdom of age and a sense of the struggle between the old world and the new offers a balance and much fun. As Fern promises her heart to the winner of the playoffs, the play serves almost as a boxing ring (Horovitz even calls for a prizefight bell to ring the transitions between scenes). The play concludes with lessons for everyone. Young and old alike question the decisions made in youth that will effect one's life forever.

The Scene: Not only have Irving and Stanley been preparing for the piano playoffs, they have been struggling to win the affection of Fern Fipps. Fern has demonstrated earlier in the play that she likes each of the boys very much and it is a difficult decision to choose between them. The boys are aggressive in their attempts to discredit each other. This is the first time we see all three of them together, due to a mistake on Fern's part about who the date tonight was to be with.

Special Note: Mr. Horovitz cautions actors to avoid any stereotypical behavior with the characters in this play. In addition, Yiddish or Eastern European accents—"or stereotyically 'Jewish' intonation" should be avoided.

THE CHOPIN PLAYOFFS

(The scene has shifted once again to Capy's Grille. Stanley is, as they say, fit to be tied. The lights widen to include Stanley and Fern, and Irving, who stands at the piano, watching Fern and Stanley. They will "act" that other students fill the imagined other tables and are overhearing Stanley's rage)

FERN: I...I'm sorry, Stanley, I got confused... I thought I made the date with Irving...

STANLEY: You told me Capy's at three, so, at three I was at Capy's. Now it's five and where am I? Still at Capy's but you're here too, and with who?

IRVING: Whom...you said "who."

STANLEY: If you enjoy life, I wouldn't, Yanover, okay?

FERN: This is a nightmare!

STANLEY: You're telling *me*? You're not the one waiting here for two and a half hours only to watch you walk in the place holding hands with this brain-damaged homo-putz!

IRVING: *(Stepping in)* This really *is* a nightmare!

STANLEY: You say something, Yanover?

IRVING: Yuh. I did, Rosen. I said that this is a nightmare.

STANLEY: You wanna step outside, Yanover?

FERN: Stanleyyy!

IRVING: Typical Rosen move: he waits for us for two hours and then right away he wants to step outside. *I* don't want to step outside. I've just been outside. But, listen, Rosen, you wanna step outside, be my guest: step.

STANLEY: Ho. Ho-ho. Ho-ho-ho. It's hard for me to sit still for your rapid-fire, slashing wit, Yanover.

IRVING: You're not sitting, Rosen, you're standing. When your knees are stiff and your *tookis* is perpendicular to the floor, you are standing. When your knees are bent and your tookis is parallel to the floor, it is then you are sitting.

*(Stanley will shove Irving. N.B.: Shove = *)*

STANLEY: Damn! I forgot...tookis up: stand*; tookis down: sit*... this man has a firm grip on the basics*...what a *thinker*...what a great goddam *mind*. Tookis up: stand.* Tookis down: sit.* *Fabulous!**

THE CHOPIN PLAYOFFS

FERN: I'm leaving before the fistfight starts again, thank you...

STANLEY: No, don't leave, Fern, please! I am not fighting! Please stay! This is my only afternoon off! I'm not clear again until Monday! *(To Irving; loud whisper)* If she leaves, Yanover, I will drop out of school and dedicate my life to your death.

IRVING: Any time, any place, any Army you wanna bring with you, pecker-face...

FERN: You both promised me! You promised me!

STANLEY: *(Sudden shift; to Fern)* We're not fighting! *(To Irving)* Are we fighting?

IRVING: Absolutely not.

FERN: Let's sit down together, then, okay?

STANLEY: But you're *my* date, Fern, dammit! *(Another fierce whisper, to Irving)* If that *tookis* of yours goes down, this foot of mine goes up...*if* you get my point...you *will*... *(Stanley twists Irving's flesh, unseen by Fern)*

IRVING: *(To Fern)* I have to go home now, really. I shouldn't stay. I've, uh, got to help my father with inventory...

STANLEY: You have a father? Gosh, I thought you were found under a rock, putz-face...

IRVINGL At least I was *found*, shit-for-brains! You've yet to be discovered...like Pluto...and I don't mean the planet, Rosen. I mean Goofy's friend, the dog...

STANLEY: This is the goddam limit, homo-head! My foot is heading for your anus, and I don't mean the planet, either!

FERN: *(Starts to sob. Her shoulders shake. She moans, rasps, shouts)* Will you two *stop*...will you two please stop...will you two please please *please* stopppp? *Will you? Will yoooo?*

IRVING: We're not fighting, Fern...

STANLEY: Not at all...

FERN: That's not it! *(Moans; sobs)* Oh, Goddd...

IRVING: We're really not fighting, Fern. Look at us...

STANLEY: There's not reason to cry...

IRVING: I apologize, Fern, I really do... Don't cry...

FERN: *(Crying openly)* I'm not crying...

THE CHOPIN PLAYOFFS

IRVING: We really weren't going to fight...not in front of you.

STANLEY: Honest to God...not in front of you...

FERN: *(Sobs)* That's not it... That's not why I'm upset...

STANLEY: What's it, then?

IRVING: Why are you upset?

FERN: Because...I can't...tell you apart!

IRVING: You can't tell who apart?

FERN: You and Irving.

IRVING: I *am* Irving.

FERN: *(Sobs) You seeee?*

(Stanley and Irving stare at each other a moment)

STANLEY: You can't tell me apart from Irving Yanover?

FERN: No, I can't. I really can't. You both play piano, you both crack jokes, you're both depressed all the time, you're both Jewish, you're both skinny, you're both conceited...

IRVING: Rosen has dandruff.

FERN: Oh, my God! That was really *cruel*!

STANLEY: I'll kill you for that!

IRVING: Rosen is round-shouldered.

FERN: So are you. You're much more round-shouldered than he is.

IRVING: I am not!

STANLEY: You are, Yanover!

FERN; You are so!

STANLEY: Practically a hunchback...

IRVING: An hunchback...

STANLEY: How about *an* hit in the head, Yanover?

FERN: *No fighting!*

IRVING: Irving started it. I didn't. Don't blame me.

STANLEY: Don't blame me, either, Fern: blame Rosen!

FERN: *Oh, my God...* I really can't tell you apart: it's true! *It's trooooo...* *(She sobs)* Every night, before I go to sleep, the phone rings and it's one of you...as soon as I hang it up, I know the other one will get mad at me...because the other one has been calling and calling, waiting for the line to stop being busy... *(Pauses)* Just the same, just exactly the same... *(She sobs, again)* You dance the same, you kiss the same, you both like to hold the same hand, you like the same books, the same movies, the same records, you're both terrible athletes, A+ students, neither of you smokes, nor drinks, both of you crack bad jokes endlessly...and you both talk about Chopin all the time...and ... you both...upset me *so much*! Ooooo! *(She sobs, again)*

STANLEY: Fern Fipps, this is really insulting. It's not insulting for Yanover ot be mistaken for me, but I am...insulted deeply. Deeply!

FERN: I knew I made the date with you, Stanley, but I got confused and thought you, Irving, were Stanley...that's why I was late, Stanley.

IRVING; And our date was tomorrow, Fern... I was supposed to practice in Music Hall today, so I can cream Rosen come the playoffs.

STANLEY: Come the playoffs, dear boy, the cream will be Rosen. The *creamed* will be Yanover. *(Stanley threatens to hit Irving)*

FERN: NO FIGHTING! YOU PROMISED! YOU PROMISED ME, BOTH OF YOU!

(Stanley and Irving face each other, fists ready)

IRVING AND STANLEY: We're not fighting!

FERN: I can't stand it! *I'm going to end up hating both of you!*

STANLEY: This is your goddam fault, Yanover!

FERN: ...I like being with both of you, but I can't be with both of you...and I can't choose one over the other because I can't tell you apart...

STANLEY: Loookkk, I have a simple solution, Fern...

FERN: *(Sobs again)* What is it?

STANLEY: How about the concert? Maybe the better man should win you in the playoffs, Fern. Let the winner really *win*.

IRVING: Aren't you kinda' making a mistake there, Rosen?

STANLEY: I hardly think so, Yanover...

IRVING: Oh, really?

STANLEY: Oh, really...

FERN: Oh, that's such a good idea, Irving.

STANLEY: Stanley...

FERN: *(To Irving)* Stanley, I mean...

STANLEY: Me, Fern, me...

FERN: Ooooo, my God! The playoffs aren't until the end of June.

THE CHOPIN PLAYOFFS

It's only May 10! How will I ever *live* till the end of June?

IRVING: Until then, you go out with only me, and after that the winner...Irving.

FERN: Until then I'll go out with you, Irving, one week and you, Stanley, the next week, and then you, Irving, the next week, and so on... *(Seriously)* Please, say "yes"? *Please*!

STANLEY; Yes, I say "yes"...

IRVING: I really hate this. I want you to know that I really and truly hate this... Yes, okay, yes.

FERN: *(Thrilled)* I...am...sooo...*relieved*!

SPRING AWAKENING
by Frank Wedekind
translated by Tom Osborn
Martha (14-15) - Thea (14-15) - Wendla (14-15)

The Play: Frank Wedekind's *Spring Awakening* is a pre-expressionistic tragedy about young people searching for knowledge about sex. Set in the bourgeois society of late 19th-century Germany, the hypocritical morality and stultifying attitudes of the children's parents and teachers choke them off in the very springs of their lives. The story focuses on two friends, Melchior and Moritz, who are just beginning to experiment with sexual activity. Like their fellow classmates, they only receive vague, foolish answers to their questions. Wendla and her girlfriends find it even more difficult to gain information. She and Melchior begin to fall in love, and, after succumbing to a moment of passion, Wendla becomes pregnant—yet she does not understand why. Her horrified mother arranges an abortion for the girl, and she dies. Moritz, confused by his sexual feelings, begins to fail in his studies and doesn't graduate. Troubled and disturbed, he commits suicide. There is no sympathy from his father and teachers, however, only contempt. Later, Melchior, who has been sent to a reformatory, is driven to escape and find Wendla's grave. The specter of Moritz appears and encourages the boy to join him in death, but a stranger—the force of life—intervenes.

The Scene: Martha, Thea and Wendla are strolling along the street arm in arm.

Special Note: Students may want to look at Eric Bentley's translation of the play, as well as Edward Bond's.

SPRING AWAKENING

(THEA, WENDLA and MARTHA come along the street arm in arm)

MARTHA: Are your shoes wet?

THEA: They're soaking.

MARTHA: So are mine.

WENDLA: Doesn't the wind burn your cheeks.

THEA: Can you feel your heart?

WENDLA: Let's go on the bridge. Ilse told me the river's nearly over the wall. It's full of trees and bushes. The boys have got a raft out. She said Melchi Gabor was nearly carried off yesterday.

THEA: And he's a marvellous swimmer.

MARTHA: He'd need to be.

WENDLA: If he wasn't a good swimmer he'd have drowned.

THEA: Your hair's coming loose, Martha, your hair's coming down.

MARTHA: Oh let it come. My hair's a big nuisance—all day and all night my hair. I can't cut it short like you, I can't wear it loose like Wendla, I can't have a fringe. And all the time I've got to do it specially, because one of my aunts is coming to visit.

WENDLA: I'll bring some scissors tomorrow. In scripture you'll recite Lord now lettest thou thy servant depart in peace—and I'll snip it off.

MARTHA: For God's sake, Wendla, they'd beat me till the blood came. Pappa would beat me and Mamma would lock me in the coal-cellar for three nights.

WENDLA: What does he beat you with, Martha?

MARTHA: I do think they'd miss me, though, if I wasn't there, even a hopeless lump like me.

THEA: Oh Martha.

MARTHA: And you're allowed a blue ribbon, aren't you—bright blue, to thread round the top of your petticoat.

THEA: Pink satin. My mother says pink goes best with my jet-black eyes.

MARTHA: Blue goes like jewels on me. You're so lucky. My mother pulled me off the bed by the hair—I fell on the floor. She comes to pray with us each evening, you see...

WENDLA: I'd have run away long ago.

MARTHA: 'There you are'—she was shouting at me—'that's just what I mean—there you are—but you'll learn, you'll learn all right.'

THEA: What did she mean?

MARTHA: I don't know.

THEA: Do you, Wendla?

WENDLA: I'd have asked her.

MARTHA: I was screaming on the floor. Then Father came in. He tore my petticoat right off me. I ran out of the front door. 'What did I tell you'—he was shouting too. I wanted to go out in the street like that, to show them...

WENDLA: You didn't, did you, Martha?

MARTHA: It was too cold. I'd got the door open. They put me in a sack for the night.

THEA: I couldn't sleep in a sack.

WENDLA: I wish I could sleep in your sack for you one day.

MARTHA: They beat me too, you know.

THEA: Don't you suffocate?

MARTHA: My head stays out. It's tied under my chin.

THEA: And then they beat you?

MARTHA: Not always. Only for something special.

WENDLA: What do they beat you with, Martha?

MARTHA: Whatever's around—all sorts of things. Does your mother think it's wrong to eat bread in bed?

WENDLA: No, she doesn't.

MARTHA: I still believe we mean something to them—even if they never say so. When I have children I'll bring them up like weeds. Nobody bothers about weeds—but they grow thicker and higher than all the flowers in our garden. They don't need sticks to keep them up. Not like the roses. They get more feeble every summer.

THEA: When I have children I'll dress them all in pink, pink hats, pink dresses, pink shoes. Except their stockings, they'll by jet black. And when we go out they'll walk ahead of me in a column. What will you do, Wendla?

WENDLA: How do you know you'll have children?

THEA: Why shouldn't we have them?

SPRING AWAKENING

MARTHA: Aunt Euphemia hasn't got any.

THEA: She's not married, stupid.

WENDLA: Aut Bauer was married three times and she hasn't got one.

MARTHA: Would you rather have boys or girls, Wendla?

WENDLA: Oh, boys, boys.

THEA: I'd like boys too.

MARTHA: So would I.

THEA: Girls are a bore.

MARTHA: If I could choose I'd never be a girl.

WENDLA: I think that's a matter of opinion, Martha. Every day I think how happy I am being a girl. I wouldn't change places with a Prince. But I still only want boys.

THEA: That doesn't make sense, Wendla.

WENDLA: Of course it does, because it must be hundreds of times more exciting being loved by a man—than by a girl.

THEA: Do you think Forestry Commissioner Klein loves his wife more than she loves him?

WENDLA: Yes, I do think so. Klein's got self-respect...he's proud of himself because he's Forestry Commissioner but that's all he's got. Mellita is full of joy because he's made her into ten thousand times more than what she'd be alone.

MARTHA: You're proud, aren't you, Wendla?

WENDLA: There's nothing wrong with that.

MARTHA: I wish I could be proud like you.

THEA: Look at the way she walks, the way her head looks up in the air—that's pride all right.

WENDLA: Well I want to be a girl. If I wasn't a girl I'd kill myself, quickly, for the next time...

(MELCHIOR passes by and waves to them)

THEA: He's got a lovely profile.

MARTHA: That's how I think of the young Alexander going to school, with Aristotle.

THEA: Oh Lord, Greek history. All I know is Socrates lying in his bath being sold a donkey's shadow. That was by Alexander, wasn't it?

WENDLA: He's supposed to be third best in his class.

THEA: Professor Breakneck said he could be first if he tried.

MARTHA: He's got a nice profile, but his friend has got more dreamy eyes.

THEA: Moritz Stiefel? He's so stupid.

MARTHA: We've always got on quite well.

THEA: He's embarrassing to be with. At Hans Rilow's party he gave me some chocolates. They were all melting. He said he'd forgotten them in his trouser pocket.

WENDLA: You know what, that time—Melchi Gabor told me he didn't believe in anything. Not in God, or a future life. He didn't believe in anything any more in the whole world.

WHAT I DID LAST SUMMER
by A.R. Gurney, Jr.
Charlie (14) - Ted (16) - Bonny (14)

The Play: Set during summer vacation, 1945, on the Canadian shores of Lake Erie near Buffalo, New York, this warm-hearted memory play is the coming of age story of fourteen-year-old Charlie Higgins. World War II is just winding down, and Charlie Higgins and his mother and sister are attempting to carry on with their lives as best they can while Mr. Higgins is serving in the Pacific. Charlie's mother, Grace, has been finding it increasingly difficult to make Charlie behave, so she has decided to send him to boarding school in the fall. But Charlie rebels; he takes a part-time job to earn spending money rather than tutor Latin. He approaches Anna Trumbull, a Tuscarora Indian know in the area as the "pig woman." Anna is a bohemian spirit devoted to organic living and self expression. She finds a kindred and impressionable spirit in Charlie, whose mother, it turns out, was once one of Anna's prize students. Much to Grace's consternation, Anna stretches Charlie's mind and soul by teaching him painting and sculpture, and filling him with radical ideas about life which eventually cause him to reject the conservative values of his family. This crisis results in a showdown between Grace and Anna in which the conflicting values of Materialism and Idealism are brought into sharp focus. At the end of the summer, Charlie leaves the tutelage of Anna Trumbull with a new sense of himself and his purpose in life.

The Scene: Charlie and his friend Ted have been vying for the attentions of Bonny. Bonny has opted for the more experienced and older Ted, however, despite the disapproval of her mother and father. Ted is waiting in his car for Bonny to show up for their first date.

WHAT I DID LAST SUMMER

(Ted comes on from U.L. singing "Pistol Packin' Mamma." He gets into his "car," adjusts the "mirror," combs his hair, and then waits impatiently. Bonny backs On nervously from U.L.)

TED: *(Rolling down the "window," leaning out.)* Come on.

BONNY: He's not here yet.

TED: Who? Don't tell me you asked Charlie!

BONNY: He said he'd meet me in the driveway right after supper.

TED: You and your buddy system... You'd think a guy could ask a girl for a date without her bringing along another guy.

BONNY: Charlie's not just another guy.

TED: Do you think you could at least wait for him in the car? Or would your dad think you were necking with a Canuck?

BONNY: I can wait in the car, Ted. *(Ted gets out, crosses around the front and opens the door for her. She gets in uneasily. She sneaks a peek in the "mirror" while he crosses back.)*

TED: *(Getting into the "car.")* Did you tell your folks you were going to the Cyclone?

BONNY: I decided not to. I told them we were all going to see *Dumbo.*

TED: "All." I love that "all."

BONNY: They're at least letting me drive in your car, Ted. That's something, at least.

TED: Yeah well, look. Here comes your buddy. *(Charlie comes on from U.L.)*

CHARLIE: Sorry.

TED: Where were you?

CHARLIE: I fell asleep.

TED: Asleep? At eight in the evening?

CHARLIE: I was tired. O.K.? I've been working for two women. *(Charlie starts to get in next to Bonny. Ted reaches behind Bonny, to pull forward the "seat.")*

TED: Get in back, O.K.?

CHARLIE: How come I can't sit in front?

TED: It's a floor gearshift. Get in back.

BONNY: He's just gotten his license, Charlie.

WHAT I DID LAST SUMMER

TED: I just want him in back.

BONNY: Be reasonable, Charlie. *(Charlie reluctantly gets into the back, shoving Bonny forward by the "seat." Bonny closes the "door.)*

TED: And we are off. To the Cyclone! *(He starts up the "car.")*

CHARLIE: *(Leaning forward, between them.)* Don't you think you better put on your lights first, Ted?

TED: *(Quickly putting the "lights" on.)* I was planning to do that.

CHARLIE: *(Sitting back.)* Oh yeah. Sure. Right. You bet. *(They drive.)*

TED: So, Charlie. How's the Pig Woman?

CHARLIE: Fine.

TED: Is it true she doesn't wear any underpants?

BONNY: Oh honestly...

CHARLIE: No.

TED: No she doesn't? Or no it's not true?

CHARLIE: She wears underwear, Ted.

BONNY: Of course she does.

TED: How do you know, Charlie? Have you looked?

CHARLIE: Knock it off, Ted. O.K.?

BONNY: Yes, Ted. Stop teasing. Really. *(They drive.)*

TED: What does she pay you, Charlie?

CHARLIE: Never mind.

BONNY: My father says it's rude to talk about money.

TED: Hey look. I'm just a poor Canuck who wants to know what the rich Americans are paying their help this summer.

CHARLIE: She's not rich.

TED: That's why she only pays a quarter.

CHARLIE: There are more things in this world than money, Ted.

BONNY: Yes, Ted.

TED: Such as what?

BONNY: Look out for that car! *(Ted swerves. They all lean. Ted staightens the "wheel.")*

CHARLIE: Jesus. Drive much?

TED: I saw him.

CHARLIE: Uh huh. You betchum, Ted.

WHAT I DID LAST SUMMER

TED: I want to know what the Pig Woman gives you that's more important than money, Charlie.

CHARLIE: Things you wouldn't understand, Ted.

TED: Such as what? *(Silence from Charlie.)*

BONNY: Such as what, Charlie?

CHARLIE: Whose side are you on, Bonny?

BONNY: I'm just curious, Charlie. What does she give you?

CHARLIE: She...teaches me things.

TED: *Teaches* you? You mean, like a...*teacher*?

BONNY: What does she teach you, Charlie?

CHARLIE: She... I don't have to tell.

TED: You don't have to ride the Cyclone, either. *(He stops the "car." They all jerk forward.)* Maybe we'll just sit here by the side of the road until we hear about those wonderful, secret, piggy things.

BONNY: Oh, Ted.

CHARLIE: Fine with me. Maybe there are more important things than riding some dumb machine in an amusement park.

BONNY: Oh, Charlie.

TED: O.K. We sit.

CHARLIE: You know what amusement parks are, don't you? Amusement parks are places where people fritter away their potential.

TED: Fritter away their what?

CHARLIE: Potential. Potential.

BONNY: What does that mean, Charlie?

CHARLIE: It means that everyone's got this potential, if they only use it right. I've got it, you've got it, Hitler's got it, even Ted's got it.

BONNY: Is that what she teaches you, Charlie?

CHARLIE: Sure. And she's trying to bring mine out.

TED: Yeah well tell her I got some potential right here in my pants.

BONNY: That's disgusting, Ted.

CHARLIE: Yes, Ted. Knock it off. There are ladies present.

TED: Want to make something out of it, Charlie.

BONNY: Oh stop!

TED: Or don't you have enough potential?

CHARLIE: I'll make something out of it, Ted.

WHAT I DID LAST SUMMER

TED: O.K., then let's get out of the car, you dumb little creep.

CHARLIE: *(Pushing against Bonny's seat.)* O.K., you crude Canadian townie hick!

TED: *(Leaping out of the "car.")* You'll be gumming your food, buster!

BONNY: Oh God!

CHARLIE: *(Holding his ground.)* I'm not scared of you! *(They square off. Bonny is out of the "car" by now, and comes between them.)*

BONNY: Oh stop! Please! Ted, you're two years older!

CHARLIE: Just a year and a half. *(They face each other. Then Ted backs off.)*

TED: You're lucky there's a woman around, Charlie.

CHARLIE: *(Making his knees shake, like a cartoon character.)* I'm scared, Ted. Help. Gasp. Shriek. *(He starts Off L.)*

BONNY: How will you get home, Charlie?

CHARLIE: Who has to go home? I've got other places to go besides home! *(He runs Off. Bonny returns to the "car." Ted tries to close the "door" for her. She slams it shut herself.)*

TED: *(To Bonny; through the "window.")* Still want to go to the Cyclone?

BONNY: I don't know... *(Ted moodily gets into the "car." Elsie comes out with her book, settles D.L in chair to read.)*

TED: Or do you want to just sit out here, in the middle of nowhere?

BONNY: Maybe you'd better take me back, Ted.

TED: Knew it. Home to Daddy, eh? *(They drive. Bonny looks out the window. Ted turns on the "car radio." Music comes up: a wartime song like "Praise the Lord and Pass the Ammunition.")*

THE YOUNG AND FAIR
by N. Richard Nash
Mildred (19) - Drucilla (19) - Nancy (17) - Lee (17)

The Play: *The Young and Fair* is set at Brook Valley Academy, a fashionable school for young women (the cast requires 21 women). The story centers around a successful alumna of the school, Francis Morritt, who returns to enroll her younger sister, Patty. They soon discover that Sara Cantry, owner of the school, has been having some difficulty appeasing the members of the board of directors—one of whom has a daughter, Drucilla Eldridge, who is a student. Drucilla is a mean-spirited, jealous and manipulative girl who will stop at nothing to gain power over her schoolmates. Using the prestige of her father's position, she spreads rumors about two of the girls (both of whom are innocent), hoping to have them expelled. When one of the girls refuses to be blackmailed, she goes to Sara Cantry, who finds herself caught up in a struggle between right and wrong but unable to act. Francis and her sister are unwilling to compromise, however, and they help the girl overcome Drucilla's unscrupulous tactics.

The Scene: Drucilla, who has formed a secret Vigilante Committee (the "Vidge"), has just entered Patty's room followed by Mildred. Dru claims to be searching for objects that Patty has stolen.

THE YOUNG AND FAIR

(The R. side of the stage is illuminated quickly and we see: THE BEDROOM. No one is there. A knock on U.C. hall door, then Dru streaks into the room, wild-eyed and out of breath. She looks about her disconnectedly, then goes quickly to one of the bureaus and opens a drawer. Abruptly, hallway door opens and Mil, also breathless, stands on threshold.)

MIL: Dru! For Pete's sake, what are you doing?

DRU: I'm going to search every bedroom—until we find the thief. I'll show Miss Morritt the Vidge can do what she can't!

MIL: Dru, you'd better get out of here!

DRU: No! I'm going to show them all that there's a *need* for the Vidge——

MIL: But you'll get in trouble!

DRU: I'll risk it!

MIL: Do you have any idea who the thief is? You said you had a suspicion.

DRU: I had to say that, stupid—to show the girls I knew what I was doing. *(Going toward bureau again.)* Come on—let's get started.

MIL: Oh, Dru! I'm sure Lee didn't take anything—and if you suspect Patty, you're off your trolley!

DRU: I don't suspect anybody, I told you! I only hope—I hope Patty did do it!

MIL: Don't talk so crazy! You know darn well she's not the kind to——

DRU: How do we know she *didn't* steal those things? And I tell you—if she did—she and her sister will be out of here so fast——!

MIL: You're doing this out of spite! You're just trying to get back at Miss Morritt!

DRU: Why shouldn't I? She's trying to trim me down to a nobody! It's her against me! She's got to leave this place—or I've got to! And anything I can do to get her out——

MIL: *(Frightened.)* I don't want to have anything to do with this! *(She starts for U.C. door.)*

DRU: Wait a minute! *(Sincerely affected.)* You're walking out on me...?

243

THE YOUNG AND FAIR

MIL: *(Unhappily.)* Dru, let's call it off—forget about it!

DRU: *(Quietly.)* What are we calling off? Our friendship?

MIL: No, of course not! I mean *this*—all this sneaking around and——

DRU: Miss Morritt was right. When it comes to a showdown, I've got nobody. I've got to do it alone!

MIL: *(Desperately.)* Dru, don't you understand? All this business—it makes me feel scared and—sick. If you gave a rap about me you wouldn't ask me to——

DRU: I do ask you! *(Then, quietly.)* I ask you to prove that Miss Morritt was wrong—that I do have friends—that they'll stick to me!

MIL: Oh, Dru!

DRU: Well?

MIL: *(Quietly, trembling.)* No... *(with an outcry.)* No! It costs too much to be your friend, Dru—it costs too much! *(Mil rushes out of room U.C. Dru stands there, immobilized, in an agony of loss and frustration. What to do? She paces, starts for U.C. door as if to make it up with Mil—and give up the whole project. But she can't. As last, quieting the turmoil inside her, she makes her decision: Dru goes toward bureau and resumes her search.... Suddenly, offstage, the sound of running footsteps. Dru shuts drawer, frightened. She freezes as she hears knock on U.C. door.)*

NANCY'S VOICE: Lee! *(Dru looks around for an escape, she races toward closet down R. At this precise moment, Nancy enters and sees closet door closing.)*

NANCY: Lee! Lee—is that you? *(Dru comes back into room cautiously. She is about to make an excuse for her presence here when Nancy, who is carrying some objects in her hand, makes a panic-stricken movement to hide them behind her back. Dru sees this.)*

DRU: *(Measuredly.)* Hello, Nancy.

NANCY: *(Tense.)* Hello. I heard voices in here. I thought it was Lee.

DRU: What do you want Lee for?

NANCY: I—just wanted some—some advice. But it's nothing—I'll come back. *(She makes a jerky movement toward U.C. door. Dru steps quickly into her path.)*

244

THE YOUNG AND FAIR

DRU: Wait a minute... There's no rush, is there?

NANCY: *(Stopping tensely.)* I'm in a hurry—I——

DRU: What for? What are you so nervous about?

NANCY: I'm not nervous. Please let me go by.

DRU: *(Quickly.)* What have you got behind your back?

NANCY: *(Retreating.)* Nothing.

DRU: Let me see it, huh? You'd better give it to me, hadn't you?

NANCY: *(Breaking away in panic.)* It's not yours!

DRU: *(Suddenly making a grab for Nancy.)* Give it to me!

NANCY: *(Struggling—crying out.)* Please—let me alone! *(She tries to break away but Dru, stronger, subdues her. The struggle is over—and Dru has objects in her hand.)*

DRU: *(With a gasp.)* My God! The pen and the fraternity pin and my money—everything! *(As Nancy collapses on bed.)* So *you've* been doing the stealing...

NANCY: *(In a frenzied confusion.)* I don't know—I don't know—— *(She begins to sob.)*

DRU: You'd better come along.

NANCY: *(Resisting.)* Where? Where are you taking me?

DRU: Miss Cantry. *(She tries to shepherd Nancy toward U. C. door.)*

NANCY: No—please—she'll send me home!

DRU: I'm sorry, Nancy. But the Vidge set out to find the thief. Well, we've found her.

NANCY: Please——! I won't take anything again—I promise! My mother—I don't know what she'll do to me! Please help me out!

DRU: Look, I can't go protecting a girl who——

NANCY: I'll do anything you say—anything!

DRU: I'm sorry it's you, Nancy—but it had to be somebody. *(Suddenly, struck by inspiration, she drops Nancy's arm.)* Wait a minute... Why does it have to be you?

NANCY: You will help me, won't you?

DRU: Be quiet—let me think! *(Suppressing her excitement.)* What did you come into this room for?

NANCY: Miss Morritt asked if I'd taken the things. And I said no——

245

DRU: *(Quickly.)* Did she believe you?

NANCY: I think so. But then I got scared. I didn't know what to do. I thought Lee would tell me what to do.

DRU: *(Quietly—with studied friendliness.)* Nancy, you know you're in a tough spot. Not only could you be sent home—you could be arrested.

NANCY: Please help me——

DRU: If I do, liable to get me in trouble.

NANCY: No—no, it won't!

DRU: If I protect you, you've got to back me up. Because I'd be taking a big chance for your sake.

NANCY: *(Snatching at the straw.)* Of course—I understand—I'll back you up.

DRU: And you'll have to stay in with me until the very end. It would be bad for both of us if something went wrong. *(With elaborate solicitude.)* And it would be still worse for you, Nancy.

NANCY: I know—I'll do whatever you say.

DRU: All right... Here—take this stuff. *(As Nancy obeys, Dru quickly moves to Patty's bureau. She opens second drawer, searches around, then comes up with a stationery box.)* Put the things in this stationery box.

NANCY: But it's Patty's!

DRU: Never mind that—do as I tell you! *(As Nancy complies.)* Now put the box in this bottom drawer.

NANCY: It's Patty's bureau—I couldn't do that!

DRU: *(Impatiently.)* All right—if you don't want me to help——! *(Nancy puts box in drawer.)* Shut the drawer. *(As Nancy shuts drawer, we see Patty and Lee enter the Main Hall from R. Lee starts U. C., through archway.)*

PATTY: *(Calling.)* Hurry up, Lee. We'll miss the main feature.

LEE: I'll only be a minute.

NANCY: *(Frightened.)* Lee's coming in!

DRU: Oh, dammit! *(Quickly improvising.)* Go round the bend in the hallway. When Lee comes in here, stand outside the door. Listen to everything that goes on in here. *(Nancy goes. Dru quickly surveys room. In Main Hall Patty has picked up a book and is reading. Lee breezes into bedroom U.C. On seeing Dru, she halts. As if in slow motion, she puts down the books she is carrying.)*

LEE: What are you doing in our room?

DRU: I'm making a search of all the rooms in Fairchild.

LEE: Did you get Miss Morritt's permission to do that? Or Miss Cantry's

DRU: I have the permission of the Vidge. That's enough.

LEE: The Vidge doesn't exist. And you can't search in here. *(Dru smiles.)* Oh, for goodness' sake, do you think we stole your money?

DRU: I don't think anything. But I'm going to fine-tooth-comb this school. Every single room.

LEE: I won't allow you to touch a thing in here.

DRU: Then you make the search while I watch.

LEE: You won't get me to search anything!

DRU: If you're innocent, why do you object to it? *(A moment.)* Now don't waste time or I'll make it pretty tough for you. *(Quietly.)* And believe me, I can!

LEE: *(Apprehensively—in a strained voice.)* It's useless anyway—none of the stolen property is here!

DRU: *(Casually.)* All right—let's see. Why don't you start with that bureau——?

LEE: I can't go rummaging in Patty's things——

DRU: *(With studied impatience.)* Oh, don't be silly. You're *clearing* her by doing it.

LEE: *(Opening top drawer of Patty's bureau.)* There! There's nothing in any of these drawers. You can see for yourself. Scarves—sweaters—three blouses—nothing else.

DRU: *(Offhandedly.)* Okay—try the next one.

LEE: *(Opening second drawer.)* It's all her art stuff. Brushes, paints—— *(Suddenly she comes upon the stationery box. She opens it and, seeing its contents, gasps. Quickly collecting herself, she closes drawer. In a tight voice:)* Nothing there.

DRU: *(Quickly.)* What was in that box?

LEE: Nothing. I tell you—nothing! *(But Dru has now opened drawer*

247

herself, she pulls out box. Opens it.)

DRU: Holy——!

LEE: *(Quaking.)* She—but—where did they come from?

DRU: They came from Abby and Selma and me!

LEE: Patty can't—she doesn't know anything about those things!

DRU: Maybe they just sneaked in by themselves!

LEE: Or maybe they were sneaked in by somebody else! By you, perhaps! *(Abruptly moving toward U.C. door.)* I'm going to ask Patty whether she knows anything——

DRU: Wait, Lee! *(Suddenly her tactics change. Almost sympathetically.)* I had no intention of searching the rest of the school. I knew the search would stop here.

LEE: *(Infuriated.)* Of course you did!

DRU: *(Building, block by block.)* I knew it would stop here because I was tipped off about Patty.

LEE: *(Savagely.)* Tipped off! By whom—Mil Cheaver?

DRU: *(Measuring each word.)* No—by somebody else. Somebody in this school saw Patty with that fountain pen this morning!

LEE: You're a liar!

DRU: The girl came into this room without knocking. Patty was standing in front of this bureau—with the pen in her hand. When Patty saw the girl she quickly opened that drawer. And then she was furious at the girl for barging in!

LEE: I don't believe it!

DRU: If I ask the girl who saw her with the pen to come in her will you believe *her?*

LEE: No, I won't!

DRU: Maybe you will when you see who the girl is. *(Dru goes swiftly to U.C. door, looks down the hall and beckons to Nancy. Without an instant's pause:)* I know how you feel about this, Lee—and I don't blame you. But somebody did steal that stuff——

LEE: Not Patty——

DRU: Listen, you can never be sure of anybody! Who can tell what's eating Patty? Maybe there's something wrong with her—something we don't know about——

THE YOUNG AND FAIR

LEE: Don't say that! *(Nancy is now at U.C. door. Lee's back is to Nancy, but Dru sees her.)*

DRU: *(Indicating Nancy.)* All right, Lee—look! *(Lee turns and sees Nancy.)*

LEE: *(Shaken.)* Nancy!

DRU: *(Gently, to Nancy.)* Nancy, tell Lee what you told me. Didn't you see Patty with that pen this morning?

NANCY: *(Her eyes down—faltering.)* Yes.

DRU: Where was she standing?

NANCY; It was—I—in front of the bureau——

LEE: *(Going to pieces.)* Nancy, you must be wrong! Are you sure it was this fountain pen? Don't make a mistake, Nancy!

DRU: *(As Nancy hesitates.)* No—don't make a mistake.

NANCY: Yes...it was that one. I'm sure of it.

LEE: Nancy—listen——

DRU: Don't, Lee. Can't you see how this is getting her all upset? She didn't want to have to tell, did you, Nancy? *(Nancy shakes her head. She is unstrung.)* Go on back to your room, Nancy. *(Nancy leaves, U. C.)*

LEE: *(Breaking out.)* I can't belive it! Something must be wrong——!

DRU: Of course! Something is wrong—with Patty. Otherwise, I couldn't believe it myself.... Now, what are we going to do about it?

LEE: *(Crying out.)* I'm not going to do anything!

DRU: But we've got to! You and I have got to take that box to Miss Cantry!

LEE: Me?—I won't!

DRU: I'm not asking you to lie or anything. I just want you to——

LEE: You're asking me to call Patty a thief!

DRU: You needn't call her anything! Just tell Miss Cantry that you and I discovered the stolen property in Patty's stationery box.

LEE: *(Desperately.)* I won't!

DRU: What if you're asked? Will you lie?

LEE: If I have to—yes!

DRU: Lee, don't be a fool! Why make yourself her accomplice? *(In a movement of flight, Lee starts for U.C. door. Dru stops her.*

249

THE YOUNG AND FAIR

Ominously:) If you lie, you know what'll happen, don't you?

LEE: You can't do anything to me.

DRU: Oh, yes, I can! I'll show them what a liar you really are! You lied to get into the school! You know you people aren't allowed at Brook Valley! I'll expose you—as a liar!

LEE: *(Wildly.)* What's Patty got to do with that? You can't persecute Patty because of me!

DRU: *(Quietly.)* Look here, Lee. The stolen articles were found in this room. This is Patty's room—but it's also *yours!* *(Insinuating.)* If Patty didn't steal those things, who did?

LEE: You don't think I did?

DRU: No, but there might be others who'd think so. There are lots of people around here who wouldn't throw you out because you're a Jew—but they'd jump at the chance to throw you out as a thief!

LEE: *(She grips two ends of bureau C., and hangs over it, shaking.)* Oh, God!

DRU: Now, remember. All I'm asking is that you tell the truth. That's all—the truth—you discovered the box in Patty's bureau. If Patty's innocent, she'll be able to prove it! *(In hallway, Patty walks to arch U.C. and calls:)*

PATTY: Lee, where are you?

DRU: *(Rapidly—in a whisper.)* Now listen to me—don't sacrifice yourself!

PATTY: Lee!

DRU: You don't want to see her now, do you?

LEE: *(At wit's end!)* What'll I do—what'll I do——

DRU: Come on. Come into my room. She won't see you. Come on—we'll talk about it some more—come on—— *(Lee hardly hears Dru. She behaves as though she were sleep-walking. Dru gets stationery box, takes Lee gently by the arm, leads her out.)*

253

PERMISSION ACKNOWLEDGMENTS